I dedicate this book to the flower of my life—Bridget Jourgensen.
—LAURENCE KOTLIKOFF

To Cheryl and the joy of seeing you every day.
—PHILIP MOELLER

To my grandchildren: Bella, Joe, Will, Finn,
Bridget, Anderson, and Hadley.
—PAUL SOLMAN

GET WHAT'S YOURS

THE SECRETS TO MAXING OUT YOUR SOCIAL SECURITY

Revised and Updated

Laurence J. Kotlikoff,
Philip Moeller, and Paul Solman

SIMON & SCHUSTER

New York London Toronto Sydney New Delhi

Simon & Schuster
1230 Avenue of the Americas
New York, NY 10020

This Simon & Schuster hardcover edition May 2016

SIMON & SCHUSTER and colophon are
registered trademarks of Simon & Schuster, Inc.

For information about special discounts for bulk purchases,
please contact Simon & Schuster Special Sales at
1-866-506-1949 or business@simonandschuster.com.

The Simon & Schuster Speakers Bureau can bring authors to your live event.
For more information or to book an event contact the Simon & Schuster Speakers
Bureau at 1-866-248-3049 or visit our website at www.simonspeakers.com.

Manufactured in Italy

10   9   8

Library of Congress Cataloging-in-Publication Data is available.

ISBN 978-1-5011-4476-9
ISBN 978-1-4767-7231-8 (ebook)

CONTENTS

GET WHAT'S YOURS

Revised and Updated

1

WHY WE BOTHERED

The first version of this book began with a catchy true story of a simple Social Security strategy: how, during a break in the exercise coauthors Larry and Paul refer to as "tennis," Larry made a completely legitimate $48,000 for Paul in less than two minutes by instructing him on how to get *his*. The rest of the book guided readers through the various steps and strategies necessary to get *theirs* as well, using other real-life stories, plausible hypotheticals, and humor, to the limited extent we could make Social Security amusing.

The book's deep purposes were broad: to make our fellow Americans aware of how little they knew about the country's most important retirement program; to make them aware of how critical it was to their own financial future to understand the system's basic contours, as well as its nooks and crannies; and finally, to demystify Social Security's paralyzing complexity so that literally anyone could navigate it.

But when it comes to getting what's yours, our main objective was to convey—no, to beat you over the head with—one strategy above all others: patience, and the huge potential dollar return from waiting to collect massively larger benefits starting at older ages, regardless of your age, marital status, or earnings history.

A VIVID EXAMPLE OF THE
PATIENCE PAYOFF

Consider a 62-year-old couple who both stop working at that age, each having earned above Social Security taxable FICA limit—the maximum taxable amount—from age 22 on. They would jointly receive about $50,000 a year if they both began taking benefits at 62 (the earliest age at which you can collect). To generate the same amount of annual income from investments, assuming a return of 2 percent a year above inflation, they would need a nest egg of over *$1.3 million*—more than many upper-middle-income retirees have saved by retirement age. (The net worth of a typical household headed by someone aged 65 to 69 is only a fifth of this amount and much of it is in the value of their home.)[1]

Of course, $1.3 million is a lot of money. But—and here's the key takeaway—it's *much smaller* than what the couple can get by maximizing their Social Security benefits. Because, if they make the right decisions, they can increase the value of their lifetime Social Security "asset" to more than $1.7 million!

All the couple must do is wait until age 70 to start collecting their retirement benefits. If they do, Social Security will pay them benefits that are a whopping 76 percent higher than their age 62 benefits. And yet, according to the latest data, less than *2 percent* of Americans wait until 70 to collect. (In Chapter 2, we will note some important exceptions to our Patience Rule. But we will also demolish the arguments of those who think they know better than to wait.)

AN UNFORTUNATE EVENT

Less than nine months after the first edition of *Get What's Yours* was published, the government decided to rewrite Social Security rules. On November 2, President Obama signed into law the "Bipartisan

Budget Act of 2015." Under the arguably disingenuous heading "Protecting Social Security Benefits," the new law modifies several former provisions, most prominent among them the simple "file-and-suspend" strategy Larry had shared with Paul across the net. After six months from the signing of the bill, the "file-and-suspend" strategy would be severely restricted. This book will tell you all about the new provisions and help you understand the extent to which they will or won't affect you.

Thanks to the new law, the 62-year-old couple we mentioned can no longer collect one full spousal benefit between full retirement age and age 70 while waiting until 70, as Larry had advised Paul over tennis. Still, many married couples and divorcees remain eligible over the next 4 years to follow Paul's strategy.

But here's the good news, and a key reason we felt compelled to rewrite and present this revised edition of *Get What's Yours*: the strategy that earned Paul and his wife $48,000 may still work for many couples and divorced individuals both of whom were 62 or older by January 1, 2016, but not yet 70, and who are not the same age. There are, by our rough reckoning, millions of you out there, millions of Americans who will be "grandparented in" and therefore still able to employ the strategy Larry advised Paul to adopt. And while our 62-year-old couple, who turned 62 too late, will lose roughly $60,000 because of the new law, they will still gain about $400,000 from maximizing strategies still in effect.

Moreover, the rest of the book's suggestions and strategies remain true and invaluable: be patient; become aware of and then learn how to take all the benefits to which you're entitled (and may never have heard of); *time* your various benefits to make the most of them; and overall, understand Social Security's rules well enough to make the best decisions for you and your family, since you really can't rely on Social Security to do it for you.

Social Security's unreliability was something we knew about

when writing *Get What's Yours*, but we have had it impressed upon us time and time again since publication as plaintive readers write to us to complain of having been given bum advice. One reader even gave us a single star on Amazon for having given her "wrong advice," because her local Social Security office assured her we were wrong. We weren't, and Larry got the review removed and, we hope, straightened out the reader's benefits. In defense of Amazon reviewers, however, another one said he had learned a great deal from our book—and identified himself as a Social Security representative.

But since the strategy Larry shared with Paul—and that coauthor Phil Moeller and his wife, Cheryl, are using—still applies to millions of Americans for the next four years, what exactly *is* it? Here's the original story.

BAD TENNIS, GOOD STRATEGY

Back in 2010, as Larry and Paul had taken a break from what they optimistically call tennis, Larry launched into a harangue, as he often does; this one was about Social Security's maddening complexity. Paul listened with his skeptical journalist's ear. Or, maybe, since it was a Larry harangue, just half-listened.

Then Larry popped the question: how old were Paul and his wife and when did they plan to take their Social Security benefits?

Proudly, Paul told Larry not to worry: he and his wife had it all figured out. They would both wait until 70, when Paul would get something like $40,000 a year instead of the $30,000 or so if he took his benefits earlier at 66, his *"full"*—but not *"maximum"*—retirement age, which was in fact just around the corner. Paul had for years been reading and filing away those annual greenish statements from the Social Security Administration with their "Estimated Benefits." He'd been reading his wife's, too.

How old are you and Jan? Larry asked.

Paul's wife would soon turn 67; he, 66.

Here's what you do, said Larry, never at a loss when it comes to speaking in the imperative. Jan should apply for her Social Security retirement benefit now, since she is *already* 66, but then "suspend" it. That is, she makes herself eligible for the benefit by officially registering with Social Security, on the phone or in person at her local office. But Jan then tells Social Security she is not *taking* her benefit right away but *suspending* it until some time in the future. In other words, she "files and suspends."

Then, said Larry, when you (Paul) turn 66, you also call or visit Social Security and register with the system. But you apply not for your own benefit, but for a *spousal* benefit. A spousal benefit is fully 50 percent of what Jan is entitled to at her full retirement age—66, in Jan's case.

Paul was confused but intrigued.

Spousal benefits? Paul had vaguely heard of them. He had, however, never imagined he or his wife was eligible for any, though had you asked him why not, he couldn't have told you. Was he entitled to them?

Yes, said Larry, so long as you're not yet taking your own benefit. Then, Larry continued, when Jan hits 70, she does as originally planned—she calls or visits Social Security again and says she now wants to take her retirement benefit, at which point it will start at its highest possible value.

And what do *I* do at 70? Paul asked.

Just what you *planned* to do originally, said Larry. You contact Social Security and tell them you're switching from the spousal benefit to your *own* benefit.

And where's the extra money? Paul asked.

Well, said Larry, during the four years you wait, you would earn about $12,000 a year—half of Jan's full retirement benefit. Meanwhile, your own benefit would have grown by 8 percent a year, for a total of 32 percent (reaching the amount Paul's greenish statements had estimated if he waited until 70).

Spousal benefits for four years. That should indeed be almost $50,000, just as Larry had quickly estimated. And importantly, it would give Paul and Jan a cushion as they waited until 70. Suppose they faced sudden, unforeseen expenses?

An aside is in order here. Larry is a world-famous scold, or, he will tell you, a dead-on Cassandra, with respect to Social Security's insolvency. Advising people like Paul to take extra benefits from the system while himself decrying the system's funding shortfall was not what Paul expected to hear (more on that in Chapter 17). But Larry believed it wasn't fair that some beneficiaries got more than others simply because *they* knew the system's rules while so many others didn't. (And Paul and Phil agreed with him. Which is why we wrote *Get What's Yours*.)

Fast-forward. Jan filed and suspended—by phone. The person she talked to couldn't have been nicer. Paul turned 66. He filed for a spousal benefit. The Social Security representative on the phone had never heard of file-and-suspend, checked with her supervisor, and came back on the line to thank him for enlightening her about a strategy she could now share with everyone who called thereafter.

We are dedicated to getting you every dollar to which you're entitled, she said, or words to that effect.

When they hit 70, both Paul and his wife called again, were again reprocessed—graciously, competently, and within minutes, though his wife was nonplussed when asked if she'd ever been a nun.

ANOTHER COAUTHOR AND SPOUSE
WILL STILL GET WHAT'S *THEIRS*

The tennis court strategy is what Congress is doing away with. But fortunately our third coauthor, financial journalist Phil Moeller, was born in 1946, and his wife, Cheryl Magazine, is four years his junior. Lucky for them both because, by a stroke of pure chronological circumstance, Cheryl was born before the clock ran out on 1950, meaning she was safely beyond 62 before the ball dropped in Times Square and rang in the year 2016. Beating the ball meant Cheryl was grandparented in. To her, the old rules still apply.

And what about Phil? Happily for him, he had gone a-courtin' as roughly a third of American men appear to have done, looking at data from the Census Bureau, and married a woman at least four years younger than himself. (The median difference in the United States is a man *two* years older than his wife.) Phil, of course, was dutifully waiting until 70 to collect his own maximum Social Security benefit, 32 percent higher than had he begun taking his benefit at age 66. (As coauthor of a book whose main advice is to wait as long as possible before taking Social Security, he would have run the risk of public censure—and coauthor abuse—had he done otherwise.) So just as Phil turns 70 and begins collecting his maximum benefit, Cheryl turns 66, files a *restricted application*, and begins collecting just her *spousal benefit*: half of Phil's "full retirement benefit," the amount he was eligible to collect when *he* turned 66, and just what Paul had done when he began collecting on Jan's record.

Phil and Cheryl are the perfect couple—at the very least for spousal benefit eligibility under the new rules. The four-year spread in age means that Cheryl can begin taking spousal benefits just as cradle-robbing Phil turns 70, and she can receive them for the full four years until she herself reaches that lofty level. Crucially, for readers of *Get What's Yours*, the same holds true for *any* spouse four or more years younger than the person to whom they're married— think college senior marrying high school senior—but remember: the younger spouse has to have been at least 62 before January 2, 2016, to be eligible under the old rules.

Phil and Cheryl are also the perfect couple because, were she only *three* years younger—a freshwoman when he was a senior, for example—she would already be 67 when Phil turned 70 and thus get only *three* years' worth of spousal benefits; if a sophomore to his senior, two years; just a junior, well, you do the math. The reason they are allowed to do this is that Cheryl made the age-62 cutoff. Under the new law, older spouses who file and suspend can't provide their spouse or any other dependents with benefits while their retirement benefit is in suspension. Admittedly, the estimate you're about to read is a rough one, but of the nearly 30 million or so Americans born between 1946 and 1953, there figure to be millions of couples in a situation analogous to Phil's and Cheryl's and others grandfathered differently under the new law. Someone you know is surely among them.

SOCIAL SECURITY VERBATIM

YOU'RE RIGHT THERE (AND WE'RE RIGHT HERE)

"The regulations that require a notice for an initial determination contemplate sending a correct notice. We consider that an initial determination is correct even if we send an incorrect notice."

ALL QUOTES FROM OFFICIAL SOCIAL SECURITY RULES

A PERVERSE TWIST THAT THE
NEW LAW ENCOURAGES

The new law encourages divorce, as we'll explain in Chapter 11. It's true that Paul and Jan would have benefited had *they* gotten divorced, because each could have taken spousal benefits on the other's record. But the way the law reads now, the *only way* for same-aged couples who were 62 by January 1, 2016, to do what Paul did (collect a full spousal benefit while waiting till 70 to take his retirement benefit) is to get divorced two years before they reach full retirement age—an amicable divorce (amicable to the point of intimate, even). Then, after six years of equally amicable cohabitation, they can reunite, maybe even throw a new wedding to celebrate. Want to guess how much they could afford to spend on the event just from having collected spousal benefits on each other for the four years between full retirement age (66) and age 70? If both were top earners, $128,000 in 2016 dollars. If they were not top earners, but getting only the *average* benefit these days—$15,000 a year—they would still have collected $60,000 over the four years.

WHY WE SO DISLIKE THE NEW RULES

Even though we're coauthors and friends, we disagree about many things. We even disagree about many things with respect to Social Security, as Chapter 17 makes vividly clear. And we disagree about the new rules, as Chapter 4 will make apparent. But we do *not* disagree about the process that led to them; we think it was too fast, too opaque, and, therefore, unsurprisingly, ill-considered, at least with respect to the details. And whether it's God or the devil in the details (lexicographers differ), it's clear that in Social Security, the details can make all the difference.

When Social Security was last revised by Congress back in 1983, the retirement age was extended by two years—from 65 to 67. But the full extension was phased in over *44 years*. By contrast, the ability to provide benefits to relatives or to receive benefits from relatives based on a suspended retirement benefit filing was phased out for most people over a period of less than six *months*, and the ability to take spousal benefits at age 66 while letting your own benefit grow until 70 has a four-year phase-out.

Some such plan was mentioned in the president's budget as submitted in March 2014. The exact language: "the Budget proposes to eliminate aggressive Social Security claiming strategies, which allow upper-income beneficiaries to manipulate the timing of collection of Social Security benefits in order to maximize delayed retirement credits." But there was no mention of eliminating Social Security provisions in the budget issued *this* year, no public hearings or debate. Just rumors, mere days before the budget bill passed, that certain claiming strategies were on the chopping block.

Indeed, we know the final language was seat-of-the-pants because, after Larry pointed out (in his *PBS NewsHour* weekly online Social Security column, "Ask Larry"[2]) that the original language would eliminate some benefits that people were *already collecting*, the bill was amended—amended, Larry was told by a high-ranking Social Security official, because the implication of the language hadn't been realized until he pointed it out. But better late than never, and current file-and-suspenders can thank goodness, or the deity of their choice, for the eleventh-hour amendment.

An estimate we used in the first edition of *Get What's Yours* was that if all spouses and divorced spouses were to take advantage of the strategy, it would cost the system $9.5 billion per year. A key argument against file-and-suspend is that high earners were likely to be the primary beneficiaries of this strategy. But there is recent evidence from Stanford economist John Shoven and coauthors that shows the rich aren't much more likely to delay their claiming than the poor.

Let us tell you about someone who doesn't fit the stereotype, a Boston University employee Larry knows well whom we'll call Alice. Alice was born in 1951 and works two jobs for a total of 80 hours a week. She's been doing so for the last 15 years. Her husband can't work because he needs to stay home with their severely disabled child. Alice makes a modest combined income in the two jobs, but spread over three people, she and her family are hardly even middle income.

Alice had planned on filing and suspending her retirement benefit at 66 so her husband could collect a spousal benefit and her son could collect a disabled child benefit while she waited till 70 to collect her retirement benefit. She had planned to quit her second job thanks to these extra benefits. But because she did not turn 66 in time, she no longer can. If she can't keep working at her current pace, however, she'll have to take her retirement benefit early. This will activate the benefits for her husband and child, but will also mean a permanently lower retirement benefit for her. How many Alices are there out there?

For some other features of the law that seem unfair and/or arbitrary, if not downright perverse, please read Chapter 4.

WHAT IS STILL TRUE ABOUT
GET WHAT'S YOURS

The premise of this revised and updated edition of *Get What's Yours* is the same as that of the first: to guide you through Social Security to get the benefits you paid for all your working life and to which you are entitled. Remember, before we published the book, the world had been divided into two random camps: those few people who happened to know Larry (or had learned the strategy independently, through other Social Security mavens), and the vast majority of Americans, whom one might call the strategically uninformed. It was for them that we wrote, hoping especially that we would reach readers least in the know and most dependent on Social Security for their livelihood in old age. That is still the case.

We had written a book to help people understand how to maximize the Social Security benefits they had earned and therefore, we believed, deserved to get. And we figured that since the three of us—the economist and the two journalists—had spent years studying Social Security and making economic complexity in general intelligible to the public, we were the right folks for the job.

WHY ELSE WE BOTHERED TO WRITE THE BOOK, AND NOW A NEW EDITION (WHICH WE DIDN'T EXPECT WOULD BE NEEDED QUITE SO SOON)

Social Security is, far and away, Americans' most important retirement asset. And that's true not only for people of modest means. Middle-income and upper-income households actually have the most to gain, in total amounts, from getting Social Security right. Toting up lifetime benefits, even low-earning couples may be Social Security millionaires. And except for the Bill Gateses and Warren Buffetts of the world—whose percentage of the population was exceedingly modest last we checked—Social Security is a *very* meaningful income source.

So this book is for nearly every one of you who's ever earned a paycheck and wants every Social Security benefit dollar to which you are entitled—entitled because you paid for it. You earned it. It's yours. It can be yours even if you never contributed a penny to the system but have or had a spouse, living or dead, who did. It may be yours even if you spent some or all of your career working for employers who did not have to participate in Social Security.

Perhaps you wondered, when you got your first paycheck, what the huge deduction for that four-letter word "FICA" referenced. If you learned that it stood for the Federal Insurance Contributions Act, you might have been none too pleased at first, but then assuaged by hearing that these "contributions"—week after week, month after month, year after year, out of every paycheck (up to a limited amount of income)—would lead to higher retirement benefits.

Even those of us who aren't superrich, but have earned and saved a lot, view Social Security as a critical lifeline. We realize, after the crash of 2008, that no assets—not our homes, not our bonds, and certainly not our stocks—are safe from life-altering declines. We realize that even our private pensions, if we have them, may hinge on our former employer staying in business and inflation not eroding the pension's purchasing power. (It's the rare private-sector pension that boosts payments to protect against inflation.) We also know that we could, with plausible medical breakthroughs, live to 100 or longer.

But isn't Social Security a bigger deal for the poor? Not necessarily. To be sure, Social Security benefits are a crucial lifeline for lower-income beneficiaries. And, yes, Social Security benefits rise less for higher earners than do their FICA tax contributions, for reasons we'll explain later. But benefits do rise with both time and earnings, and they involve *very* big sums.

THE BEST SEX IN THE BOOK

One more story, to illustrate why Social Security is so damnably complex—and can be to the point of absurdity. This morbidly humorous tale comes from our Technical Expert, Jerry Lutz, who spent his entire career with Social Security and reviewed this book for accuracy.

One day, while Jerry still worked for Social Security, a claims representative approached him with a question. A new claimant's husband had died of a heart attack on their honeymoon while having sex. They clearly were married for less than 9 months, the threshold for receiving survivor's benefits. But one of the exceptions to the 9-month duration-of-marriage rule involves "accidental death." Up until then, Jerry had considered "accidental" to mean something like a car wreck. But his job was to research tough cases like this one.

So he searched the vast Social Security rule book and found POMS GN 00305.105, which describes an accidental death in part as follows:

A "bodily injury" occurs whenever the outside force or cause affects the body sufficiently to interfere with its normal function.

The cause of the bodily injury is:

"External" if it originated outside the body. An external force can include an injury suffered due to weather conditions or exertion.

NOTE: By exertion we mean an activity that involves at least moderate effort for the average person. Routine activities, e.g., standing, do not constitute exertion for purposes of finding accidental death. Circumstances which more readily lend themselves to a favorable finding of accidental death include:

- an unexpected heart attack occurs during moderate exertion;
- an unforeseen event negates the voluntary nature of an activity, e.g., an exercise machine breaks down while exercising;
- some unintended, unexpected, and unforeseen result occurs during exertion, e.g., a fall or slip while running; or
- a crisis or sudden peril requires strenuous exertion.

"Moderate exertion"? Arguably. "Unintended" and "unexpected"? Indubitably. And so, based on the claimant's testimony and her husband's death certificate, widow's benefits were eventually conferred, but the determination was anything but simple.

10,000 OF YOU TURN 66 EVERY
SINGLE DAY (INCLUDING SUNDAY)

That's right: 10,000 baby boomers are reaching retirement age every day. Each of them needs to know precisely how to get Social Security's best deal. But Paul's best moves—or Larry's or Phil's, for that matter—aren't necessarily yours. The Social Security system is governed by 2,728 core rules and thousands upon thousands of additional codicils in its Program Operating Manual, which supposedly clarify those rules. In the case of married couples alone, the formula for each spouse's benefit comprises 10 complex mathematical functions, one of which is in four dimensions.

This book contains minimal math, excepting the "simple" formula presented in this note.[3] Rather, it explains in the simplest possible terms the traps to avoid and basic strategies to employ in maximizing a household's Social Security retirement, spousal, child, mother/father, survivor, divorce, and disability benefits. That covers a whole lot of ground, which is why this book is not as succinct as we (and you) might like.

We will point out Social Security's windfalls and pitfalls—explain obscure benefits and more obscure penalties; benefit collection strategies like *file a restricted application* (take one benefit while letting your retirement benefit grow) and *start, stop, start* (starting benefits, stopping them, and restarting them). We'll also describe Social Security's *deeming* rules (being forced, in some cases, to take certain benefits early at a very big cost) and related gotchas that can handicap you financially for the rest of your life.

We'll explain Social Security's significant incentives to get divorced, to get married, or to live in sin, depending on your circumstances. Do you know about Social Security's hidden payoff for working late in life? About the Earnings Test (deduction of benefits at certain ages from earning too much) that isn't necessarily a test at all? Do you know that you generally get the Earnings Test deductions back in full, inflation-adjusted, if you live to full retirement age and beyond? How about the Family Maximum Benefit (the limit to benefits your family can collect based on your work record)? It's actually not a maximum. It's also unfairly low for poor, disabled workers.

Throughout, we'll emphasize the often huge payoff from waiting to collect benefits. But we'll also explain lots of situations where it's best *not* to wait. We'll even throw in the mythical man with four ex-wives who could theoretically collect divorced or widower benefits on each of them. The ever-surprising and often frustrating Social Security sudoku puzzle goes on and on. We're here to solve it.

We're also relieved that you came to us to learn about Social Security and aren't relying solely on Social Security's advice. Frankly, Social Security is not the first place we'd send you to learn how to maximize your lifetime benefits. With the exception of the system's small number of technical experts (including Jerry Lutz, mentioned above), many of Social Security's official or phone support staff are insufficiently trained or too beleaguered to dispense uniformly correct information or advice about the system's ins and outs. And they aren't supposed to give advice anyway. We're going to provide specific examples of people losing lots of money by believing or following what the well-meaning folks at Social Security told them. Unfortunately, the local Social Security office is single-stop shopping for most retirees making their benefit decisions. And many of them are waiting pretty late in the game before even thinking about managing what for most retirees is their largest financial asset.

At the surface level, Social Security is complex because it has so many seemingly crazy rules. At a deeper level, its complexity reflects social policy that, when translated into practice, produces results that often defy common sense. An example is paying survivor benefits, based on the work records of ex-spouses, to the divorced who remarry, but only if they remarry after reaching age 60. Get remarried at 59 and 364 days and you're out of luck. Another perversity is paying benefits to mothers (or fathers) of young children if their spouse is collecting retirement benefits, *but only if the parents are married.* If the parents are divorced and under 62, too bad.

The result is a government retirement system that few if any can decipher without the kind of help provided here. And yet, for most people, Social Security is their *only* retirement option. Moreover, given the virtual disappearance of company pensions, except for those grandparented under old plans, and the failure of most Americans either to contribute or contribute fully to 401(k), IRA, and other retirement accounts, Social Security is, well, pretty much it for pretty much all of us.

Our book is organized around general lessons, supporting examples, specific game plans tailored to your situation, and answers to actual questions posed to Larry in his enormously popular "Ask Larry" column, which appears weekly on Paul's *PBS NewsHour* Making Sen$e website (http://www.pbs.org/newshour/making-sense/).

A warning that we'll issue up front and reiterate throughout the book: we will often repeat ourselves. The worst that can happen, we figure, is that you'll simply skim and skip ahead. Much worse would be your forgetting some of your key options and thus nullifying, at least for yourself, the whole point of *Get What's Yours.* And for those of you who might think the repetitions betray a lack of confidence in our readers, know that we authors ourselves still check our notes on these items when we hit the key age milestones, despite having written about Social Security for years.

PAUL AND JAN GOT WHAT'S THEIRS. PHIL AND CHERYL WILL GET THEIRS. TIME TO GET WHAT'S YOURS

This book was born of Paul's first Social Security epiphany with Larry. We wrote it to help people like you, who don't happen to know Larry, get every last penny Social Security owes you. We've spent a huge amount of time trying to come up with clear, correct answers to questions we all face so you don't have to. And we've now rewritten it to account for the sudden changes made to the system in the budget bill signed into law on November 2, 2015. Thus there is a new chapter on the new law, and a new one on Medicare and Social Security, drawing upon Phil's new book, *Get What's Yours for Medicare*. We have also included new horror stories we've heard about Social Security's inconsistencies and bad advice, about the new treatment of the disabled introduced in late 2014 as the book had already gone to press, and new secrets we discovered since the book came out.

Finally, we think that even though "entitlement" has become a dirty word in policy debates, it's more than legitimate for you to feel *entitled* to your benefits. It's a feeling deeply rooted in all those years of FICA payments, buttressed by the annual Social Security statements itemizing your past contributions and projecting your future benefits, and guaranteed by our politicians' unwavering promises to defend the system and what it owes you. The promises may be suspect, but you have been forking over payroll taxes your entire working life; you deserve to get what you paid for; and it's the law.

LIFE'S BIGGEST DANGER
ISN'T DYING, IT'S LIVING

As a prospective retiree, what should you be most afraid of? Golf elbow? Dr. Phil fatigue? Driving your spouse to drink? Driving your spouse at all, given slower reflexes? Dementia? Death? Death is surely a top candidate, right?

From this book's point of view, it's none of the above. And when it comes to death, your greatest fear should be the very opposite. It should be the fear of *immortality*. Or, failing that, fear of an epically long life. That's because if you're the typical American who has saved less than $10,000 on average by the time you're within ten years of retiring, the longer you live, the greater the danger of your "golden" years turning to lead, weighed down by penury and its attendant anxieties. According to a recent survey, more than one in five Americans believe they will die in debt.[1]

To be brutally candid, if you're old and poor, you will face rejections by rising numbers of doctors who don't take Medicare or Medicaid. Your children may face crippling debt to buy you a long-shot cure that no insurance—public or private—will cover. You won't leave the house without a companion for fear of falling, yet won't be able to afford one, or even an Uber.

In other words, the greatest danger you face is *outliving your savings*, which brings us quickly to this chapter's punch line: the best way for millions of people to avoid a miserable financial future is *to wait* to collect Social Security. This is the optimal strategy emphasized throughout this book. And it is as true in this edition of *Get What's Yours* as it was in the first: be *patient* in taking certain benefits because they can be bigger—*massively* bigger—if you bide your time.

Clearly, many Americans have *already* outlived their savings and therefore exist more or less hand-to-mouth, saddled with debt. If you fit this description, you may have no option but to take whatever you can get from Social Security as soon as possible. Ditto if your health or luck or gene-pool draw rules out a long life. We recognize that there are many special circumstances that support early claiming of benefits.

But for the rest of you—millions upon millions of our fellow Americans—we counsel patience. And for those of you who took retirement benefits early and think it's now too late, we're here to tell you that even under new Social Security rules, you retain the option of suspending your benefits at Full Retirement Age (66 for current retirees) and starting them up again at or before age 70. Moreover, even those cursed with a terminal medical diagnosis should think twice before collecting. Medical breakthroughs are happening all the time. More important, as we'll explain, collecting early can cost your current and even ex-spouses big bucks in lower survivor benefits.

EARLY CLAIMANTS BEWARE!

Most of you will have a clear and Hamlet-like choice when it comes to timing benefits: to wait or or not to wait. And if you are *not* waiting until 66 or 70 to take benefits that will be much higher, adjusted for inflation, than the amounts available at an earlier age, you are, in our opinion, tempting a barrage of slings and arrows from outrageous fortune, or you're simply nuts.

Remember that, crucially, this isn't just about *you*. The benefits of your "dependents"—children, spouse, ex-spouse (if you were married for 10 years), and surviving spouse (if you were married for 9 months)—*depend* on your work record. And in the case of survivor benefits available to current and ex-spouses, these benefits depend on precisely when you decide to collect your own retirement benefit.

Amazingly, however, at least to us, Americans do *not* wait long enough to collect their highest possible benefits. Indeed, hardly *any* of you do. Take a gander at this table,[2] pulled from an annual report from the Social Security Administration, which seems to issue nearly as many reports as it has beneficiaries. It reports the percentage of people who take their full retirement benefit at different ages.

RETIREMENT BENEFIT CLAIMING AGES

(percentages rounded to nearest percent)

	MEN								
Year	Number	62	63	64	65	66	DI*	67–69	70+
2009	1,452,000	44	7	7	12	15	13	3	1
2010	1,387,000	43	8	7	11	16	13	4	1
2011	1,340,000	41	7	8	10	14	14	5	1
2012	1,419,000	37	7	7	12	16	15	5	1
2013	1,447,000	35	6	6	11	18	17	6	2
2014	1,433,000	35	6	6	10	17	17	7	2
	WOMEN								
Year	Number	62	63	64	65	66	DI*	67–69	70+
2009	1,288,000	50	7	7	10	9	12	4	2
2010	1,248,000	48	8	7	10	9	12	4	2
2011	1,238,000	47	7	8	10	10	12	4	2
2012	1,316,000	42	7	8	11	11	14	5	2
2013	1,347,000	40	6	7	11	12	15	5	3
2014	1,339,000	40	7	7	10	12	16	6	3

* DI = Disability payments are automatically converted to retirement payments at Full Retirement Age.

The three of us were taken aback by the numbers in the far right-hand column of this table. A minuscule 1 to 3 percent of people wait until 70 to take their Social Security retirement benefit—when it's 76 percent larger than at 62 and 32 percent larger than at 66. (Or at most, as interpreted by the authoritative Institute on Aging, at Boston College, about 3 percent of people.) On our first book tour for *Get What's Yours*, when we asked interviewers or audiences to estimate the percentage of people who wait until 70 to take their retirement benefit, we almost never got a figure below 10 percent. The average guess was around 20 percent. So why do so few of us wait?

The obvious reason, as already mentioned, is that lots of people need whatever money they can get as soon as they can get it. Rainy day funds are pretty much nonexistent for most Americans. More than 60 percent of Americans have no emergency savings for things such as a $1,000 emergency room visit or a $500 car repair, according to a survey of 1,000 adults by personal finance website Bankrate. Approximately 62 percent of Americans have less than $1,000 in their savings accounts and 21 percent don't even have a savings account, according to a survey of more than 5,000 adults by Google Consumer Survey. In fact, according to a Federal Reserve report,[3] 47 percent of respondents said they either wouldn't be able to cover an unexpected $400 expense, period, or would have to cover it by selling something or borrowing money.

So when a storm hits, our finances are understandably swamped, we find ourselves underwater, and we begin bailing. Sure enough, after the Great Recession of 2008, more people claimed Social Security early. As the economy slowly improved, early claiming percentages declined to longer-term trend levels. But as you can see from the chart, something like *40 percent* of us still take our Social Security retirement benefit the moment it becomes available.

As we'll discuss, for some households, taking retirement benefits even as early as 62 can actually be optimal. But for the vast majority of us, taking our retirement benefit early comes at an enormous cost—not to our current self, but to our future selves.

BUT THIS IS EXACTLY *WHY* PEOPLE OUGHT TO WAIT

Our point is simply this: if you haven't saved enough by the time you approach retirement, voluntary or *in*voluntary, the *last thing* you should do is claim early, thereby depriving your future self of even *more* savings for old age. We repeat the key number from the last chapter: the difference between taking your benefits at age 62 and waiting until 70 for a couple can be worth as much as $400,000 in savings.

That much money prompts this list of Suze Orman–like options for those who "can't afford to wait." (We hope Ms. Orman would approve.)

- If you're thinking of voluntary retirement, work a few more years.
- Get a second job.
- Cut your spending.
- Move to a cheaper location.
- Downsize your home.
- Consider a reverse mortgage.
- Draw from your retirement account(s).
- Borrow from friends or family.

Regrettably, however, regardless of their other options—regardless even of the economy's overall health—people who lose their jobs in their early 60s tend to file early for Social Security to replace their lost income. So do people who work in physically demanding jobs, who tend to file early because they're worn-out, their jobs have become too demanding, and/or they don't think the job will survive even if *they* do. And people who began work when they were young also tend to file early, presumably saying to themselves, "Enough is enough; I've paid for years and years for these benefits. I finally want to see them in my hands." Finally, it turns out, early filers also are more likely to have traditional pensions than those who don't file early. Why these people file early is anybody's guess. Maybe they feel they can better afford reduced Social Security benefits, in which case we suggest they read this chapter twice.

But here's what's so revealing. It turns out that the when-to-file decision can be shaped by *how it's explained to you*. To abbreviate lots of research, people who are asked to frame their Social Security benefits decision from the vantage point of being 62 are greatly influenced by the fear of losing four years of benefits if they wait until age 66. If, however, they are asked to make the decision from a 66-year-old's perspective, more people will wait to that age (or something close to it). A similar behavioral wild card is whether the advice people receive about filing for Social Security emphasizes how much money they could *lose* by not filing early versus the possible *gains* they would see if they delayed filing.

This illustrates a principle that behavioral economists have long known: while we humans do like to make money, our fear of *losing it* is an even more powerful driver of our decisions. And when making the decision as to when to draw Social Security benefits, "loss aversion" can be catastrophic.

Finally, "[t]he use of 'break-even analysis' has the very strong effect of encouraging individuals to claim early," according to a study by top economists on how behavioral framing affects claiming decisions.[4] Yet despite the fact that break-even analysis is utterly inappropriate, the Social Security Administration itself has routinely nudged people toward early claiming. Until several years ago, the agency actually described the claiming decision as a "break-even" calculation.

Okay, what *is* break-even analysis? A simple version might go like this, if you'll bear with us for a bit of simple arithmetic. Your benefit at age 66 is projected to be $1,000. If you begin taking benefits at 62, they will be only $750 a month. By waiting until 66, you'll have passed up 48 months of benefits at $750 a month. That's $36,000 in total.

What do you get for waiting? Your benefit at 66 will net you an extra $250 a month for the rest of your life. But $250 a month is only $3,000 a year. So it will take you 12 full years, until age 78, before you'll make up the $36,000 you left on the table by not filing at age 62. At that point—at age 78—you will have "broken even." As we will stress shortly, calculating your benefit collection options this way is conceptually bankrupt, as you yourself may be if you use break-even analysis. Yet when Social Security explained the timing decision this way, it caused people to claim benefits 12 to 15 months sooner than people who were simply told that it will cost the program the same amount of money regardless of when people claim benefits. In other words, break-even analysis made people worry that delaying benefits was some kind of gamble. Social Security has since shifted its communication approach to a somewhat more value-neutral perspective. Perhaps that's one reason people have begun to wait a little bit longer, although, as you'll soon see, Social Security's posted explanation still leads people perilously astray.

Now, maybe we're naïve, but it is hard to accept the idea that more than 60 percent of American men and women were so financially strapped that they *had to* claim benefits before reaching their Full Retirement Ages—97 percent or more before age 70. And recent research supports our skepticism. One study found that nearly 40 percent of those who claimed benefits early came to regret their decisions.[5]

Can we overcome this bias? Yes, but doing so may require us to delve into a deeper, darker explanation of how we make decisions.

Psychologists might loosely call it economic multiple personality disorder, best dealt with if understood. Here's the argument.

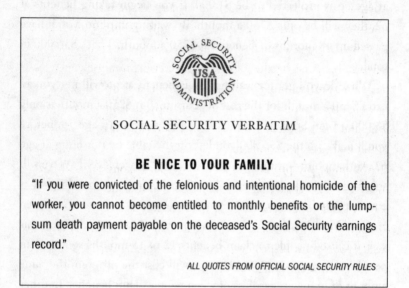

SOCIAL SECURITY VERBATIM

BE NICE TO YOUR FAMILY

"If you were convicted of the felonious and intentional homicide of the worker, you cannot become entitled to monthly benefits or the lump-sum death payment payable on the deceased's Social Security earnings record."

ALL QUOTES FROM OFFICIAL SOCIAL SECURITY RULES

HOW MANY PEOPLE ARE YOU, ANYWAY?

We tend to think of ourselves as being one person—one unitary self. But Hamlet was of two minds. The eighteenth-century Scottish philosopher David Hume wrote: "I cannot compare the soul more properly to anything than to a republic or commonwealth, in which the several members are united by the reciprocal ties of government and subordination." The nineteenth-century poet Walt Whitman famously noted: "I contain multitudes." The twentieth-century psychologist Paul Bloom wrote an article for the *Atlantic* titled "First Person Plural."

It's by now a commonplace in psychology: multiple selves contend over one body and its consciousness. Think of your last sudden bout of "road rage." Who *is* that person controlling your behavior in such an outlandish way? Recall New Year's resolutions routinely broken by Groundhog Day. Or, more dramatically, picture the alcoholic whose long-term morning self takes a dose of the medication Antabuse so that he or she will vomit when the impulsive "alcoholic" self takes over and tries to knock down a stiff one in the afternoon.

What is the relevance of multiple selves to the timing of Social Security benefits? It's the difficulty of exercising impulse control—of delaying gratification. The classic example is a Stanford experiment in which psychologists put one marshmallow in front of young children and offered them a choice: they could eat it now or wait a few minutes and get a second one.

You know the problem as well as we do. If your self of the moment can't be coaxed to care enough about your future self (or selves), "you" will overindulge in the here and now.

And so it is with Social Security. Your multiple selves duke it out inside your brain to protect their own living standards, using their own very different time horizons.

BE THE BEST SELF YOU CAN BE

But let's be clear: this book is written for only one of your selves—the reflective, rational long-term thinker, the one who would actually incur the pain of reading a book about Social Security, the one who realizes the organism it inhabits could conceivably live to age 100 or beyond. This "adult" self is located in the youngest part of the brain—the prefrontal cortex, which evolved after the parts we share with reptiles. Our reptilian self rules our reflex emotions while the prefrontal "you" tries not to drive while tipsy, or to smoke, or to hang glide. And, unless the organism formerly known as you is in dire need or facing imminent and sure demise, it doesn't automatically take Social Security retirement benefits early. Because to do so would be to ignore that self's fiduciary responsibility to, well, all your future selves.

Admittedly, there's a philosophical problem here. You might say: "Why should I care about any of my future selves? What have they ever done for *me*?" If that's your attitude, this chapter has little to offer.

But, in moments of reflective repose, as you presumably are in at this very moment, you might feel as protective of your doddering, possibly drooling, almost surely weak-kneed and ever-feebler future self or selves as the authors of this book feel protective of *theirs*. If this is the case, you will not want to let him, her, or "them" suffer the fate of outliving "your" savings.

Such discussion inevitably leads to a next question: how long might the bunch of yous live? Social Security has its own actuaries to estimate such probabilities and posts an Actuarial Life Table. Here's a summary:

	MEN		WOMEN	
Age	Death Odds*	Years Left	Death Odds*	Years Left
40	0.22%	38.23	0.13%	42.24
50	0.53%	29.35	0.33%	33.02
60	1.10%	21.27	0.67%	24.3
70	2.45%	14.03	1.84%	16.33
80	6.16%	8.1	4.39%	9.65
90	16.84%	4.02	13.11%	4.85
100	35.38%	2.12	29.95%	2.49

* Probability of dying within one year.

We reproduce, in the notes, an expanded table.[6] If you consult it, you will see that a 60-year-old woman faces odds of only two-thirds of a percent that she will die in the next 12 months. On average, she has another 24.3 years to live, or until she is older than 84. Remember that these are averages, so by definition many people will live longer and some of them much longer. For a 65-year-old couple, the odds are 50 percent that at least one spouse will live to 94 and 25 percent that he or she will live to the age of 98![7] And who can forget Jeanne Calment, the Frenchwoman who lived to a documented age of 122? (Some say it was the red wine.) The Census Bureau predicts we could have more than four million centenarians by midcentury.

And thus our bottom line: *don't count on dying on time!*

RED WINE AND OTHER PREMATURE BURIAL ANTIDOTES

Note that if you believe these 2009 Social Security projections, your "break-even" for waiting to collect until 70, even if you're thinking only of the benefits for yourself, is somewhere in the low 80s. (And no, you don't have to factor in inflation, since all Social Security benefits are adjusted for the cost of living.) To make the point in simple arithmetic, if you were to start drawing your "full" retirement benefit of, say, $20,000 a year at age 66, you'd have taken a cumulative sum of $80,000 by age 70. But your "maximum" benefit, earned by waiting until 70, figures to be about $26,000 a year. (It might be even higher if you keep working at age 66 and raise your Social Security earnings base.) So at a minimum, you'd be getting an extra $6,000 a year. But even at "only" $6,000 a year extra, you can see that in barely 13 years, you'd have earned back the $80,000 you passed up in years 66–70.

"But wait," you might be thinking, "I would be earning money on that $80,000 if I socked it away. That's worth something, isn't it? Shouldn't I be calculating the break-even point based on a reasonable expectation of returns I can get on that money if I invested it?"

Yes, we agree that what you can earn in the market matters. But break-even analysis, whether or not you incorporate that issue, remains the wrong way to think about this decision.

And yet, unfortunately, we've come across many, indeed, far too many people who are absolutely convinced that the break-even period is relevant for thinking about when to take Social Security benefits. Many software programs, including "leading" commercial ones (but not Larry's, he is quick to note), display break-even analysis. And as recently as 2008, the Social Security Administration told its public claims representatives to use a break-even framework to help potential retirees decide when to begin taking benefits, as we mentioned earlier.[8]

WHY BREAKING EVEN IS BREAKING BAD

Associated with the focus on break-even is the notion that "I can take my Social Security benefits early and invest them in stocks and make more money than I'll get from Social Security." And a related proposition is that we should run Monte Carlo computer simulations to see the chances of doing better on the stock market by taking our benefits now.

Viewing Social Security as an investment rather than as an insurance policy encourages thinking about it in terms of break-even approaches. Our advice: *Don't do it!*

If you insist on evaluating an insurance policy as an investment, based on break-even analysis, consider your house. Think about whether it makes sense to buy homeowner's insurance on a break-even basis. How? Compare the money it costs you in premiums to buy the insurance with the cost if your house burns down, multiplied by the vanishingly small chance that it will. If this so-called expected value of the policy is less than the premium, the insurance "investment" fails the break-even test.

Now, we guarantee that the expected payoff from "investing" in your homeowner's policy is less than the premium the insurance company charges you, meaning that you can't break even buying homeowner's insurance. The reason is that the insurance companies charge "loads" to cover administrative and other underwriting costs. Thanks to these loads, the total payoffs from homeowner's insurance, life insurance, car insurance, health insurance, etc., are always less than the premiums charged. Therefore, if you focus solely on the break-even, you should never buy any insurance at all.

But that would be crazy. You don't analyze standard insurance this way because you are focusing, properly so, on the worst-case scenario—your house burns down, your car is totaled, you get cancer.

Very few of us can afford to play the odds of catastrophe. And you're in no better position when it comes to Social Security longevity insurance.

In the longevity sphere, the worst-case scenario is, to reiterate, living too long—living to your maximum possible age of life, and, as a result, outliving your savings and income. Social Security provides insurance against this worst-case scenario. This insurance is safe against inflation and against default. It's also dirt cheap. There is no close substitute for it in the market.

OUR EARNEST EFFORT TO HELP YOU
KEEP MORE OF WHAT'S YOURS

Now, after this plea, if you're still stubbornly tempted to take Social Security benefits at age 62 and invest them on your own, please consider that you're not liable to beat its rate of return anyway.

Let's assume you're the average investor since, on average, those of you reading this probably *are*. Well, over the 20 years from 1991 to 2011, the average American investor actually *lost money*, after accounting for all costs and inflation. The reason would seem to be following the crowd—buying when stocks and bonds are flying high, and selling when they tank and sink to new lows. This, of course, is exactly the opposite of investing's Golden Rule: Buy low, sell high. But on average, we cannot be trusted to do so.

The average American's rate of annual loss over this period was –0.4 percent, however, so based on this, you shouldn't *subtract* anything from that $80,000 you'd have been paid by Social Security for waiting four years. But unless you're sure you can beat the average investor, which probably means you're illegally trading on insider information, you shouldn't *add* anything, either.

Still tempted? Then let us remind you of the discoveries of behavioral economics over the past several decades, which help explain the fact: individual investors, on average, *lose money*, after you adjust returns for inflation.

The main message of behavioral economics, which is really a branch of psychology: Human beings consistently overestimate their own powers. This bias even has a name: "illusory superiority" or, on public radio, "the Lake Wobegon effect," after Garrison Keillor's famous description of the imaginary Minnesota town where "all the women are strong, all the men are good-looking, and *all the children are above average.*" Documented examples abound.

In a survey of faculty at the University of Nebraska, two-thirds rated themselves in the top 25 percent for teaching ability. Nearly 90 percent of MBA students at Stanford University rated their academic performance in the top half of the class.

Nor is this a new phenomenon. Back in 1976, 70 percent of students taking the annual SATs thought they were in the top half of their peers with respect to leadership ability. Getting along with others? A full 85 percent put themselves above the median, and—we love this—25 percent rated themselves in the top 1 percent.

And while "illusory superiority" is a worldwide phenomenon, it's especially acute for those of you contemplating the investment of Social Security money—Americans, that is. A famous survey of drivers half a century ago found that 69 percent of Swedes considered themselves above average in driving skill. Americans? *Ninety-three* percent! Safe driving? Seventy-seven percent of the Swedes called themselves above average; 88 percent of the Americans did.

Twenty-five years later, American self-delusion had hardly budged. Asked to rate themselves by eight different measures, including skill and safety, only one driver in five thought himself or herself *below* average.

Applied to the world of investing, the widespread recognition of the consequences of illusory superiority can be expressed in only two words: mutual funds! Mutual fund investment managers—and these are the highly paid "experts" of investing, remember—regularly fall short of where they think they will end up. The results of their actively managed investment funds routinely fail to match even market averages. As a result, low-cost index funds sprang up to purchase large numbers of securities whose performance will match market averages. They do not actively manage their holdings and have no illusions about their superiority. But they have become the dominant standard for retirement plan holdings. If so many of the experts have thrown in the towel on coming out ahead, why should anyone expect Social Security recipients to fare better?

DON'T OVERESTIMATE YOUR ABILITY TO MAKE FINANCIALLY SAVVY DECISIONS

This evidence on overoptimism may come as no surprise, but it should give all of us pause. To repeat, Social Security's Delayed Retirement Credit adds 8 percent a year to lifetime benefits between the ages of 66 and 70—*after inflation*, though with no compounding. Even if you love taking risks and therefore ignore our point about insurance, you should protect yourself against self-delusion.

Finally, speaking of risk, we are obliged to report that as your brain ages, the decision-making part—the prefrontal cortex, home to the previously rational self—starts to deteriorate, at age 50 or so. Not quickly, we gratefully add, but inexorably. Here's an excerpt from an interview Paul did with brain researcher Dr. Jordan Grafman at the National Institutes of Health some years ago: "I think the way people have to make decisions when they get older is to be much more cautious about new ventures. And that's where they might need to work with other people, to collaborate, to take the advice of other family members or advisors."

Therefore, said Grafman, when it comes to investing, we should all do so more conservatively as we age, "because since the prefrontal cortex is probably not functioning as effectively as it did when you were younger, you're going to be more prone to impulsive decision making." That, of course, is precisely what Social Security protects us from.

So look again at the longevity table in the notes at the end of the book and observe that if you made it to age 66 as a man in 2009, your life expectancy was about 83; as a woman, more like 86. But think about this: these are *averages*—many will die before these ages and the rest later. So the critical question is: Can you afford to take the chance that you'll be among those who outlive your actuarial life expectancy? Or would you rather take out old-age insurance against that eventuality, which is just what waiting until 70 to take higher Social Security *is*: extra old-age insurance. Moreover, these averages have risen every year since 2009, especially among more educated and affluent groups.

ARE WE NEAR A TIPPING POINT FOR LONGEVITY?

Consider the longevity forecast of Ray Kurzweil, the fabled techno-whiz who at age 28 invented the first machine that could speak what it read, vastly enhancing the lives of blind Americans like Stevie

Wonder who could afford it and eventually benefiting us all. As a 60-something adult, Kurzweil now takes 150 pills a day, and has written, among other books, *The 10% Solution for a Healthy Life*, *Fantastic Voyage: Live Long Enough to Live Forever*, and *Transcend: Nine Steps to Living Well Forever*.

His goal, he told Paul during an interview, "is to get to a point in the future where the progress is so rapid that we're adding more time to life—your remaining life expectancy—than is going by. That will be a point where the sands of time are running in rather than running out—a tipping point. And that's only 15 years away by my calculations."

WE PLAN TO BE HERE AT 100

Speaking for our own frontal lobes, we three authors are planning to live to at least 100. Larry's conservative ESPlanner and Maximize My Social Security financial software defaults to age 100 for planning purposes. And when another of us—Paul—used the ESPlanner software to determine the adequacy of his and his wife's accumulated savings, he plugged in 110, just to be safe. As for Phil, his trim physique speaks volumes, and he also swears that after an hour on the elliptical, he knows exactly what being 100 feels like.

We're not suggesting you plan on living forever or even to 110. But waiting for your maximum benefit at 70 instead of grabbing your earliest available benefit at 62 will be worth 76 percent more in benefits every year right through eternity if you and Uncle Sam make it that far, due to the 7 to 8 percent a year Social Security pays you to wait.

Say you're the typical Social Security recipient who would take the average yearly benefit of $15,936 for Americans in 2015, according to the Social Security Administration website. That amount would account for about 40 percent of your pre-retirement income.

Waiting until 70 would then be worth about $5,000 a year after break-even at age 83. That adds another 13 percent to your pre-retirement income. Every year. For life. So now imagine you live until 90. That's an extra $35,000 in constant (inflation-adjusted) dollars ($5,000 a year × 7 years). Live till 100 and it's $85,000 in present dollars. Live till 110: $135,000. Jeanne Calment (122): $195,000.

And if, instead of the *average* benefit, we consider the *maximum*, we're talking about a difference of $10,142 a year, in which case *double* all the totals in the previous paragraph.

We have embraced a model of human behavior based upon a competition among various internal "selves." So our advice is to enfranchise one of them—the adult within, the long-term planner, the *life preserver* self. Keep reminding yourself: you are the guardian of your future self.

ONE OF OUR READERS IS SUCKERED INTO (ALMOST) TAKING EARLY

Here's how one of Larry's readers, "Steve," expressed the allure of early benefits in an email to the *PBS NewsHour* Making Sen$e column. First, he acknowledged that "the advice from every financial planner is not to take Social Security benefits early but to wait at least until full retirement, and even longer, because your benefits will be reduced.

"Yet here's what Social Security says," wrote Steve:

> As a general rule, early or late retirement will give you about the same total Social Security benefits over your lifetime. If you retire early, the monthly benefit amounts will be smaller to take into account the longer period you will receive them. If you retire late, you will get benefits for a shorter period of time but the monthly amounts will be larger to make up for the months when you did not receive anything.[9]

"So," asked Steve, "if I'm worried about the government being able to make full Social Security payments down the road . . . [w]ouldn't it be better to get as much in the bank now rather than rely on promises of future payment from a clearly broke federal government? And if it's the same total benefits over my lifetime, how am I penalized financially for taking it early?"

Well, let's take the Social Security statement first. As it happens, some experts dispute that the system as a whole is neutral with respect to claiming dates. A 2012 study by economists John Shoven and Sita Nataraj Slavov found the system was not actuarially fair or balanced but tilted in favor of people who delayed taking benefits.[10]

But more important is the fact that Social Security would post such a statement, even if the system *were* neutral. Here's Larry's intemperate but, his coauthors feel, entirely legitimate response to the Social Security statement, written as a letter to the acting commissioner of the Social Security Administration:

> If you were in my class and you wrote, "As a general rule, early or late retirement will give you about the same total Social Security benefits over your lifetime," I would, quite frankly, flunk you. Let me explain. You are running an insurance company. Insurance company executives do not generally say on their websites that, "As a general rule it doesn't matter whether or not you should buy insurance." But this is precisely what your statement implies. First, there is no general or average rule that applies to retirees taking Social Security. Any given retiree is only going to die once. A "general" rule suggests that what happens on average, as in across a large group of retirees, matters to a given retiree. It doesn't. Any given retiree can't play the averages. By analogy, as a general rule your house won't burn down. But if you were running a property insurance company, you would know enough to fire anyone who posted on your website that, as a general rule

your house won't burn down, so don't buy home owners coverage.

To repeat, Social Security is just like a public insurance firm. [*We remind you that this was Larry publicly addressing the acting SSA commissioner online.*] Like any insurance firm, you can play the odds and count on the averages. But your clients can't. That's what insurance is for. They will die exactly once. It could be as late as age 100. Or 122. So they need longevity insurance. You are in the business of selling longevity insurance. When someone waits to take dramatically higher retirement benefits starting at 70, they are giving up eight years of reduced benefits (since they could start their retirement benefits at age 62). These eight years of benefits not taken represent the premium they are paying you for the increase in benefits past age 70 that you will pay them.

Larry then addressed the writer, Steve, telling him to ignore the statement by Social Security and approach his longevity risk as he would any other kind of risk that needs to be insured against.

As for Steve's fear that his retirement benefits will be cut, he indicated that he was 57, which means he was born in 1958. That makes him a baby boomer—an American born between 1945 and 1964. How likely is it that, in the current political environment, a president and Congress will cut back on his Social Security? Ever see the video of the late and powerful Chicago congressman Dan Rostenkowski besieged by seniors when he dared suggest that they be denied certain benefits? As the *New York Times* described it, he "was booed and followed down the street by a group of screaming elderly people Thursday as he left a meeting with community leaders opposed to his stance on a program intended to protect the elderly from the high costs of extended illnesses. Several dozen people shouted 'Liar!' 'Impeach!' and 'Recall!' when Mr. Rostenkowski, the Democrat who heads the House Ways and Means Committee, left a community center in the North Side district of Chicago that he has represented for 30 years. The group briefly blocked his car, hitting it with picket signs and pounding on the windows." And that was back in 1989. Imagine the incivility that might greet an anti–Social Security politician these days.

Finally, what about Steve's thought that he might be better off investing the money? We've done almost all we can to shoot down that argument earlier in the chapter, but let us add one timely reminder. As we write this edition, putting early Social Security benefits in the bank will yield a zero or negative or very low rate of return. Investing the money in the stock market will produce a much higher expected rate of return, of course: an annualized return of just under 7 percent a year above inflation since 1871.[11] But the return comes with huge risk. The stock market has had runs of *negative* returns that lasted more than a decade. What happens if you need the money and the market has just crashed by 90 percent, as it did from 1929 to 1933? Or by more than 50 percent, as it did from 2007 to 2009?

By contrast, Social Security's return—the benefit increase that comes from waiting—is substantial and, critically important, it's risk-free. Let us end this chapter then by repeating our favorite harangue. By being patient and taking your Social Security retirement benefit at age 70, you get guaranteed benefits that are 76 percent higher than those at age 62. (This deal's not quite as good for those born after 1954.) Plus, if you are married or divorced after having been married 10 or more years, the higher benefit will likely be passed to your spouse or ex-spouse if you predecease them. It is one of Uncle Sam's all-time best deals. We urge almost all of you to take it.

Okay, but who, precisely, *shouldn't* wait to collect their retirement benefit at 70 if they want to maximize their lifetime benefits?

Keep reading for the answer.

SOCIAL SECURITY—
FROM A TO ZZZZZZZZ

Getting yours—*all* of what's yours—requires understanding not just general facts but also a slew of specific details about Social Security and its benefits. To do this we will need to suspend what Phil calls the "just-tell-me-what-to-do" syndrome, which he encounters again and again when he gives public speeches about Social Security. Yes, we live in a busy and complex world, we're pressed for time, and we may have become so used to getting communications in short bursts that even Twitter's 140 characters seem gabby.

Unfortunately, with Social Security, the initial answer to nearly every significant benefit question is, "It depends." Later chapters will provide details about various claiming decisions, given your own particular circumstances. But first, we're going to describe the basics, as well as provide some essential details. We are aware that Social Security's basic rules are less engrossing than, say, J. K. Rowling or E. L. James (though one reviewer called the first version of this book "the new *Over-50 Shades of Grey*"). But the rewards are likely to be more enduring. And for memory-challenged recidivists, there is a Glossary with key terms at the back of the book. For those already in the know, jumping ahead to Chapter 4 to learn about the major 2015 changes to Social Security law will not get you expelled from our book.

SOCIAL SECURITY HAS LOTS
OF DIFFERENT BENEFITS

Here is a list of different benefits, one or more of which almost surely apply to *you*:

- retirement benefits;
- spousal benefits (how Paul's and Phil's wives got theirs in Chapter 1);
- spousal benefits for those caring for an eligible child or children;
- child benefits for minor kids of retirees;
- child benefits for disabled children of retirees, regardless of the child's age;
- divorced spousal benefits.

We're not done. There are also a set of survivor benefits, including widow(er) benefits for surviving spouses, child survivor benefits, divorced widow(er) benefits, mother and father benefits for surviving parents caring for young or disabled children, and parent benefits for parents of deceased workers who were financially dependent on the deceased worker. Finally, there are disability benefits.

YOUR WORK RECORD CAN GENERATE
BENEFITS FOR BOTH YOU AND OTHERS

The first thing you need to know is how to qualify for your own Social Security benefit. The answer is simple: to be eligible for benefits on your own work record, you need to acquire 40 quarters of coverage. One way to do this is to work in covered employment for 10 years. Those quarters don't have to be consecutive. You can work, trek Nepal for 15 months (or 15 years, for that matter), return home, and start racking up more quarters. But they have to be in "covered" employment—jobs where Social Security payroll taxes, aka "FICA contributions," are deducted.

An interesting secret is that the 40 quarters don't have to be 40 periods of covered employment of 3 months each. (This wasn't the case before 1978, when the system considered what you earned every 3 months, rather than simply what you earned in a given year.) Indeed, the phrase "quarter of coverage," like lots of Social Security's lingo, is misleading. Today to get a quarter of coverage you need to earn $1,260 on which you paid Social Security taxes. To get 4 quarters of coverage in a year—the most quarters of coverage you can get for working in a single year—you need to earn 4 times $1,260 or $5,040 during the year. *But you can do so all within a single 3-month period* (a quarter in regular-speak) *if you earn $5,040 in that quarter.*

What if you get paid $5,040 for working for just one hour and then hit the beach for the rest of the year? That, too, will suffice to get you 4 quarters of coverage for the year. Oh, and by the way, the $1,260 figure rises each year with growth in economy-wide average wages.

This point is a very big deal for people approaching retirement age who are shy of the 40 quarters they need to qualify for a retirement benefit, but who can't work a full year. The other key point is how little you need to make to accumulate 4 quarters—just $5,040 in a calendar year.

Once *you* qualify for benefits, your current spouse, your ex-spouse(s), your young children, and your disabled children may qualify to receive benefits based on your aforementioned work record. Moreover, when you die, your work record can continue to provide benefits—known as *survivor* benefits—to your loved ones, or even not-so-loved ones, including dependent parents. Stated differently, if you've earned your 40 quarters, so has your corpse.

There's a flip side to this coin. You *yourself* may be able to receive spousal benefits, divorced spousal benefits, survivor benefits, divorced survivor benefits, child benefits, child survivor benefits, or parent benefits based on the work records of *your* current or former spouses, be they dead or alive, your children, be they dead, or your parent, be they dead or alive.

Clearly, then, a lot is riding on your covered earnings record. If you don't know it, you can and should get it from Your Social Security Statement. Go to this Web address—http://socialsecurity.gov/myaccount/—which the agency calls "my Social Security." You will need your Social Security number and must have a valid email address, a U.S. mailing address, and be at least 18 years old. You'll also need to enter personal information that only you know, so when you use your online account, Social Security will ask you some security questions that only you can answer. The agency is sensitive to hacking and other security concerns, so you may need to spend some time figuring out what's called a "strong"—in encryption terms—password. You also can sign up for an additional level of account security, but it will take extra time and also involve text messages to your cell phone.

There are also a number of earnings records you should have a right to see, but that you aren't able to easily access or access at all. If you're already collecting a retirement benefit, you can't pull up your own earnings record online. Yes, that seems very strange. However, you should be able to get Social Security to mail you your earnings record if you call them or get them to print it out at their local office. *Just don't forget the thermos. You could have a long wait.*

What about the earnings records of your spouse, or your ex-spouse, or your dead spouse, or your dead ex-spouse, or your dead parent, or your dead child? Obtaining those records, even though they can help you determine what benefits you're now owed or may be owed in the future, isn't possible for you, for privacy reasons. You can, however, get estimates from Social Security about the actual or potential size of these benefits once you have proven your connection to the worker in question. Thus a widow will need to provide marriage and death certificates.

Once you've set up your account, either download or print out the current copy of Your Social Security Statement. It features Social Security's year-by-year record of the wage earnings on which you (and your employers) have paid Social Security payroll taxes. Not only will you then know your contribution record but you'll also get an estimate of the Social Security benefits to which you're entitled. (Unfortunately, as discussed in Chapter 6, these estimates can be very badly biased.) If there are mistakes in your earnings record, which can happen for a host of reasons, you should take steps to correct them.[1]

A WORD ABOUT SOCIAL SECURITY LINGO

Social Security uses elaborate and, we think, often confusing terms to describe its benefits and how they're calculated. Still, this language may be crucial to getting your best mix of benefits. For example, you might not think there is much practical difference between the words "eligible" and "entitled." Hah! No soup for you! The agency uses "eligible" to mean that you are qualified due to age or other circumstances to file for and collect benefits. "Entitled" means you have actually done so and are collecting benefits or have suspended your retirement benefit. It is easy to confuse these meanings but if you do, that could cost you.

We are going to adopt the agency's terms for this book, not because we like them but because their plain-language equivalents are often foreign to agency representatives. Arming you with indispensable rules of thumb won't do you much good if Social Security doesn't know what you're talking about and immediately dispenses with them (and you). So we will be providing a commonsense grounding of the system, but in *Social Securitese* as well as English.

AIME IS NEVER HAVING TO
SAY YOU'RE SORRY

The first of these terms is your AIME. It stands not for "love" in French, but for your Average Indexed Monthly Earnings. (Social Security's penchant for capital letters can be especially governmental and mind-numbing.) Average Indexed Monthly Earnings may be a mouthful, but all it really means is your "earnings base" (sometimes just called "base")—your covered wages and self-employment income subject to Social Security FICA taxation—the ones itemized on Your Social Security Statement.

You may not realize it—and if you earn the average U.S. wage income of something a bit north of $45,000 a year, why would you?—but the Social Security or FICA or "payroll" tax of 12.4 percent (combined for you and your employer) applies to wage plus self-employment income only up to a certain limit, sometimes called the "tax max" by Social Security. For example, the 2016 maximum or ceiling on Social Security's taxable earnings was set at $118,500. Social Security looks at your covered earnings each year, forms a special average of these earnings—that's your earnings base or AIME—and plugs this base into a formula to figure out your full retirement benefit.

How exactly is the AIME calculated? Social Security takes each of your past years' covered earnings, up through age 60, and adjusts them—"indexes" them—to reflect the rise in average wages each year—from the year you earned them to the year you turn 60. Indexing keeps average benefits more closely aligned with average real-wage levels and avoids harming people who earned more money earlier in their careers.

So, for example, say you made $20,000 in 1981, when you were only 25 years old. This year, at age 60, you expect to make $80,000. That's four times as much in unadjusted terms, but wages have gone up a lot during the past 35 years. Indexing evens out the value of wages you earned earlier in life so that they are credited with their fair share of the lifetime earnings on which your Social Security benefits are based.

Indexing, in this case, will blow up the $20,000 by 3.5 times to $70,000 before these and other indexed years of earnings—as well as covered earnings after age 60, for which there is no indexation—are ranked to find the largest 35. The 35 are then averaged and divided by 12 to determine Average Indexed Monthly Earnings. Without this indexing, people who earned more when young would be penalized relative to those who earned more when old. That's because those who earned more when old did so when wages in general were higher.

As we'll explain later, the fact that post-60 earnings are not indexed can be a big incentive to continuing to work past normal retirement age.

But what, you might ask, if you don't *have* 35 years of covered earnings? Suppose, for example, you have only 20 years of covered earnings? In this case, Social Security will say you have 15 years of zero earnings and include those zeros in its average. This means that working more years, up to 35, can make a huge difference. If, for example, you have just 10 years of covered earnings and add only one more, you'll raise your base by 10 percent and increase your lifetime Social Security benefits dramatically!

SOCIAL SECURITY VERBATIM

BE REALLY NICE TO YOUR KIDS

"If you are a minor convicted of intentionally causing your parent's death, you *may* [our emphasis] be denied survivor benefits on the earnings record of your parent."

ALL QUOTES FROM OFFICIAL SOCIAL SECURITY RULES

WE DARE YOU TO GUESS WHAT THESE LETTERS STAND FOR

The next acronym of note is your Primary Insurance Amount, or PIA. That's your basic benefit itself, based on your work record of covered earnings. The PIA is also equal to what's called your full retirement benefit, the retirement benefit you receive if you start collecting Social Security at what the law defines as your Full Retirement Age (FRA).

A few words here about the age of eligibility. While for Social Security it begins at age 62 or even earlier, depending on specific benefits and when you choose to take them, for almost all of you, FRA will be at least 66. For anyone born before 1938, FRA was 65. For those born between 1943 and 1954, which includes much of the baby boom, it's 66. And for people born in 1955 and later, FRA will start rising in 2021 by two months every year until it reaches 67 for anyone born in 1960 or later. Here's the full table, as it appears on the Social Security website.

FULL RETIREMENT AGE

Year of Birth	Age
1937 and earlier	65
1938	65 and 2 months
1939	65 and 4 months
1940	65 and 6 months
1941	65 and 8 months
1942	65 and 10 months
1943–54	66
1955	66 and 2 months
1956	66 and 4 months
1957	66 and 6 months
1958	66 and 8 months
1959	66 and 10 months
1960 and later	67

Source: Social Security Administration.

THE PIA BENEFIT FORMULA
IS HIGHLY PROGRESSIVE

The formula that determines your full retirement benefit, or PIA, based on your lifetime earnings base, or AIME, is progressive. This means it gives lower-wage workers—those with low earnings bases—a disproportionately better deal. In 2016, for example, the full retirement benefit formula is 90 percent of the first $856 of your monthly earnings base, plus a much lower 32 percent of the base above $856 through $5,157, plus a mere 15 percent of the earnings base over $5,157. These different percentages are applied at what the agency calls "bend points," which are adjusted each year based on the growth in economy-wide average earnings.

Bend points are complicated enough in their own right, but here's another wrinkle that nearly no one knows but which will affect the calculation of your benefits. If you begin taking Social Security this year, for example, you might think your benefits will be calculated using the 2016 bend points. How silly of you! Nope, the bend points used to calculate your retirement benefits and, generally speaking, auxiliary benefits available to others based on your work record, are those in effect during the year you turned 62. This is the case regardless of when you take your retirement benefit and when auxiliary benefits are first collected. For example, if you begin claiming benefits in 2016 when you turn 66, your benefits will be calculated using the 2012 bend points. Social Security does, however, adjust your benefit level for the amount of inflation between age 62 and the year you or your auxiliary beneficiaries are collecting.

If you're like most people, your eyes may have started to cross. But if you're not sure you believe that the Social Security benefit formula is progressive, here's an example. Say you turned 62 in 2016 and begin taking your full retirement benefit at age 66. If your AIME is $3,000, you will collect, apart from any future inflation adjustments, 90 percent of $856 plus 32 percent of $2,144 ($3,000 less $856), or a monthly full retirement benefit of $1,456.

Now imagine you have two brothers, also 66, named Billy and Whitey. Billy worked as a plumber and made more than you. In fact, his AIME is twice as big—$6,000. His full retirement benefit (we'll spare you the math) is $2,273. And Whitey, who sold liar loans most of his career, has an AIME that's three times larger than yours—$9,000—and a full retirement benefit of $2,723. So even though Billy's AIME is twice yours, his full retirement benefit is only 56 percent (not 100 percent) larger. And even though Whitey's AIME is three times yours, his full retirement benefit is only 87 percent, not 200 percent, larger.

To make things even more complicated, adding a touch of what one might call gallows math, Social Security calculates your PIA differently if you happen to have died before age 62. Indeed, if you leave behind a surviving spouse or ex-spouse, it will make two different calculations and give your survivor the higher of the two resulting death-related PIAs. The two calculations are intended to respond to the fact that if you *are* dead, you've potentially had a shorter covered earnings history, which could make the standard full benefit measure uncomfortably and perhaps unfairly low for dependents, past or present.

Given that you're dead, you won't, presumably, care much about this. You also probably didn't buy this book. But members of your family and even ex-family may care, especially if it means they'll collect more survivor benefits.

A GREAT BENEFIT OF SOCIAL SECURITY BENEFITS: THEY'RE INFLATION-PROOF (PRETTY MUCH)

Starting January 1 of each year, Social Security raises all the benefits it's paying out by the rate of inflation that occurred between the prior two Octobers, as measured by a widely used version of the Consumer Price Index. There have been proposals to use a different price index to set this annual Cost of Living Adjustment, or COLA, which would lower the COLA adjustment by a modest amount each year. There was a huge hue and cry, however, because even small changes in the COLA will have a meaningful impact on retiree benefits over time. And as virtually all Social Security recipients know, there was no COLA at all for 2016, despite overwhelming real-world evidence that the prices of drugs and other things seniors buy actually rose that year and, in some cases, by sizable amounts.

Still, neither the lack of a COLA nor possible adoption of another index on which to base future COLAs changes the fact that Social Security does a good job of maintaining the real buying power of the dollars it pays out. And this is a big, big deal.

SOCIAL SECURITY'S FULL RETIREMENT BENEFIT FORMULA IS INDEXED TO ECONOMY-WIDE WAGE GROWTH

To further ensure that Social Security benefits grow through time in proportion to workers' wages, Social Security annually raises the dollar amount of those bend points in its PIA formula—the $856 and $5,157 amounts mentioned earlier—by each year's growth in economy-wide average wages.

Incidentally, since the system also indexes Social Security's taxable earnings ceiling to growth in economy-wide average wages, as wages have become more unequally distributed across the workforce in recent years, a larger share of total wages has moved above the ceiling—from 10 percent in 1983, according to Social Security, to 19 percent today.

This is putting even more pressure on Social Security's long-term finances, which we'll discuss in Chapter 17. But this book is about getting what's yours, not fixing the system or bemoaning its fate. And so we press on.

EARLY BENEFIT REDUCTIONS

If you take retirement, spousal, or survivor benefits early (before Full Retirement Age), they will be subject to an Early Retirement Reduction for every month you do so. The reduction is hefty. For example, taking your own retirement benefit at 62 rather than at FRA currently entails a 25 percent lower monthly payment. Taking your *spousal* benefit at 62 entails a 30 percent reduction. And taking your *survivor* benefit at 60, instead of waiting until FRA, currently means a 28.5 percent reduction. Disabled widows can collect as early as age 50 with the same 28.5 percent reduction, though this reduction goes away at FRA for workers who become disabled before becoming widowed.

For those born after 1960, which includes all our kids, the hits for taking their own retirement benefits or spousal benefits at age 62 are larger: 30 percent and 35 percent, respectively. This is because the FRA for these folks will be 67, not today's 66. That adds another 12 months of benefit reduction to the hits, because the early benefits age will remain 62. In the case of survivor benefits, things are different. The hit is fixed through time. The monthly reduction factor is adjusted over time to ensure that it never exceeds 28.5 percent.

DELAYED RETIREMENT CREDITS

Through its Delayed Retirement Credit (DRC), Social Security raises your personal retirement benefit for *each month* you wait to claim beyond Full Retirement Age (FRA) and the raises continue right through to age 70. Remember, the FRA is 66 for those born between 1943 and 1954. The DRC is 8 percent a year, or 0.67 percent a month, until you turn 70.

To put both rules in round numbers, if you were due a monthly $1,000 retirement benefit at age 66, it would be reduced 25 percent to $750 if you claimed benefits at age 62. It would rise 32 percent (four times the 8 percent annual increase) to $1,320 if you deferred benefits until age 70. The difference between $750 and $1,320? A whopping 76 percent!

To put it in monetary terms and plugging in pretend numbers just to make the point, suppose you are now 62 and are eligible for a reduced early retirement benefit of $20,000 a year starting immediately. If you wait until 70 to start collecting, you'll get an extra $15,200 a year—just for being patient and thinking long-term. The new patience-earned benefit will be $26,667 a year starting at age 66; $35,200 starting at age 70. You might think about it this way: if you manage to live to 100, God willing, that would be $15,200 a year more after age 70 than had you started at age 62—an extra $456,000 in today's dollars (since the benefits will be inflation adjusted) for waiting past 62, in return for giving up eight years' worth of benefits at $20,000 a year: $160,000 in total.

Of course, just adding up annual benefits doesn't take account of the fact that a dollar received in the future is not as valuable as having that dollar today. But we're just trying here to give you a general sense of the payoff from waiting to collect.[2]

In 2014, the last year for which data are available, an astounding (to us) 35 percent of men and 40 percent of women filed for Social Security benefits at age 62; *another* 22 percent of men and 24 percent of women filed before reaching their FRA of 66. And to our near disbelief, only 2 percent of men and 3.3 percent of women waited until age 70 to file. That is, almost *none* of your and our fellow Americans. Even so, these numbers reflect a steady trend toward later claiming ages—a welcome event.

And, to gild this lily a bit more, waiting, as we've already pointed out, also can mean larger widow(er) benefits for spouses and qualified ex-spouses (divorced after at least 10 years of marriage).

Increasing the FRA to 67 will also have an effect on DRCs— Delayed Retirement Credits. They will apply to a maximum of only three years, not the current four years. So, the maximum value of the DRCs will be reduced to 24 percent from 32 percent.

WITHDRAWING YOUR RETIREMENT BENEFIT

Your timing of retirement benefits is crucial—both for the size of your own payments and of those you might collect on the earnings record of a current or ex-spouse, dead or alive. It also may affect benefits others can collect based on your work record. Because of its importance in everything that follows, keep in mind that Social

Security gives you a year from the time you file for a retirement benefit to say, "Yikes. I made a mistake. I want to pay back what I received so far and be treated as if I never applied for a retirement benefit." Unfortunately—and this is something most people don't know, or ignore at their peril—what you'll need to pay back includes any Medicare Part B premiums and tax withholdings that were deducted from your Social Security payments.

SUSPENDING YOUR RETIREMENT BENEFIT

When you *withdraw* your retirement benefit, as we've just outlined, you tell Social Security to treat you as never having filed for a retirement benefit. When you *suspend* your benefit, however, you tell Social Security to treat you as having filed for your retirement benefits, but to put them on hold until you restart them. You can suspend your retirement benefit only at or after you reach Full Retirement Age. You also can't be above age 70.

When you suspend your benefit, you start to accumulate DRCs, which, as noted, total 8 percent per year. These credits don't compound, so your age 70 benefit is 32 percent (4 years times 8 percent) larger at 70 than at 66, assuming your FRA is 66 and you suspend your benefit on your 66th birthday.

Suspending your benefit after April 2016, however, comes at a cost: you won't be able to provide spousal or child benefits while your benefit is in suspension. You also can't collect any benefits on anyone else's record. Importantly, qualified ex-spouses can still collect divorced spousal benefits whether or not you respond.

When disabled workers reach Full Retirement Age, their disability benefit turns into their full retirement benefit. They can suspend their retirement benefit, but they can't withdraw it.

IN DESPAIR BECAUSE YOU'VE
ALREADY LEFT MONEY ON THE
TABLE? ALL IS NOT LOST.

In the course of reading this book, you may well come across a benefit to which you were already entitled but have not applied for. Thanks to "retroactivity," you can apply today and usually receive up to 6 months' worth of that benefit *retroactively*, in the form of a lump sum. This retroactivity, however, applies only to what are known as "unreduced" benefits, which in this case are those you're entitled to starting at full retirement age.

So, if you applied for benefits at the age of 66 and 4 months, you would get a lump sum equal to only 4 months of benefits. Likewise, if you applied at the age of 66 and 8 months, the most you would receive is a lump sum for 6 months of benefits.

SOCIAL SECURITY VERBATIM

THE CASE OF THE MISSING CORPSE

"In a disappearance case where the body is not recovered, you must clearly prove the death of the missing person. Submit all available evidence, including: statements of persons having knowledge of the situation; letters or notes left by the missing person that have a bearing on the case."

ALL QUOTES FROM OFFICIAL SOCIAL SECURITY RULES

THE FULL MONTY ON YOUR
FULL RETIREMENT AGE

Later chapters will discuss further the significance of your FRA. The agency also calls this, on occasion, your *normal* retirement age. But for many of us contemplating the end of work, this age is neither full nor normal. Not anymore. By the time you reach 66, your life expectancy is about 84. Nearly a third of people aged 65 through 69 are still in the labor force, up from 26 percent in 2002 and 21 percent in 1992. More to our point, perhaps, 20 percent of Americans aged 70 to 74 are still in the labor force, too. We could go on, buffeting you with statistics. But for now, please just keep in mind that taking benefits before, at, or after your FRA can have an enormous impact on your lifetime benefits.

As we've said, taking benefits *before* Full Retirement Age reduces them, while waiting past this age (but not beyond your 70th birthday!) *increases* them.

Reaching FRA also spells the end of the Earnings Test, which we will discuss shortly. Social Security uses its Earnings Test to at least temporarily claw back benefits you take before FRA if you earn too much.

SPOUSAL BENEFITS

The full, or maximum possible spousal benefit equals one-half of your spouse's full retirement benefit. Stated differently, the spousal benefit equals half of what your spouse's retirement benefit would equal were they to take it at FRA. So whether your spouse takes their retirement benefit early or late doesn't directly impact the size of your spousal benefit, except for this big but: you can't collect your spousal benefit unless your spouse is collecting their own retirement benefit or suspended their own retirement benefit before the end of April 2016. Now for an even bigger but. You can't collect a spousal benefit by itself—what Paul did—unless you reached 62 before January 2, 2016. (More on this in Chapter 4.) If you are eligible to collect your spousal benefit (that is, you satisfy the big but) but weren't 62 in time, you'll be forced to take your retirement benefit at the same time as you take your spousal benefit. This is a key feature of a provision called deeming. We call it the deeming demon, since Social Security won't pay you both benefits. They'll pay you, roughly speaking, the greater of the two. This means you'll lose one of the two benefits.

To make matters even more crazy complex, if and when you collect a spousal benefit, Social Security will disguise the fact that it's wiped out all or virtually all of your retirement benefit by telling you that you are, in fact, receiving your retirement benefit plus an excess spousal benefit. Social Security uses this excess benefit language whenever you are taking or are forced to take your retirement benefit while also taking an auxiliary benefit, like a spousal or survivor benefit.

But the sum of your retirement benefit plus your excess benefit either exactly equals your auxiliary benefit or is very close. So don't be fooled. If you are receiving an auxiliary benefit, all those taxes you paid over your entire working life in order to raise your own retirement benefit are making little or no difference to what you are being paid each month. Hence, you may think you are collecting your retirement benefit when you basically aren't. Or you may think you are receiving your auxiliary benefit when you aren't because your excess benefit is zero. *This is one of the toughest things about dealing with Social Security—knowing what the payment you receive actually represents and what it doesn't represent.*

DIVORCED SPOUSAL BENEFITS

Divorced spousal benefits are calculated like spousal benefits, and are based on the full retirement benefit of the ex. To collect a divorced spousal benefit, you have to qualify. This means you have to have been married for 10 or more years and not be remarried. In addition, your ex either has to be at least 62 and you must have been divorced for two or more years, or your ex must have filed for their retirement or disability benefit.

And just like spousal benefits, divorced spousal benefits are reduced if you take them before FRA, but not increased if you take them after FRA. Finally, any divorced person not grandparented under the new law (not 62 before January 2, 2016) who takes their divorced spousal benefit will be deemed also to be filing for their retirement benefit. So a large divorced spousal benefit can disappear entirely if your own retirement benefit is larger.

Even if you were 62 on time, if you take your divorced spousal benefit early (before FRA), you'll get hit by deeming and be forced to take your retirement benefit early as well. In this case, your full divorced spousal benefit will be transformed into a reduced (because you took it early) excess divorced spousal benefit.

Yes, by now our heads are spinning, too, which is why the next chapter is devoted to explaining the new law.

EXCESS SPOUSAL BENEFITS

Your excess spousal benefit is the difference between 50 percent of your spouse's full retirement benefit (PIA, or Primary Insurance Amount) and 100 percent of your own full retirement benefit (PIA). If this difference is negative, the excess spousal benefit will be set to zero. And, thanks to the progressivity of the PIA benefit formula, this difference will often be negative if both spouses have decent-sized earnings.

In other words, it's not hard for 100 percent of your PIA to exceed half of your spouse's even if they're earning a lot more than you.

If your excess spousal benefit is positive, it too will be reduced if you take it early. Also, here's a little-known secret: when you suspend your retirement benefit and then restart it, the formula for your excess spousal benefit changes. It becomes 50 percent of your spouse's full retirement benefit minus 100 percent of your own full retirement benefit, augmented by any Delayed Retirement Credits you received during the period your retirement benefit was suspended.

And there's that other gauntlet: to collect an excess spousal benefit, your spouse has to be collecting their retirement benefit or have suspended it before April 30, 2016.

EXCESS DIVORCED SPOUSAL BENEFITS

This benefit is calculated in the same manner as the excess spousal benefit. Ignoring DRCs, it's the difference between half your ex's full retirement benefit and all of your own full retirement benefit.

The additional gauntlet here is the same as for full divorced spousal benefits: your ex-spouse has to (1) be over 62 and have been divorced from you for at least two years or (2) have filed for their own retirement or disability benefit. The new law seemed to let ex-spouses block the payment of divorced spousal benefits simply via the act of suspending their own retirement benefits. When the Social Security Administration eventually recognized the perversity of this new loophole, albeit after the fact, it closed it with new regulations (another example of fire-ready-aim).

THE DEMON KNOWN AS DEEMING

Unless you have been grandparented under the new law, if you take your spousal benefit, you are deemed also to be filing your retirement benefit regardless of whether you are under or over Full Retirement Age. In other words, you are forced to take your retirement benefit, too.

Social Security will then give you your retirement benefit plus what, to repeat, they call your excess spousal benefit (which is often zero). This pretty much comes down to your getting the larger of the two benefits.

This works the same way for the divorced who were married for 10 or more years. They too are deemed, but, in this case, they are deemed to be taking their excess divorce spousal benefit.

Why is deeming the devil's work? Because getting an excess rather than a full spousal benefit is almost the same as simply getting the larger of your full spousal benefit and your retirement benefit. This basically means that you lose one of the two benefits, which is no fun.

Furthermore, deeming works in two directions. If you file for your retirement benefit, and you are subject to deeming, you'll be deemed to be filing for your spousal or divorced spousal benefit as well if you're eligible. In this case you'll get just your excess divorced spousal benefit.

Being eligible comes back to meeting the above caveats concerning excess spousal and excess divorced spousal benefits. If, for example, your ex-spouse is 61 when you file for your retirement benefit at, say, 62, you can't be deemed because you can't collect an excess spousal benefit on the ex's work record. The ex-spouse is not old enough yet for you to do so. But as soon as they are old enough, you will be deemed. This is yet another feature of the new law.

Fortunately, deeming does not affect survivor or divorced survivor benefits. But you can still get stuck with only an excess survivor(s) or an excess divorced survivor benefit if you don't play your cards right.

WIDOW(ER) BENEFITS: WHEN ARE THEY AVAILABLE AND HOW ARE THEY CALCULATED?

Widow(er)s and divorced widow(er)s—the latter need to have been married for 10 or more years—can collect their survivor benefits as early as 60, or as early as 50 if disabled.

What's the actual amount a widow or widower, including a divorced survivor, might get as a survivor's benefit? We're not glad you asked, because it depends on a whole bunch of things.

Thing 1 is when your spouse or ex-spouse dies. If they die before age 62 Social Security calculates their PIA, on which survivor benefits are based, in two different ways and uses the larger of the two numbers.

Thing 2 is whether your deceased spouse or deceased ex-spouse took their retirement benefit early (and, with apologies for repetition, by early we mean before FRA). If they did, this can lower your survivor's benefits, which are calculated based on a special formula. It's called the RIB-LIM, which stands for Retirement Insurance Benefit Limit. (The formula is about survivor's benefits, but the acronym refers to retirement benefits. Go figure.)

The RIB-LIM formula seems to have been designed to drive us crazy. It's the smaller of two numbers, one of which is the larger of two numbers.[3] We kid you not.

If you're in RIB-LIM world, your survivor or divorced survivor benefit will depend on whether you take your benefit early and also how early. If you take it as early as possible—at 60 (50 if you are disabled)—you'll get 71.5 percent of your former spouse's PIA. If you take it closer to Full Retirement Age, you'll get the larger of the reduced retirement benefit your spouse was collecting or 82.5 percent of your spouse's PIA.

The important thing to remember if you are in RIB-LIM world is that at some point before full retirement age, waiting to collect your survivor benefit won't get you higher benefits. We'll discuss this further via an example in Chapter 10.

Now for thing 3, which occurs if your spouse or ex-spouse died without having taken their retirement benefit early. In this case, your survivor or divorced survivor benefit, before any reduction due to your having taken this benefit early, equals your dead spouse or ex-spouse's PIA if they died before FRA. If they died after FRA, your survivor's benefit is the actual benefit, inclusive of Delayed Retirement Credits, they were receiving when they died or would have received had they applied for benefits the day they died.

Clearly, applying for benefits the day you die is a challenge. (Still, it may be easier than mastering the RIB-LIM formula.) Fortunately, if you die after FRA not having filed for your retirement benefit and you don't make it to the local office before you check out, Social Security will pretend you did.

DO YOU KNOW ABOUT CHILD-IN-CARE SPOUSAL BENEFITS?

Spouses with children under age 16 or disabled children, regardless of the disabled child's age (provided the child became disabled before 22 and stayed disabled), can collect what are called child-in-care spousal benefits, provided their spouse (the worker) is collecting her or his retirement or disability benefit or suspended that retirement benefit before April 30, 2016. The spouse can be any age and still collect this benefit. Nor is there any reduction for taking this benefit early, that is, before the spouse is at Full Retirement Age. And, unlike normal spousal benefits, child-in-care spousal benefits don't trigger deeming of your own retirement benefit.

The child-in-care spousal benefit is 50 percent of the worker's

PIA. But this benefit is subject to another nasty gotcha called the Family Maximum Benefit, which we will explain below.

What about divorced spouses who were married for at least 10 years and have the worker's children in their care? Can they get divorced child-in-care spousal benefits? No and yes. It's no if they are under 62, yes if they are over 62.

EVER HEARD OF MOTHER (FATHER) BENEFITS OR DIVORCED MOTHER (FATHER) BENEFITS?

There are also child-in-care benefits for surviving spouses and surviving ex-spouses (and there is no duration of marriage requirement here as there is for divorced benefits). These are called mother or father benefits. Again, the child has to be under 16 or be disabled before 22 and stay disabled for the benefit to continue to be provided. This benefit is 75 percent of the deceased spouse's or the deceased ex-spouse's PIA. But it, too, is subject to the Family Maximum Benefit. As with child-in-care spousal benefits, the surviving spouse or ex-spouse can be any age. Nor is there any reduction for taking this benefit early, that is, before Full Retirement Age. In the case of a surviving spouse or surviving ex-spouse who is aged 60 or older, they have the choice of receiving the larger of either the mother/father or the survivor benefit.

HOW ABOUT CHILD BENEFITS?

Children of living parents taking their retirement benefits or who suspended their retirement benefit before April 30, 2016, can receive 50 percent of their parents' PIA. The children need to be under 18 (19 if they are still in elementary or high school). Or the children can be disabled provided they are single, were disabled prior to age 22, and didn't earn enough money after age 22 to keep them from being viewed by Social Security as no longer disabled. This disabled child benefit can continue as long as the child remains unmarried and disabled.

Once the parent or parents die, a child who would otherwise qualify for a child or a disabled child benefit can collect a child survivor benefit. This is 75 percent of the deceased parent's PIA. And, as with the disabled child benefit, disabled children can continue to collect their child survivor benefits if they don't marry or earn too much money. Indeed, they can be 90 years old and still collect these benefits.

Are your children, or any you know, eligible for benefits through their retired, disabled, or deceased parents? If they are, the basic rules specify half of the parent's primary amount; if the parent is deceased, the benefit is larger: 75 percent. More complicated provisions kick in for situations where both parents' benefits may be the basis of the claim and for multiple-child households.

EVER HEARD OF PARENT BENEFITS?

Our guess is no. Well, if you were paying for more than half of, say, your mom's support and you pass away, she can collect a parent benefit equal to 82.5 percent of your PIA. If she is collecting benefits on her own, she will, however, receive only the larger of the two benefits.

BE AWARE OF THE FAMILY
MAXIMUM BENEFIT

As we've noted, there is usually a "however" with Social Security's rules, and there's *a huge* one here: the Family Maximum Benefit

(FMB). Child, ex-spouse, and survivorship benefits could cause overall Social Security payments to exceed a certain ceiling known as the Family Maximum Benefit. If that happens, payments to all beneficiaries would be reduced to bring total family payments under the ceiling. Benefits going to exes, however, aren't subject to the FMB.

Where two or more earners have filed for retirement or disability benefits, or have died, there's another "however": It's possible ancillary benefits based on their earnings records would be subject to a higher *combined* Family Maximum Benefit. The rules for computing this higher maximum are, as you might have guessed, very complex.[4] But if you're in this situation, be aware that these higher limits might be available, and ask Social Security about them.

We'll note another twist here. Your Primary Insurance Amount (PIA) is calculated by plugging your average earnings (AIME) into what is a decidedly progressive formula. The Family Maximum Benefit is pretty much the opposite. Surprisingly, it's calculated by plugging your Primary Insurance Amount into a formula that is *regressive*—one that treats high earners disproportionately better than low ones. If your PIA is very low, your total Family Maximum Benefit will be only 150 percent of that amount. With a somewhat larger PIA, however, the maximum rises to 187 percent. It then ebbs, ending up at 175 percent of your primary benefit. But even a 175 percent family maximum for those with the highest full retirement benefit for themselves is considerably more than the 150 percent for workers with the lowest PIA.

The way this benefit is calculated doesn't make sense to us. But while there is nothing you can do about it, the application of this maximum can affect your optimal Social Security claiming decisions.

Also, if you're disabled, there's a different, potentially far more restrictive FMB, which we'll tell you about later. For very low earners who become disabled, this FMB is *zero*, apart from what the disabled worker herself receives. We feel this is even more unfair than the low-income FMB.

Finally, and this is really important, the worker's own full retirement benefit (even if they suspended it before April 30, 2016) is counted against the Family Maximum Benefit, but only when the worker is alive. Once they die, their family members will be able to collect more because (1) survivor benefits are higher and (2) the decedent's PIA no longer counts against the Family Maximum Benefit.

ALSO BE AWARE OF THE EARNINGS TEST

If you are collecting retirement benefits and have not yet reached your FRA, your Social Security benefits may be reduced if you also have outside wage earnings (investment and pension income does not count). Even earnings at jobs where you didn't pay Social Security payroll taxes are included.

Now, don't get too worked up here. In most cases (and we will explain the exceptions), this is just a cash flow issue since Social Security will, over time, restore these reductions starting when you reach FRA.

That said, there are two trigger levels—one for the years before you reach FRA and a second for the year in which you reach it. For someone whose FRA is 66, their Social Security benefit would be reduced by $1 for every $2 in earnings (including earnings in noncovered employment) that exceeded $15,720 while they were aged 62 to 65. During the year they turn 66, their benefit would be reduced by $1 for every $3 in earnings that exceeded $41,880, but only those earnings received before reaching FRA are counted. These are 2016 trigger levels; the levels are changed every year to reflect national wage trends.

The Earnings Test may also affect your spousal benefits or

divorced spousal benefits or survivor or child benefits, if your outside earnings exceed the trigger levels. Those benefits also will be reduced if your spouse (the worker) is collecting retirement benefits, has not reached FRA, and earns more than the trigger levels.

Benefit reductions are not prorated during the year but front-loaded. This can play havoc with your budget. For example, if your outside earnings reduced your $18,000 annual benefit to $12,000, your $1,500 monthly payment would not be reduced to $1,000 for an entire year. Instead, you would get *no* Social Security payment for 4 months and then the $1,500 payment for 8 months.

At FRA Social Security bumps up benefits lost to the Earnings Test. However, spousal benefits and survivor benefits received by people because they have minor or disabled children in their care are *not* restored if they are reduced because of the Earnings Test. Equally important, and perhaps even more confusing, if you are collecting one type of benefit before FRA and switch to a different benefit after FRA, you won't recoup the benefits you lost due to the Earnings Test.

A YEAR OF GRACE NOTES FOR THE EARNINGS TEST

If you file for your retirement benefits early and are hit by the Earnings Test, Social Security's grace year rule may help you—during your first year only of collecting benefits—by not counting any earnings you made in the months before you began collecting benefits. For the months after you began collecting, the rule permits the Earnings Test to be applied on a monthly and not annual basis (meaning that the annual earnings limits would be divided by 12 and compared with your monthly earnings). To illustrate, assume you began collecting benefits early in July, had made $50,000 in the first half of that year, and had no outside earnings the second half of the year. Under grace-year provisions, you would not be hit with Earnings Test benefits reductions.

'CAUSE I'M THE TAXMAN, YEAH, I'M THE TAXMAN

Federal taxes may be due on up to half of your Social Security benefits if what's called your "combined income" is more than $25,000 a year ($32,000 for joint filers). If you make between $25,000 and $34,000 ($32,000 and $44,000 for joint returns), you may owe federal taxes on up to 85 percent of your benefits. You will never pay federal income taxes on more than 85 percent of your benefits. These combined income thresholds are not adjusted for inflation, so over time more and more people have seen their Social Security benefits subjected to federal income taxes. Combined income is defined as the total of your adjusted gross income plus any nontaxable interest you receive (from, say, municipal bonds) plus *half* of your Social Security benefits.

Social Security will withhold federal income taxes from your benefit payments upon your request. The agency will let you select one of four percentage withholding amounts—7, 10, 15, or 25 percent. You can request withholding when you apply for benefits and can change this amount later by filing IRS Form W-4V (available at http://www.irs.gov/pub/irs-pdf/fw4v.pdf).

YOUR BENEFITS—WITH STRINGS ATTACHED

When Social Security says you can get a benefit, there are always strings attached. Here are some examples.

- **Retirement Benefits**—you have to be 62 or over to collect.

- **Spousal Benefits**—you have to be 62 or over to collect and your spouse has to have filed for his or her retirement or disability benefit. You need to have been married at least a year to qualify for spousal benefits on a new spouse's work history.

- **Divorced Spousal Benefits**—you have to be 62 or over to collect, as does the spouse on whose benefits you're collecting, unless they are collecting disability benefits. You also have to have been married for at least 10 years, not be currently remarried, and you must be divorced for at least 2 years if your ex has not filed for their own retirement or disability benefit.

- **Widow(er) Survivor Benefits**—you have to be 60 to collect, but only 50 if you are a disabled widow or widower and didn't remarry before age 60 (50 if disabled). And, apart from death caused by accident, you normally need to have been married for at least 9 months. Depending on your year of birth, the FRA used in calculating your survivor benefits can be 4 months earlier than the FRA used in calculating your retirement and spousal benefits.

- **Divorced Widow(er) Survivor Benefits**—you have to be 60 or over (50 or over if you are disabled) to collect on a deceased ex to whom you were married for at least 10 years provided you didn't remarry before 60 (50 if disabled).

- **Spousal Benefits if You Have a Child of the Retired Worker in Your Care**—you can be any age and collect a spousal benefit if your spouse has filed for a retirement or disability benefit and you are caring for his or her children who are under age 16 or disabled. If one or more is disabled, then you may collect regardless of their age(s) provided the disability began before age 22.

- **Mother/Father Benefits if You Have a Child of Your Deceased Spouse or Deceased Ex-Spouse in Your Care**—you can be any age and collect this survivor benefit based on your deceased spouse's or deceased ex-spouse's work record if you are caring for his or her children who are under age 16 or disabled (regardless of their age provided the disability began before age 22 and continued, uninterrupted, thereafter). To be eligible, you cannot currently be remarried. But you need to have been married only a second (not the standard 9 months for survivor's benefits or 10 years for divorced survivor's benefits) to qualify for this benefit.

- **Divorced Spousal Benefits if You Have a Child of the Retired Social Security–Entitled Spouse in Your Care**—you have to be 62 or older to collect, provided you were married for 10 or more years, are not remarried, your ex is 62 or older or is entitled to disability benefits, and you are caring for his or her child or children who are under age 16 or disabled (regardless of their age provided the disability began before age 22).

- **Child Benefits for Children of Disabled, Retired, or Deceased Workers**—if your parent is entitled to a disability or retirement benefit or is deceased, you are eligible for a child benefit or a child survivor benefit if you are either under age 18 (19 if you are still in elementary or secondary school) or are disabled (provided your disability began prior to 22).

As indicated, the Social Security stars have to be carefully aligned for you to collect certain benefits. If, for example, you're 62 and your husband is 22, you'll be 102 before you can collect a spousal benefit based on his work record, unless he becomes entitled to disability benefits or dies. That's because your husband has to file for a retirement or disability benefit before *you* can collect a spousal benefit and your husband has to be at least 62 (which is 40 years from now) to file for a retirement benefit.

This chapter lays out the contours of the system. But it doesn't tell you how to *get what's yours*—maximizing your family's lifetime Social Security benefits. The next chapter gives you three basic rules we've developed to guide your decisions. If you follow them, you shouldn't go wrong. Easier said than done, as you now know. Before we move on, though, we want to review a few basics about claiming benefits.

SOCIAL SECURITY CLAIMING BASICS

Before people make a decision, it is natural to want to know what others have done. Product reviews and rankings abound. Social media have made crowdsourcing a near-obligatory act for growing numbers of us before we actually sign on the dotted line or, more likely, open an app that will sign on our behalf. And while the three of us sometimes feel we would like to take Social Security out to the woodshed, the program does a thorough job of measuring what people do and building an extensive statistical record of how Americans actually use Social Security.[5] (For a look at the numbers of people getting Social Security and their benefit levels see the end of the Glossary.)

SOCIAL SECURITY IS NOT A
RETURN OF YOUR TAX DOLLARS

You can pay Social Security taxes on every penny you earn and end up with no more benefits than someone who never worked a lick. Thanks to Social Security's spousal and survivor benefits, spouses who don't work and never did can receive benefits—reasonably large ones, even—based purely on their living or dead or ex-spouse's earnings record. Yet if you're a spouse or ex-spouse who *did* work and paid Social Security taxes year after year, you may end up with no extra benefits than had you never worked at all. That's because, if you're simultaneously collecting a spousal or survivor benefit based on your mate's or ex-mate's earnings record as well as your own retirement benefit, Social Security will give you the *larger* of your own retirement benefits or those that come via your spouse or former spouse.

Curiously—some might say "deviously"—Social Security hides the fact that if you get only your spousal or survivor benefits, you aren't really getting anything back for all your *own* contributions. Say your spousal or survivor benefit is $1,000 a month and your own retirement benefit is $800 a month. Social Security will give you the $1,000, but they will tell you you're getting your own $800 benefit plus a $200 redefined excess spousal or survivor benefit.

MECHANICS OF APPLYING FOR BENEFITS

You can transact with Social Security on the phone on certain matters, including filing for your retirement benefit. (Both Paul and Jan did so effectively and hassle-free.) You can file online, as Phil did, successfully, or you can file in person. If you do go to your local office though, *make sure that you enter in writing in the Remarks section of the application form exactly what you want to do and also what you do not want to do.* Be sure to specify when you want your benefits to start. You can file well before, or even after, you wish benefits to begin. Then have the Social Security office date your application and hand you a copy. Keep your copy in a safe place. You may need it to appeal a mistake that Social Security makes in handling your case. From readers of our book and Larry's PBS column, we know this happens a lot more often than you'd think.

PROTECTING YOURSELF FROM SOCIAL SECURITY'S MISTAKES

In the Remarks section of your application, make absolutely sure to put in writing when you wish to have your benefit begin, which Social Security calls your entitlement date(s). Suppose, for example, you have accumulated Delayed Retirement Credits by either waiting to collect your retirement benefit or by suspending your retirement benefits. If you don't specify in the Remarks section that you don't want your benefits to begin retroactive up to 6 months (which means 6 months less in Delayed Retirement Credits and a permanently lower monthly check), Social Security will automatically provide you retroactive benefits.

Some widows have been very badly hurt because they mistakenly filed for their own retirement benefit at the same time as they filed for their widow's benefit. As we will discuss in Chapter 6, this mistake can cost widows enormous amounts of money from age 70 on.

If you are still able to file at FRA just for your spousal benefit while letting your own benefit grow (this is called filing a restricted application), you need to also specify this in the Remarks section. Specifically, you need to write, "I wish to exclude [BLANK—you would fill in retirement benefits in this situation] from the scope of this application." Alternatively, you can write, "I filed on [DATE] for all benefits for which I may be eligible except [BLANK—again, in this situation you would enter retirement benefits]." But we must point out that the top of the application form asserts that you are filing for all benefits for which you are eligible, which is absolutely *not* what you want to do here. So it is essential to clarify your intent in the Remarks section.

WHEN TO APPLY FOR BENEFITS, WHEN WILL BENEFITS BEGIN, AND WHEN YOU'LL GET PAID

You can file for benefits up to four months before you are eligible to collect them. But you need to be crystal clear as to when you want your benefit to begin. Social Security views you as having attained a given age the day before you actually have your birthday. This can matter. And it can matter differently when you take early retirement.

For example, when it comes to collecting retirement benefits when you first turn 62, you need to be 62 for a full month before you can receive benefits for that month. If you are born on January 1, you are viewed as turning 62 on December 31, and you can collect your early retirement benefit for the month of January, that is, you can collect for all 12 months of the year. The same is true if you turn 62 on January 2. But if your birth date is January 3 through January 31, you'll receive your retirement benefit starting with the month of February. So you'll receive payments for 12 months if your birth date is January 1 or 2 and 11 payments if your birth date is January 3 to 31. And each of these payments will be sent to you a month in arrears, which is how Social Security pays—a month late.

Now, with all this information behind us, let's look at the new law passed in November 2015 and how it may affect you.

THE NEW SOCIAL SECURITY LAW

The budget bill that President Obama signed into law on November 2, 2015, made sweeping changes to Social Security law. Fortunately, as we've told you, it didn't change the main way, for most people, to maximize lifetime Social Security benefits, which is simply to wait to collect benefits at their highest possible values. But it eliminated or greatly impaired three benefit-collection strategies for people who weren't grandparented under the old law.

First, the new law gutted the *file-and-suspend* strategy. This is the collection strategy that Paul used and that Alice, the Boston University employee, discussed earlier, had planned to use (but now can't because she's a year too young).[1] Second, the bill decimated the *suspend-now-and-in-an-emergency-unsuspend* strategy. Third, the legislation prevented people in the future from taking full advantage of the *start*, *stop*, *start* strategy.

We'll clarify the latter two strategies momentarily. But first, a few comments about how this all went down. The author (or authors) of the new Social Security provisions, constituting only a few sentences in the Bipartisan Budget Bill of 2015, operated on Social Security's rules with a meat cleaver, not a scalpel. Furthermore, the new provisions appear to have been written in a rush. Here's why we believe this.

A draft of the bill, which contained a long list of provisions, including some to keep paying benefits to the disabled and to limit Medicare Part B premium increases, was released on Monday,

October 26. It was voted on and signed into law just one week later. Consequently, Congress had no time to hold hearings on the bill, including its Social Security provisions. Nor, to our knowledge, were there any public hearings about the Social Security provisions leading up to the bill.

It's a safe bet that very few members of Congress understood exactly what the new Social Security rules entailed or how many low- and middle-income families, like Alice's, would be hurt. (For some reason AARP, the massive lobbying group for "retired people," whose eligibility begins at age 50, applauded the new rules and even sent out emails to its members asking them to thank Congress for passing the law, a law that would deny benefits to most of them.)

When Larry and Phil read the bill's draft language, they both realized that, as written, it wouldn't just cut benefits for people in the future; it would cut benefits for people already collecting benefits. That is, the bill killed strategies that Americans were *already employing*. The bill was eliminating these benefits *in retrospect*—something with no precedent in Social Security "reform."

The next morning, both of them wrote about the changes, Larry in his weekly *PBS NewsHour* column, "Ask Larry" (on Paul's Making Sen$e page on the *NewsHour* website) and Phil in one of his pieces for *Money* magazine. Larry's column's title, carefully chosen to get Congress's attention, read "Proposed Budget Bill Would Have Devastating Effects on Millions' Social Security Benefits." It pointed out that the bill, as drafted, would lead, after six months, to major reductions in the payments that hundreds of thousands, if not millions, of people were already receiving.

Within a day, the bill was amended to include two grandparenting clauses. In communicating about these clauses with a senior official in Social Security, Larry was told that (1) the 2015 edition of our book had led to the new restrictions and (2) that his column had led to the amendments.

This is a sad commentary on our democracy, though it seems to be business as usual in Congress these days. A bill gets rewritten with no public debate at the eleventh hour, written so hurriedly in this case that it has to be rewritten at 11:57, eliminating benefits under this ironic heading: "Protecting Social Security."

AN OUTRAGE OR LONG OVERDUE?

The main argument against strategies like file-and-suspend is that they were loopholes, never intended to be used as they have been. A second argument is that they disproportionately benefit people who don't really need them.

The arguments aren't crazy. As the highly respected Boston College retirement scholar Alicia Munnell wrote on Paul's Making Sen$e website, "The problem with these loopholes is that they run counter to the intent of the Social Security program and cost money. Social Security is designed to replace income lost when a worker retires, becomes disabled or dies. To achieve income adequacy goals, Congress provided a spouse's benefit to supplement retirement income for one-earner couples. The spouse's benefit was not intended as a bonus for high-income couples that could game the system to their advantage." Munnell elsewhere admitted she and her husband had themselves taken the benefit Paul and Jan had, but felt uneasy about having done so.

And as we mentioned at the outset, President Obama's fiscal 2015 budget, submitted to Congress in early 2014, proposed the elimination of "aggressive claiming strategies," presumably meaning file-and-suspend.

Moreover, there were surely couples who benefited from file-and-suspend who didn't need the money. But that's true of anyone who takes Social Security with sufficient savings to carry them through old age. And in denying the strategy to "high-income couples," the new law penalizes everyone, including those who need the income. We know of no statistical analysis as to who would be hurt, no evidence that the rich or superrich are more prone to use "aggressive filing strategies" than the middle class or poor. In fact, a recent study by John Shoven and other economists at Stanford suggests that the vast majority of the rich do what everyone else does—take their benefits as soon as they can get them.

We aren't the only people who have problems with the new law. Here's just one example of emails people sent Larry after the Bipartisan Budget Bill passed.

The way this is being done is horrible. I am 65, and my wife is 61. We had been planning our retirement for years with this strategy in mind, thanks to you. Now, because she is a few months shy of turning 62 this year, she loses all of it, while arbitrarily, a spouse who just turned 62 gets everything.

Now to the specifics. The new law made the following big changes to Social Security.

First, apart from those who are grandparented, no one—not a spouse, not a disabled child, not a young child, not a divorced spouse, and not a spouse caring for a young or disabled child—can collect a benefit based on the work record of a spouse whose retirement benefit is in suspension.

Second, apart from those who *are* grandparented, no one who suspends their benefit can request that their suspended benefits be paid to them in a lump sum, albeit at the cost of losing their Delayed Retirement Credits going forward.

Leaving aside those that were grandparented—still amounting to millions of Americans, remember—this is the death knell for the file-and-suspend strategy. Future couples like Paul and Jan, both of whom have similar earnings records and aren't facing imminent demise, will simply wait until 70 to take their retirement benefits if they can afford to, and want to maximize their lifetime incomes. Other couples, however, who have quite disparate earnings, will be induced to take retirement benefits earlier than they'd otherwise have done in order to activate an otherwise unavailable spousal benefit for their partners.

Third, the new law prevents workers who suspend their retirement benefits from later changing their minds and taking their suspended benefits in a lump sum. This means that a worker who suspends her benefits at full retirement age in order to receive a larger benefit at age 70 won't be able to collect more than a pittance in benefits if she later finds out she has inoperable cancer and will die within weeks. (We get frequent emails and phone calls from people in situations like this.) Hence, this strategy—*suspend now and, in an emergency, unsuspend*—is also toast, except for those who had suspended their retirement benefits prior to April 30, 2016.

Finally, the bill limits how many people will pursue what we call the *start, stop, start* strategy. Under this strategy, a worker takes her retirement benefit early in order perhaps to activate child or disabled child benefits as well as child-in-care benefits for her spouse. Then, at full retirement age (66 for the past few years), the worker suspends her retirement benefit and restarts it at 70. Under the old law, her child(ren) and spouse could collect on her work record while her retirement benefit was in suspension. Under the new law, that's not possible (again, assuming she's not grandparented).

THE ADVANTAGES OF BEING
A GRANDPARENT

Actually, there are many advantages of being a grandparent, but two of them apply specifically to being grandparented under the new Social Security law.

The first pertains to file-and-suspend. The new law permits those who were 66 before April 30, 2016, to provide benefits to relatives based on their suspended retirement benefits, provided that they filed and suspended their retirement benefits before that date. It also reserves to them the right, at a later date, to take their suspended benefits retroactively in the form of a single lump sum payment. We apologize for not being able to get out another edition of this book in time for those who didn't get in under the wire.

But let's be clear: the new law does not prohibit suspending your benefit. You still can file for your retirement benefit, either early or at Full Retirement Age or even after Full Retirement Age, and then decide later to suspend it—stop taking it, that is—and let it grow during the suspended years. Thus anyone can still change their mind, even after having started taking benefits, *stop* taking them, and thus take advantage of the Delayed Retirement Credits—the extra amounts your final benefit grows during the period it is suspended. You can then reactivate your retirement benefit at 70 (or even before, if you prefer).

What the new law bars: if a person younger than 66 as of April 30, 2016, suspends her benefits, her *dependents* can't take benefits based on her work record so long as her own retirement benefit is in suspension. (There is, however, a twist with respect to divorced workers who suspend their benefits, which we'll elaborate a few pages from now.) Moreover, there are two parts to this witching hour. First, no one can collect auxiliary benefits of any kind (including, for example, disabled child benefits) on anyone's suspended retirement benefit while their retirement benefit is still being suspended. Second, the person who suspends their retirement benefit can't collect any auxiliary benefits for themselves while their benefit is in suspension.

The second grandparenting provision extends Social Security's much-dreaded "deeming" rules through age 70 to anyone who turns 62 after January 1, 2016. This is a killer. Say you turned 62 a few minutes after midnight on January 1, 2016, and wanted to take your spousal benefit—50 percent of your spouse's full retirement benefit—while you wait for yours to grow.

In the first edition, we explained the penalty of taking the spousal benefit before your Full Retirement Age (66 until 2020). By taking your spousal benefit early, you would be "deemed" to have taken your *own* benefit early, too. You would be penalized for life with lower benefits than had you waited.

The new law penalizes you in the same fashion all the way to age 70. In other words, doing what Paul did—file just for a spousal benefit at Full Retirement Age and let your retirement benefit accumulate Delayed Retirement Credits until age 70—will no longer work for those not 62 before January 2, 2016. If such folk file at 66, just for a spousal benefit, they'll be deemed to be also filing for their own retirement benefit at 66 as well.

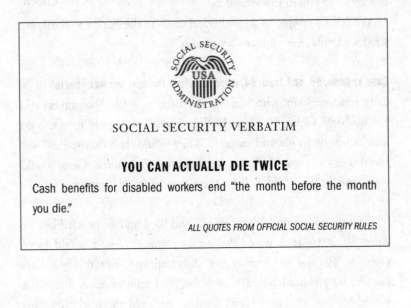

SOCIAL SECURITY VERBATIM

YOU CAN ACTUALLY DIE TWICE

Cash benefits for disabled workers end "the month before the month you die."

ALL QUOTES FROM OFFICIAL SOCIAL SECURITY RULES

INTERACTIONS OF THE
GRANDPARENTING PROVISIONS
PERTAINING TO MARRIED COUPLES

Even if you are at least 62 as of January 1, 2016, you still can't collect a full spousal benefit by itself (while letting your retirement benefit grow) unless your spouse has either already filed for their own retirement benefit or was able to file-and-suspend before April 30, 2016.

However, if your spouse has done either of these things, you can collect a spousal benefit all by itself. And, thanks to one of the aforementioned grandparenting clauses, you need only have been at least 62 years old as of January 1, 2016. In this event, you simply can wait until reaching at least your FRA and then file a restricted application for just your spousal benefit. The new post-FRA deeming rules do not apply to you in this situation.

We offer a couple of hypothetical cases in the hopes of clarifying what we know may appear very muddy.

Case 1: Gene, 66, and Joan, 64, married before the new law was enacted

Let's imagine Joan, who was 64 when the new law was signed and her husband, Gene, 66. Gene had expected to wait until Joan was 66 and he was 68 to file and suspend. They would then do the Paul and Jan thing: Joan would file for just her spousal benefits, Gene would wait, and both would collect their maximum retirement benefits at 70.

If Gene got news of the new bill and filed and suspended before April 30, 2016, they could do just as planned. Yes, it would force Gene to file and suspend earlier than expected, but this wouldn't matter; why should he care *when* he filed and suspended? And it would have no effect on Joan's filing a restricted application just for her spousal benefit.

The only way this filing and suspending early could backfire would be if Joan passed away before reaching her Full Retirement Age. In this case, Gene, having filed for his own retirement benefit (even though he'd suspended it), would no longer be eligible to take a widower benefit while letting his own retirement benefit grow. He'd have to settle for the larger of his retirement and widower benefit (since you can take only one benefit at a time).

Because filing and suspending before you absolutely need to can deprive unexpected widow(er)s of much (if not all) of their survivor's benefit, we normally wouldn't have recommended it, even though under the old law early filing and suspending would allow Gene to take his suspended benefits as a lump sum if a critical condition arose in his finances or health.

The bottom line is that the new law would force Gene, assuming he became aware of it, to act sooner than otherwise, putting him at risk of losing substantial widower benefits were Joan to die in the near future.

Case 2: Gene and Joan, married, but both were only 64 when the new law was enacted

Here's a twist on the prior example. If both Gene and Joan were 64 when the law was enacted, neither would reach 66 before the April 30, 2016, deadline for grandparenting. So while both could file for their retirement benefit and then suspend it sometime between FRA and age 70, neither could provide the other a spousal benefit while their own retirement benefit was in suspension.

True, both could still file for just a spousal benefit and defer their own retirement benefit until 70. But neither could collect a spousal benefit until the other actually began collecting their own retirement benefit. Before the new rules one spouse could have filed and suspended, permitting the other to collect just a spousal benefit. But with this option no longer available, one of them would be forced to take their retirement benefit early to permit the other to get a full spousal benefit through age 70.

Case 3: Gene, 66, and Joan are married, but she was only 60 when the new law was enacted

Under this variant, filing and suspending on Gene's part will never help Joan collect a full spousal benefit between Full Retirement Age and 70. Why not? Because she didn't turn 62 before January 2, 2016.[2] Hence, regardless of how long she waits to file, Joan will be deemed to be filing for her own retirement benefit as well as her spousal benefit if she files for either.

What if Joan doesn't have enough quarters when she reaches FRA to collect a retirement benefit on her own, or has earned next to nothing compared with Gene? In this case, the deeming won't hurt her. She'll be able to collect either her full spousal benefit, if her own retirement benefit is zero, or an excess spousal benefit that is very close to her full spousal benefit. Obviously, not being able to grow a retirement benefit worth zero or close to zero produces no loss in this case.

Gene, being 66 already, was in a position to file and suspend before the April 29, 2016, deadline. Had he done so, he would have been able to exercise his option to reclaim all suspended benefits. But, as just discussed, he would be doing this at the risk of losing the opportunity to defer his own retirement benefit through 70 and collect, until then, full widower benefits, were Joan to die before he reached age 70.

If Gene were the higher earner, we think his best move would be not to have filed and suspended. Here's why. One of the reasons, perhaps the major reason, to unsuspend one's benefits is learning that one is about to die. "My doc gives me two years at most," he might say to himself. "Best to cash in my Social Security so I can get at least some money before it's too late."

This may seem to make good sense, but actually it doesn't. The reason is that if Gene unsuspends and surrenders his Delayed Retirement Credits he will condemn Joan to a lifetime of lower widow benefits than would otherwise be the case. Now, maybe Joan is the higher earner and won't get much advantage from Gene's dying and her collecting a higher widow's benefit. But if she's the lower earner, as so many wives are, she will lose a great deal of money due to an understandable but, we think, misguided decision by Gene.

Social Security optimization is different for every household depending on their circumstances. That's why we're trying to make sure you see all the variations.

THE PAYOFF FROM BEING DIVORCED

People who divorced after being married for 10 or more years—and thus became eligible for ex-spousal benefits—have an advantage over married couples under the new law, provided they are grandparented against post-FRA deeming. If they were at least 62 before January 2, 2016, they can file for a full ex-spousal benefit when they reach their FRA and then wait till 70 to collect their retirement benefit, which will have grown all the while. They can do this only if their ex is at least 62 and they've been divorced for two years when they do this, or if their ex already is receiving retirement or disability benefits or has filed for retirement benefits and suspended them.

So then does it pay to get divorced?

In Chapter 1, we raised the notion that the new law has made divorce much more financially attractive. We're now going to reinforce this point via our final Gene-and-Joan hypothetical.

So if Gene and Joan were both 62 when the new law was enacted, should they divorce at 64?

As before, Gene and Joan were both too young to file and suspend before the end of April 2016. But, being 62 before January 2, 2016, they are both grandparented so that neither will be deemed when they reach FRA. If they remain married, as we've said, one will have to file for their retirement benefit earlier than 70 to enable the other to file a restricted application just for spousal benefits, while letting their own retirement max out until age 70.

However, as we suggested in Chapter 1, they could cook up some irreconcilable differences and get divorced at age 64. Then, at age 66, each could collect full divorced spousal benefits on the other's work record while letting their own retirement benefits grow.

If they were very high earners, this could mean $120,000 more just for getting divorced. After 70, they could reconcile those irreconcilable differences and remarry. Meanwhile, between 64 and 70, they could remain together. If anyone asks why, they could say they were attempting to patch up their relationship.

Is this legal? Even if it is, doesn't it amount to gaming the system? For the record, we aren't advising it. But we imagine some couples might try to do this because the new law has so clearly made this strategy superior, in financial terms, to the claiming options available to married couples who fit the bill.

SUMMARY

Anyone who knows about Social Security knows it is insanely complex. This, after all, is why our book did well when it first came out—because it is so hard to figure out on your own what to do. But if you are making Social Security policy, and you know the system is dealing with all kinds of people in all kinds of situations, you don't do business this way. You don't make abrupt changes that can do serious harm and wind up making arbitrary distinctions among Americans based solely on their age. You don't go into a back office at the eleventh hour and start rewriting the law, and then make it public the next day. You don't then discover that you have to amend the most egregious provisions within a few hours because someone immediately discovered things you would have seen had you taken more time.

Fixing Social Security, which certainly needs plenty of fixing, needs to be done in the light of day, in hearings open to the public, based on testimony by a range of experts, and with careful consideration of a range of options. That's what our democracy both demands and fully deserves.

In the next few chapters, we're going to discuss optimal strategies for different types of households, providing a number of numerical illustrations. As we said, one size fits none under this program. And the more concrete examples of optimization you see, the more likely you will find one that closely resembles your own situation.

THREE GENERAL RULES
TO MAXIMIZE YOUR
LIFETIME BENEFITS

Social Security's thousands of rules and hundreds of thousands of rules about its rules make our government's pension system among the least user-friendly yet devised. But we've come to help. Our goal here is to boil down all those rules into three general prescriptions for maxing out your lifetime Social Security benefit and then give you more precise directions later in the book.

THE THREE GENERAL RULES

Rule 1   *Be Patient.* Take Social Security's best deal by waiting to collect for as long as possible—taking much higher benefits over somewhat fewer years when it pays to do so.

Rule 2   *Take All Available Benefits.* Social Security has nine benefits in addition to retirement benefits. Learn about them and take them if you can. Yes, the new law has limited the availability of spousal and divorced spousal benefits. But not entirely, thanks both to the grandparenting provisions and to the wide disparity in earnings among many current and ex-spouses.

Rule 3   *Get Your Timing Right.* Which benefits you take and when you take them remains, even under the new law, a major factor in lifetime benefit maximization. You can take benefits far too early. But you can also take benefits far too late.

Let us elaborate.

RULE 1 IS LIKE THE MORAL OF AN AESOP FABLE: PATIENCE CAN PAY

Taking your benefits early can cost you dearly in many cases. Here's why. For those who aren't disabled, Social Security permanently reduces retirement, spousal, divorced spousal, widow(er), and divorced widow(er) benefits if taken "early," that is, before full retirement age.[1] And in the case of retirement benefits, it permanently raises your monthly payment for every month through age 70 that you wait to collect them.

Put another way, Social Security pays us, in most but certainly not all cases, to be patient. Here are some reasons to wait to collect. The figures pertain to those now 62.

- Retirement benefits starting at 70 are 76 percent higher than those starting at 62.
- Spousal benefits are 43 percent higher at Full Retirement Age than at 62.[2]
- Survivor benefits are 40 percent higher at FRA than at 60.

These payoffs from waiting are before Social Security's adjustments for inflation. Hence, they are *real* benefit increases—increases over and above those made simply to keep up with inflation.

REWARDING PATIENCE

Suppose you just turned 62, and like 40 percent of retirees, you take your retirement benefits right away. If you are desperate for cash because you lost your job, can't find a job, or simply can't work, collecting is obviously your only option.

But if you can wait through Full Retirement Age—by working longer, using retirement accounts, downsizing your home—you'll increase your monthly payment by 33 percent. And if you wait till 70, you'll increase it by an additional 32 percent. These two increases compound to produce the 76 percent higher age-70 starting retirement benefit we've mentioned.[3]

To really sense the size of this increase, further imagine that you make it to age 70 and that, lo and behold, you keep living, and living, and living—straight up to, well, 100. Think how much better you'll feel receiving 360 monthly payments that are each 76 percent higher than had you started your retirement benefit at 62.

Why is this reward for patience so big? Part of the answer is that it's a gift that keeps on giving. You keep living and Social Security keeps giving. The other part is that Social Security's actuarial factors that produce the 76 percent increase were legislated decades ago—in 1956, 1961, and 1983 to be precise. Real interest rates were much higher then. So were mortality rates. So, while the adjustments chosen back then were actuarially fair, they no longer are.[4] Stated differently, Social Security is being overly generous to those who wait to collect their benefits. This makes Social Security's *wait-for-more* deal one of the best financial, let alone insurance, deals going.

And for those who are married to a lower-earning spouse or were married to qualifying lower-earning ex-spouse(s), patience in taking your retirement benefit provides even larger dividends. The reason, conveyed in Chapter 3, is that if you die before your spouse or your ex-spouse(s), they will collect a widow(er) benefit equal to your retirement benefit (even after you take your own retirement benefit if the widow[er] benefit is larger).

In the parlance of the insurance industry, Social Security is providing you a joint-survivor annuity. But it's doing so at a wonderfully low price. You pay this price to the system in the form of forgoing lower retirement benefits for 8 years before age 70.

There's another really nice thing. If you missed this gravy train by taking your retirement benefit early—before full retirement—you can, even under the new law, suspend it at full retirement and restart it at a 32 percent larger value at 70. Unfortunately, thanks to the new law, you won't (unless you suspended before April 30, 2016) be able to provide your spouse (or ex-spouse) or kids benefits on your work record while your retirement benefit is suspended. But it may still be worth doing.

Unfortunately, Social Security's patience-pays deal ends at age 70. If you wait beyond 70, you'll get no higher retirement benefit when you start to collect.

There are people from whom we've heard who failed to collect their retirement benefit at 70. Some were still working and mistakenly thought they couldn't collect Social Security at the same time. Others thought Social Security's last date to start collecting was 70 and one-half (the age you generally need to take distributions from 401(k) and similar retirement accounts). Yet others thought Social Security would automatically start their retirement benefits when there was no further gain from waiting.

Social Security will pay benefits 6 months retroactively for people who file for benefits after Full Retirement Age (or even a bit before if they should have taken their widow[er]'s benefit sooner due to the RIB-LIM formula). But with Social Security benefits, it's basically use it or lose it. If you realize at, say, age 75, "Gee, maybe I should be getting my Social Security retirement benefit check and finally apply for it," you'll be out four and a half years of benefits!

This lesson, that patience pays but only up to a point, also extends to spousal and divorced spousal benefits. They are available, under the right conditions, as early as 62, but are reduced only through Full Retirement Age. If you qualify for these benefits (and far fewer will over time due to the new law), your benefits will be no larger if you wait beyond FRA to take them.

As for widow(er) and divorced widow(er) benefits, which are available as early as age 60 (age 50 for disabled widow[er]s), the reward for patience also ends at FRA, or earlier if the special RIB-LIM formula for decedents who took their retirement benefits early comes into play.

A final word on patience concerns the disabled. Their benefits are designed to penalize patience. We'll explain why in Chapter 12.

RULE 2: TAKE ALL THE BENEFITS YOU CAN GET

Rule 2—*Take All Available Benefits*—is a no-brainer. More is more. If you can get extra benefits for yourself or your family members at no cost in terms of your own retirement benefit or even at a cost, but one that's worth it, then, hey, go for it. As we keep emphasizing, it's in the contract: you paid for it; you earned it.

But the reason we make this into its own rule is that, as we related earlier in the story of Larry and Paul, you can be very smart and sophisticated (or at least pretend to be), yet be completely oblivious of what's due you. That can make you feel pretty dumb. But it shouldn't. Not knowing about Social Security's *auxiliary benefits* (all the benefits beyond the retirement benefit that might be paid on a worker's record) is a very common affliction, in part for one very understandable reason: the government hasn't gone out of its way to tell us about them.

Here's what the government might tell every American *every year*:

The FICA taxes you pay are meant to provide more than just retirement benefits. They may also provide extra financial support to your current and former spouses and to your young children and disabled children, to your surviving spouses and children, and even to your parents. There are a lot of conditions that must be met for these benefits to be paid out, but they may apply to you. So don't ignore these auxiliary benefits. And don't forget that if you are or were married, you may be able to collect benefits on your current or former spouses' earnings history.

Last we looked, there is no such annual notice. As a consequence, an unknown number of Americans are surely leaving substantial sums on the table—hundreds of thousands of dollars in some cases.

Social Security isn't just keeping many of us in the dark about auxiliary benefits. It even stopped, in 2011, sending us our annual covered earnings statements. Apparently, lots of people have objected. So Social Security now promises to send those under 60 their earnings statement, but only once every five years. Those 60 and over will get statements annually. Why 90-year-olds deserve annual statements and 50-year-olds don't is anybody's guess.

And, yes, you can pull up your earnings statement online, and you absolutely should! Why?

Because Social Security may not be crediting you for all your covered earnings either due to a clerical mistake by your employer or by Social Security itself or because your employer is pocketing the FICA taxes it's supposed to be sending to the IRS on your behalf.

And, yes, we've had people tell us this has happened to them, although the stories we've heard have all involved malfeasant employers.

RULE 3: TIMING . . . IS EVERYTHING

We've given you good reasons to wait to take benefits. But waiting may sometimes be the wrong course. Had Paul, for example, waited till 70 to take his spousal benefit, it would have gone poof.

This is due to a Social Security gotcha, actually the nastiest of its myriad gotchas.

If you try to collect two benefits at the same time, you won't get both. Instead, Social Security will give you the larger of the two benefits or something pretty close.

Since Paul's own retirement benefit exceeds his spousal benefit, he's been getting just his retirement benefit from the minute he turned 70 and started taking it.

The only reason he was able to collect nearly $50,000 in spousal benefits for four years was that he wasn't forced to take his retirement benefit during those four years. *He wasn't deemed.*

So getting your timing right can be critical not just with respect to taking your own retirement benefit, but also with respect to taking your auxiliary benefits. Auxiliary benefits is shorthand for all benefits you can collect based on the work record of your spouse, of one or more ex-spouses, or of a deceased child.

GETTING YOUR TIMING RIGHT— A SPOUSAL BENEFIT EXAMPLE

As the last chapter explained, the new law is going to coerce, via *deeming*, virtually all those who aren't grandparented to take their spousal and retirement benefits at the same time. So let's consider how a married couple in this boat needs to time its benefit collection. Things are very similar for the qualified divorced—those divorced after being married 10 years or longer.

In what follows, we're going to compare your spousal benefit with your own full retirement benefit. At its maximum, your spousal benefit is equal to half of your spouse's full retirement benefit. So, you will need to find out what your spouse's full retirement benefit is and what your own full retirement benefit is. Also, figure out what your age-70 retirement benefit will be. This table will help: www.ssa .gov/OACT/ProgData/ar_drc.html. We also recommend you and your spouse access this information by setting up your own online Social Security accounts at https://www.ssa.gov/myaccount/. And if you need any refreshers on what the terms mean, Chapter 3 provides them.

There are three cases for those not grandparented to consider.

Case 1: Your full retirement benefit is larger than half of your spouse's full retirement benefit.

In this case, we would, in general, but not always, tell you to wait till 70 to collect your retirement benefit. How come? *Because you actually can never collect a spousal benefit.* The minute you can collect a spousal benefit and actually request to do so, Social Security will *deem* you; that is, they will force you to also take your own retirement benefit. Then they will give you just your retirement benefit because your retirement benefit exceeds your spousal benefit.

So, if you are in this situation, obeying Rule 3—*Get Your Timing Right*—means that you should tell your Apple Watch or Google calendar or kids to start shouting at you when you are a few months away from celebrating your 70th.

When they do, either file online, file over the phone, or head into the local Social Security office and state your intention of taking your retirement benefit starting on your 70th birthday, when it will be as large as possible, *and not a day sooner.* Make sure this intention is written in the Remarks section of your application. Why do this? We'll tell you in Chapter 6. It's one of our Social Security horror stories.

Case 2: Your age-70 retirement benefit is less than half of your spouse's full retirement benefit.

Unlike Case 1, where you'll never be able to collect a spousal benefit, here you'll never be able to collect your retirement benefit. Yes, Social Security will claim they are giving you your retirement benefit plus an excess spousal benefit, but they'll be dissembling, to put it nicely. You'll just be getting your spousal benefit or something very close to it.

This rant aside, if you're a case 2, you should, in general, take your spousal benefit at full retirement age.

What should your timing be? Whatever day you reach full retirement. Again, www.ssa.gov/OACT/ProgData/ar_dre.html can help you figure this out.

Case 3: Your age-70 retirement benefit is greater than half of your spouse's full retirement benefit, but your full retirement benefit is less than half of your spouse's full retirement benefit.

Now we've got a tricky case, where the timing is clear only to a detailed computer program (like the one Larry offers at maximize mysocialsecurity.com). Otherwise, it's essentially impossible to determine the optimal timing on your own.

Let's say you apply for your benefits starting at Full Retirement Age. You'll get an amount that roughly equals your spousal benefit—because at FRA it's higher than your own retirement benefit—but because you've filed, *you can never collect your higher age-70 retirement benefit.*

But maybe this is the best move. After all, you will pick up 4 years of spousal benefits that you would otherwise lose were you to wait till 70. If the age-70 retirement benefit is only a few dollars more than your spousal benefit, it's surely best to take benefits at Full Retirement Age.

But what if your age-70 benefit is a lot higher—say, 30 percent higher? Then taking your benefits at Full Retirement Age is going to cost you big-time over the long haul, assuming you live a long life, which is the reality you need to plan for.

BAD-TIMING NIGHTMARES

One of our ongoing nightmares involves a spouse, say a wife, who (1) sees from her partner's online record that he can provide a large full spousal benefit, (2) contacts Social Security to collect it, (3) gets nothing except a permanently lower retirement benefit, *but thinks it's a spousal benefit*, and then (4) asks at age 70 to take her retirement benefit only to be told she's been receiving it for years and that it will never be any bigger.

This nightmare is still possible under the new Social Security rules we explained in the last chapter. Over time, we expect it to disappear, because *everyone* under the age of 62 as of the end of 2015 will be deemed to be filing for all of their eligible benefits when they file for any of them. We just hope Social Security will clearly explain these new rules, although its track record hardly fills us with hope.

A second bad-timing nightmare involves a spouse who hears from us and others that it's best to take her retirement benefit at 70 and knows nothing about spousal benefits. If she's a Case 2, she'll lose 4 or so years of spousal benefits only to find out at 70 that her total benefit is no larger at 70 than had she taken it years before at Full Retirement Age.

Our third bad-timing nightmare involves Case 3. It features the spouse who realizes his full spousal benefit exceeds his full retirement benefit, but doesn't realize that it's a lot less than his age-70 benefit. As a result, he takes benefits at Full Retirement Age when he should wait until 70.

Or he realizes that his age-70 retirement benefit exceeds his full spousal benefit and decides to wait to collect it, not realizing that he's giving up more than he's getting back by not taking his benefits at Full Retirement Age.

THIS IS JUST THE BEGINNING OF THE TIMING COMPLEXITY

Unfortunately, getting the timing straight when it comes to spousal benefits is even tougher than it sounds above because:

To collect a spousal benefit, under the new law, your spouse must first collect their retirement benefit (ignoring any grandparenting). And vice versa.

Spousal benefits are calculated so that one spouse will, for sure, fall into Case 1. So that spouse will likely want to wait till 70 to collect if he wants to collect the most. But if his partner falls into, say, Case 2 and they're the same age, she may want him to take his retirement benefit early so she can file for her spousal benefit.

Unless partners are truly focused on their mutual best interest, the new law will have introduced some irreconcilable differences—just the thing for a good pair of divorce attorneys!

SOCIAL SECURITY VERBATIM

RUSH TO JUDGMENT?

"Whenever a potential claimant visits a FO [field office] and wishes to file, make every effort to complete an application and obtain the claimant's signature."

ALL QUOTES FROM OFFICIAL SOCIAL SECURITY RULES

IMPLEMENTING THE TIMING RULE—
AN INITIAL SURVIVORSHIP EXAMPLE

We're going to provide concrete examples of Rule 3—*Get Your Timing Right*—in Chapter 9 as it pertains to spousal and divorced spousal benefits, and in other chapters as it pertains to other auxiliary benefits. But for now, we want to tell you about optimal timing as it relates to widow(er) benefits.

These are, to repeat ourselves, complicated issues even to discuss, let alone act upon. But they are extremely important to *getting what's yours*, and nowhere is this more important than to those retirees who lose a partner and must live largely on survivor benefits.

Unlike spousal and divorced spousal benefits, the new law left provisions about taking widow(er) benefits largely unchanged. In particular, there still is no deeming with respect to widow(er) benefits. This means that you can still take your widow(er) benefit before your retirement benefit or you can still take your retirement benefit first.

If you take your retirement benefit before taking your widow(er) benefit, your widow(er) benefit, when you later take it, will be regarded by Social Security as *not* your full widow(er) benefit but your *excess* widow(er) benefit. It will be the amount by which your widow(er) benefit exceeds the retirement benefit you've already been receiving. Moreover, under the new law, if you didn't suspend your retirement benefit by April 30, 2016, you can't even collect your excess widow(er) benefit while your retirement benefit is suspended.

To illustrate the importance of timing the collection of widow(er) benefits, let's consider an extended example based on a hypothetical widow named Edith, living in Vermont. Her case may not apply to you now, or ever. But it's a simple way to make clear the importance of our third rule about timing.

Edith is 62 and has spent her life as a cook at a fast-food

restaurant. She was married to Bert, a veterinarian, until last night, when, ironically, he drove into a moose near Montpelier. The moose walked away. Bert did not.

Because she's over 60, Edith would now be eligible to collect a survivor benefit. But because today happens to be her 62nd birthday, she's also freshly eligible to collect her own retirement benefit. (A cautionary reminder: both her widow and retirement benefits will be reduced if taken before 66, which is Edith's Full Retirement Age.)

Bert earned more than Edith. Once she has recovered from Bert's moose mishap, she rushes to her local Social Security office and asks to get all the benefits she can. They comply by giving her both her retirement benefit plus her "excess" widow benefit. Edith has just messed herself up royally because she has violated Rule 3: her timing has wiped out one of her benefits.

(A lengthy aside here to make a point especially close to Larry's heart. If Edith asks Social Security what happened to her own retirement benefit, they'll tell her something we find highly misleading. Rather than tell Edith that her retirement benefit has been wiped out by her widow benefit, they'll instead tell her she *is* getting her retirement benefit plus a smaller, redefined widow benefit equal to the *difference*, or excess, between her survivor benefit and her retirement benefit.)

So let's suppose Edith's monthly survivor benefit is $2,000 and her monthly retirement benefit is $1,800. Social Security will send Edith $2,000—$1,800 on her record plus $200 on Bert's record, combined into one opaque payment.

Edith worked her entire life, slinging burgers on the midnight shift at McDonald's. Her earnings record would confirm that she and the company contributed every year for 40 years to Social Security: 12.4 percent of her total earnings. Nonetheless, she would end up getting nothing extra in benefits in exchange for all those years of FICA taxes, even though Social Security would pretend that she is.

And even if Edith's own retirement benefit were not $1,800, but $1,999, her monthly $2,000 payment would not change by one red cent. Why? Because her survivor benefit would *still* be larger than her retirement benefit. Again, no matter how Social Security describes things, *if you collect a retirement and a widow(er) benefit at once, you get just one—the larger one, which is also the one that wipes out the other.*

EDITH GETS AT LEAST SOME OF WHAT'S HERS

But now watch what happens if Edith applies *just* for her own retirement benefit at 62 and waits until her FRA, age 66, to file for her survivor benefit.

In this case, Edith will actually get her retirement benefit for 4 years. As we've explained, because she starts it early, at age 62, rather than waiting until as late as age 70, it will be smaller than it might have been. But it won't be wiped out by her widow benefit for those 4 years. That's because of one simple tactic: she doesn't *file* for her widow benefit until age 66.

The beauty of this strategy is that Edith, who we imagine is in robust health, loses nothing by waiting to collect her survivor benefit until age 66. True, she will collect only $1,800 a month for four years as her own benefit instead of $2,000 as Bert's widow, and if that $200 a month is the difference between comfort and penury, she may have no choice but to collect. But were she to wait until her FRA of 66 to collect her widow benefit, it would then not be $2,000, but $2,469, over and above any adjustment for inflation. That's a 23 percent higher real benefit, year in and year out, from age 66 to her death, or from here to *eternity* if science manages to arrest or reverse the process of aging before Edith's passing. And unlike retirement benefits, widow benefits do not increase past FRA, so there's no reason for Edith to wait longer than that.

But wait! There's an even better strategy for long-lived Edith, assuming she can hold off long enough to collect her maximum benefit. She should take her reduced widow's benefit of $2,000 a month at age 62 and hold off filing for her own retirement benefit until age 70. That $1,800 retirement benefit she is entitled to receive at age 62 will grow over eight years to $3,168 at age 70. This is $1,168 more each month than her age-62 survivor benefit and $699 higher than her age-66 survivor benefit. It is, far and away, her best option.

Now take a look at Edith's scorecard in terms of following the three rules around which this chapter is built. First, by waiting to get higher benefits, Edith would be following Rule 1. Second, by waiting, she would also able to follow Rule 2 and avail herself of more than one benefit. And third, she would be following Rule 3 by getting her timing right—taking one benefit early and letting the other grow before taking it when it has reached its maximum value.

THE THREE GENERAL RULES—
ONCE MORE, WITH FEELING

"Tell them what you'll tell them, tell them, and then tell them what you told them" is the time-worn formula for good teaching, essay writing, and anything else you want people to remember. But with Social Security's bewildering maze of rules, elaborated in mind-numbing legalese, we're worried that your memory may reject our earnest efforts at repetition. So let's fall back on pedagogy's fail-safe method for imprinting lasting knowledge—terrorizing the student.

If you're an average American—and even modestly *above* average— you are facing a retirement you almost surely cannot afford, or cannot afford without a major lowering of expectations and standard of living. These days there is a fair chance that you will be forced to stop working sooner than you supposed due to a clear-the-decks boss, a hair-trigger economy, or a fickle physiology; that you will, as a consequence, find yourself involuntarily retired with far less savings than you had anticipated; and/or that you will live far longer than you had expected.

You may therefore become dependent on Social Security to an extent you never imagined. If this were to happen—and to many of you it absolutely *will*—navigating the system deftly could be a matter of (comfortable) life versus a kind death, as in "I'd rather be dead," because you're incapacitated yet can't afford the help to so much as get out of bed. That's the risk if you aren't careful and take the wrong benefit advice about what to do or not to do.

Unfortunately, much of the confusion emanates from Social Security itself. Not in what it says, but rather in what it doesn't say or doesn't say clearly enough about what you can't do or must do.

6

BE CAREFUL TAKING SOCIAL SECURITY'S ADVICE AND HELP

Yours May Be the Next Horror Story

Social Security began handing out regular monthly benefits in 1940, five years after the program was created to bolster a Depression-racked nation. It was a big change for a laissez-faire country, though it provided a safety net that would seem skimpy today: the typical Social Security payment was $17.50 a month in 1940, or roughly $300 in today's dollars.

What began as a Model T Ford program, however—one size fits all—has been expanded, amended, reformed, and socially engineered into a fully loaded Rube Goldbergmobile. It has a driver's manual a mile thick that we'd bet most of Social Security's own representatives can't follow.

Consider the story of John, one of the many Americans who email or call Larry regularly for help on their Social Security claims. (As we've written, Larry answers as many questions as he can every Monday on Paul's PBS Making Sen$e website.) It would be nice if John was an outlier, but he's not.

John was 66; his wife turned 62 before January 2, 2016. He and his wife are fairly well-off and John was still working. So they didn't need to take Social Security right away. John called Social Security and asked the person on the phone if he could file for his retirement benefit and suspend its collection so that his wife could get a spousal benefit right away.

John told the Social Security representative that he'd been the higher earner. According to John, the Social Security rep told him that he could and should file and suspend and that his wife would then get a spousal benefit. John's wife had earned more than $60,000 a year until the last 10 years, but not much of late. John and the rep figured her own retirement benefits would be very low. But they were wrong. Social Security's benefit formula is so progressive that the couple's respective benefits actually would be similar.

And if John had filed for his retirement benefit, and his wife had then filed for her spousal benefit, she would have been deemed to also be filing for her retirement benefit because she would have been filing before reaching her FRA. She'd get something close to the larger of the two benefits, which, in her case, would likely have been her retirement benefit—*not* her spousal benefit. And it would have been reduced forever because she was forced to file for it early!

The happy ending here is that John contacted Making Sen$e and a real nightmare became just a bad dream. Had he not, he and his wife could well have headed to the local Social Security office and made a huge financial mistake.

We're going to provide a few more "horror stories" at the end of this chapter. Our goal is not to pillory Social Security, which is severely understaffed and whose workers are overworked, underpaid, and, it seems, undertrained. Larry loves the idea of Social Security, but hates its implementation. Paul and Phil take a kinder view. We all three agree, though, that the people working at Social Security are trying their best to help us. Unfortunately, given the system's tremendous complexity, their well-meaning help is not always helpful. This is why we are pushing you to help Social Security help you by knowing precisely what's yours before you try to go get it.

SOCIAL SECURITY DOESN'T HAVE THE
RESOURCES TO GET YOU WHAT'S YOURS

The agency is overwhelmed with requests for advice, benefit calculations, and requests. It's hard to believe, but the agency gets 3 million requests for information every week.

Social Security services more Americans than any other agency of government, including the Internal Revenue Service. And yet it does so with shrinking staff and resources.

How big is the job? In 2014, roughly 166 million people had Social Security payroll taxes withheld from their paychecks. As of late 2015, Social Security provided payments to 42.9 million retirees and their dependents, 6.1 million survivors of deceased workers, and 10.8 million disabled workers and their dependents.

In total, the agency paid nearly $880 billion in benefits, including $747 billion in retirement and survivor benefits and $133 billion in disability payments. And yet the program's administrative expenses were less than 1 percent of the money it handled.

Consider the howls from health insurance companies when Obamacare required them to pay out at least 85 percent of their revenues in benefits. How, they lamented, are we going to run our organizations, pay our employees, and reward our owners retaining only 15 percent of our revenues?

And in the allegedly efficient *private* financial sector, the fees—in order just to *manage* your money—are often far higher.

Yes, some financial companies, like Vanguard, operate with very low overhead. Their management fees on some funds average less than a *fifth* of 1 percent. But Vanguard isn't taking in money from 160 million people and almost as many businesses a month and sending out 57 million checks. Nor is it besieged daily by millions of people asking questions and making requests.

Given its importance, you'd think the agency would receive ample resources to do its job, but the opposite is true. The Social Security Administration is under a fiscal siege thanks to congressional budget cuts. In late 2012 the agency was forced to cut operating hours at more than 1,200 field offices and began closing them at noon each Wednesday; in March 2015 it tacked an hour onto each weekday except for Wednesday. At the time, more than *180,000 people a day* were visiting those offices and the agency was handling 450,000 phone calls. Every single day. While the number of claimants has swelled due to baby boomer retirements, visits as of late 2015 were down to 165,000 a day. Agency employment in late 2015 was about 75,000, down by more than 11,000 from earlier years. In the five years ending in mid-2014, the agency had closed 64 field offices, 5 percent of its total. Yes, SSA has developed a growing ability to conduct business online. But most people want (and need) a *human being* to help them make fateful, once-in-a-lifetime financial decisions.

SSA regularly surveys consumers about their perceptions of the quality of its services. Based on its 2013 and 2014 surveys, public satisfaction rates were 66 percent for 1-800 calls, 79 percent for field office calls, and 93 percent for field office visits.

One way to look at it: the glass is two-thirds full when it comes to electronic encounters, *nine-tenths* full when the contact is human to human, face-to-face. The more journalistic appraisal, however, would be that fully one-third of all customers are *dis*satisfied online or by phone, and that office visits are the public's most successful way of meeting their needs. In a telling footnote to its 2014 report, the agency said some customer satisfaction data that year was unavailable due to a government staffing furlough.

But more to the point, how can the public know if it *should be* satisfied? If beneficiaries and would-be beneficiaries don't get a second opinion, how are they to know whether they're getting good information or being disastrously misled, even if by a very well-meaning person? The simple fact is that the SSA representative on the phone, or across from you at the table, is often overworked and undertrained.

2013 AND 2014 PUBLIC SATISFACTION WITH SOCIAL SECURITY SERVICES

SERVICE	PEOPLE SERVED	SERVICE RATINGS (%)	
		Satisfied	Excellent
1-800 Callers	53,000,000	66	22
Field Office Caller	45,000,000	79	35
Field Office Visitor	44,000,000	93	42
Card Center Visitor	1,000,000	86	31
Hearing Office Visitor	500,000	92	31
Internet Benefit Applications	3,000,000	89	27
Internet Change Address/Direct Deposit	900,000	95	42
Internet Disability Reports	800,000	81	22
Internet Requests	4,000,000	89	30
TOTAL ALL SERVICES	156,200,000	80	33

"INFORMATION," NOT "ADVICE"? TAKE IT WITH A SHAKER (OR MAYBE A MINE) OF SALT

Social Security claims that its representatives do not give *advice* to consumers. Instead, they say, they provide *information*. This would surely come as news to most of the people who ask it for help.

Moreover, what seems like the simplest Social Security question can require considerable thought by even the most knowledgeable personnel and a lengthy explanation to the questioner. Their recourse, then, is to provide one-size-fits-all answers. This is especially true in the online world, where the agency has been making much of its new public service effort.

Further, and this is very important, Social Security claiming decisions are often irreversible.

Go into nearly any retail store in this land, buy a product in error, and you will be able to return it later. But that's often not the case with mistaken Social Security claiming decisions, even if prompted by the agency's own representatives. Thus the agency's information could wind up being the most costly "advice" you ever get.

A final red flag. In the words of Social Security itself, "The fact that we determine that a claimant meets the requirements for entitlement does not preclude us from making another determination that the claimant no longer meets those requirements at some subsequent date," according to the agency's vast Program Operations Manual System, or POMS. A reasonable inference to draw: even *correct* information from Social Security may be, in the lingo of Wall Street money managers, no guarantee of future returns.

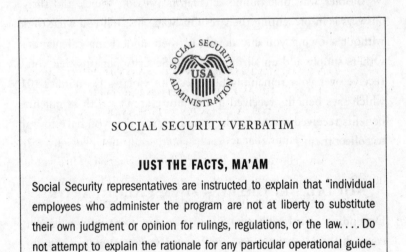

SOCIAL SECURITY VERBATIM

JUST THE FACTS, MA'AM

Social Security representatives are instructed to explain that "individual employees who administer the program are not at liberty to substitute their own judgment or opinion for rulings, regulations, or the law. . . . Do not attempt to explain the rationale for any particular operational guidelines, nor go to any great lengths to justify them."

ALL QUOTES FROM OFFICIAL SOCIAL SECURITY RULES

ESTIMATES OF YOUR FUTURE BENEFITS: WHICH SHOULD YOU TRUST?

You might think that online calculators will give you the right strategy for maximizing your lifetime benefits. Some will, some won't. This is particularly true if your situation differs from the average, as we discovered when we tested them ourselves.

There are two ways online calculators can go badly wrong. They can take in the wrong inputs, and they can make the wrong calculations with those inputs. Social Security calculators geared to be quick don't take in enough information "above the hood"—in their user interfaces—to make the right calculations "under the hood"—in their computation engines. So even if a quick calculator's computation engine is correctly programmed—*a very big if*—it can't produce accurate results.

Another way that online calculators provide "quick and dirty" answers is in presenting their results. Some just tell you what to do without showing you any details of their underlying calculations. Others simply add up all future Social Security benefits that you'll receive over your remaining lifetime. This violates Economics 101, which says benefits received in the future aren't worth as much as benefits received today, for the simple reason that you have to wait to collect them.

SOCIAL SECURITY'S OWN CALCULATORS

Depending on which Social Security source you use, you may receive different answers to your request for an estimate of future benefits. Social Security has various estimation techniques. We're all for freedom of choice but think these sources should agree with one another. It turns out they don't.

Your choices include:

- SSA's official annual statement with benefit estimates;
- An over-the-phone Social Security staff estimate;
- An in-person estimate at a local office;
- Four different online benefit calculators, each of which gives you a number.

But if the numbers vary among these seven estimate options—and they very likely will—you won't immediately know why, or which to believe, though the calculators do say that the numbers provided are estimates and that there are many reasons they might differ from your actual benefits.

Let's take a look at perhaps the most familiar of these estimates—that provided in the annual earnings statement, which Social Security calls Your Social Security Statement. It itemizes your earnings history and lays out its assumptions about your future earnings. But in presenting the retirement benefits you can collect, starting at different ages, the statement doesn't say whether the amounts are shown in today's dollars, adjusted for inflation, or in dollars of the year in which you start collecting. Nor does it say whether the benefit estimates take into account America's projected real-wage growth between the year of the statement and the year benefits collection might begin. Yet, until age 60, your benefits are indexed to this very number: the overall wage growth of American workers. And afterward, they're adjusted yearly for the cost of living.

In fact, the benefit estimates on your earnings statement assume no growth in Social Security's Average Wage Index (AWI) as well as no future inflation *whatsoever*! And this despite the fact that, since 1952, the AWI has grown in all but one year and prices have risen in all but two years.

Likewise, if you call or visit your Social Security office, they will give you benefit estimates, but won't necessarily tell you what dollars they are quoting your benefits in, or whether they are *assuming* economy-wide wage growth. And they may not know to tell you since they too are relying on calculators and reports whose underlying assumptions aren't immediately apparent.

Moreover, if you are requesting a benefit quote for when you pass age 65, they may quote your benefit net of Medicare's Part B premium payment, since this is taken out of the payment you would actually get each month. It may also be quoted net of withholding for federal income taxes.

Okay, those are the problems with Your Social Security Statement and personal advice from Social Security, either by phone or in person. But what about the four online calculators?

We went to the main Social Security calculator page (http://www.ssa.gov/planners/benefitcalculators.htm) and took each of them out for a spin.

First we followed the advice provided in Chapter 3 and created an online account at *my Social Security* (http://www.ssa.gov/myaccount/). We were then able to use the agency's own record of our Social Security earnings history (we used only one coauthor's actual earnings history). Here's how the calculators stacked up against one another:

Quick Calculator (http://www.ssa.gov/OACT/quickcalc/index.html)

It was quick indeed and it also showed results in both today's dollars (unadjusted for inflation) and in *future* dollars (adjusted to reflect the rising cost of living). We entered in $80,000 a year in covered earnings up until the year we would begin claiming benefits. This calculator said our retirement benefit at age 70 would be $2,622 in current dollars and that benefits would be $1,905 for a spouse, plus $1,429 to a qualifying child, with a Family Maximum Benefit of $3,348. The problem is, if we didn't know better, we might well have stopped there.

Online Calculator (http://www.ssa.gov/retire2/AnypiaApplet.html)

This was a lot of work, as it asked for earnings for every year since our first in the labor force. Fortunately, we were able to plug in the details from our version of Your Social Security Statement. We used the same $80,000 a year in estimated future covered earnings as before.

But here's the punch line. This nonquick calculator said our monthly retirement benefit at 70 would be $3,249! That's 24 percent more than what the Quick Calculator generated: $627 a month, *for the rest of our life*. And our spousal, child, and other family benefits—all pegged to our full retirement benefit—would be comparably higher as well.

Detailed Calculator (http://www.ssa.gov/OACT/anypia/anypia.html)

This is the most time-consuming tool to use. It requires you to download software to your computer and to enter your year-by-year earnings history again. But the software has been updated with the latest benefit computations, including the most recent annual Cost of Living Adjustment (COLA). It also was the only tool that calculated our Primary Insurance Amount, or PIA. According to the Detailed Calculator, our retirement benefit at age 70 would be $3,198 a month—an estimate not far from the Online Calculator's $3,249.

Retirement Estimator (http://www.socialsecurity.gov/estimator/)

This calculator provides benefit estimates based on your actual Social Security earnings history. It does so by asking you for identifying information, including your Social Security number. It then pulls your actual earnings history from agency computers and produces an estimate. Once you've entered this information and answered a couple of other questions, you get a result quickly. So, it's much easier to use than the Online Calculator or the Detailed Calculator. And it's accurate as well. It said our retirement benefit at age 70 would be $3,249 a month—identical to the Online Calculator.

For one last comparison, we went online to consult our current Your Social Security Statement. It said our retirement benefit at age 70 would be $3,205 a month. That was lower than the other detailed calculators. But in looking at the reason, it turns out the agency was assuming our future earnings would be smaller than our own estimates.

A MAJOR WORD OF WARNING ABOUT ALL SOCIAL SECURITY BENEFIT ESTIMATES, INCLUDING THOSE PROVIDED BY ITS CALCULATORS

As we mentioned, Social Security projects your future benefits assuming no future economy-wide growth in average wages and no future inflation. These assumptions appear to be used by all its calculators and in whatever calculators or other software staff at local offices or over the phone are using to provide you with benefit estimates. Social Security's "ANYPIA" calculator (see above) does, however, permit you to change these historical assumptions. But you need to learn how to work with the calculator first.

Interestingly, the trustees of the Social Security system don't believe in zero future inflation or zero future economy-wide wage growth. In their 2015 Trustees Report[1] they assumed inflation will be 2.7 percent after 2020 and a bit higher before then. They also assumed that average wages would grow at roughly 4 percent after 2020 and at more than 4 percent before 2020. Using these assumptions rather than the zero inflation and wage growth assumptions underlying Social Security's standard benefit estimates can produce huge biases in estimates. Take, for example, a moderate-earning

50-year-old who plans to work through age 60. These two assumptions could easily lead to a 20 percent understatement of her full retirement benefit. The younger the worker, the greater the downward bias.

Why is Social Security providing lowball benefit estimates to younger workers? Larry asked this question of a very senior Social Security official. His answer: to make sure workers didn't overestimate their replacement rate—the ratio of their benefit to their earnings right before retirement. He and others at Social Security worry that providing the true, higher benefit estimate will lead workers to compare that number not with their pre-retirement wages, but with their current wages and, as a result, overestimate their replacement rate. Such an overestimate could lead them to save too little on their own.

Social Security can also *over*estimate your future benefits. Its standard assumption is that what you are now earning is what you will continue to earn through full retirement age, at which point you will stop earning entirely. This may be true for some current workers, but certainly not for all. And those current earners with particularly high current earnings who don't expect to work through full retirement can find their benefit overestimated because the overestimates of untypically high earnings are incorporated in the calculation of the worker's AIME (Average Indexed Monthly Earnings).

Larry's Maximize My Social Security software reverse-engineers Social Security's benefit estimates as needed because he's seen how far off they can be. He's also found that biased estimates, particularly for married couples, where the estimates can be differentially biased for the two spouses, can produce inappropriate claiming strategies. As the old saying goes, "garbage in, garbage out." That goes for commercial as well as free Social Security calculators. Even if those calculators are good under the hood, they won't deliver the right advice if the inputs that are entered aren't correct.

TAKING A TEST DRIVE OF
THE AARP CALCULATOR

There are scads of free calculators out there. We're going to take a deep look into the one provided by AARP. Odds are, it's one of, if not the, most heavily used (roughly 750,000 times a year, AARP says). Also, the questions we pose about it are valid considerations in using other calculators. And the greatest shortcoming of all of them (or at least all of them we've seen, and that's a lot) is their focus on being easy to use. But as we've seen, when it comes to Social Security, simplicity is the enemy of accuracy.

AARP, as you probably know, used to be shorthand for the American Association of Retired Persons. With some 37 million members ages 50 and above, AARP pays a lot of attention to Social Security. Simple doesn't necessarily mean off base. But it could be the case here, as careful readers of Chapter 3 know.

Jean Setzfand, AARP's vice president of financial security, stresses that simplicity and ease of use were important considerations in designing AARP's calculator. She is a fan of more sophisticated calculators, which often charge fees. "Many of them are terrific," she said in an interview with us. "But they are more for a financial advisory audience. We're not targeting sophisticated investors. . . . [The AARP tool] is really for individuals who have a basic understanding of their finances."

AARP's tool gives you two ways to provide your Primary Insurance Amount (PIA), which, of course, is the building block for calculating all the benefits you and yours can get on your earnings record.

QUICK AND DIRTY—METHOD 1

Method 1 entails entering your earnings and letting the calculator figure out your PIA. If the tool solicited your exact earnings history, it would be able to calculate your PIA precisely. But instead it asks you to enter your average earnings.

But what's the meaning of "average earnings"? The instructions say, "If your earnings have gone up and down over the years, enter an average salary, even if it's different than your current salary." Okay, but is this an average salary measured in today's dollars or is it an average of the actual dollars you earned each year in the past? The website doesn't say. But it can make a huge difference to the calculated PIA. And even if you know whether to enter your past average earnings in actual dollars or today's dollars, that doesn't suffice to determine your PIA. Indeed, if you didn't work for 40 quarters in covered employment, your PIA will be zero because you won't be eligible for any benefits, period. If you do have 40 quarters under your belt and *if* you enter your average past covered earnings correctly, your PIA may still be miles off. The reason is that the accurate calculation of your PIA is based on your Average Indexed Monthly Earnings (AIME), which, in turn, is based on each year's separate level of earnings. In other words, when you made your earnings can matter—*a lot!*

Moreover, the AIME calculation only uses past *covered* earnings, not your total earnings. But the AARP calculator doesn't tell you to enter your average past *covered* earnings. It just tells you to enter your average earnings, which users will likely take to mean their total, not their covered earnings.

To understand how bad just this mistake could be with respect to getting a benefit estimate from AARP, we ran a single person—call him Dan—twice through a software program (Larry's Maximize My Social Security) that incorporates precise earnings histories. In each case, Dan's average nominal earnings are $50,000. But in one case, Dan earns exactly $50,000 each year for 40 years. In the other case, Dan earns $100,000 each year for 20 years and zero otherwise. Although Dan's average earnings are the same, his benefits in the first case are one-third larger than in the second case!

Setzfand noted that possible inaccuracies with letting people calculate their own average earnings were one reason AARP recommends that people get their actual earnings history from Social Security and plug this number into the AARP calculator. This sounds fine. But what number, we would ask, should they use?

How long will you continue to work? The AARP calculator must assume you'll work through FRA, but it doesn't say. And if you are only going to work for two more years and FRA is eight years away, well, that's yet another potential decent-size mistake entering into your PIA calculation. This is particularly the case for workers who earn above the taxable maximum after age 60. For such workers, their AIME is guaranteed to go up for each year they work after age 60 because each extra year's worth of covered earnings thrown into the pot will always be larger than the other ones in the pot.

Furthermore, without exactly correct data on your past covered earnings, it's impossible for an online calculator to properly figure out how much your benefits will rise due to your continued earnings after age 60. (This process, known as Social Security's Recomputation of Benefits, is explained in the next chapter.) It's also impossible to properly calculate Social Security's Windfall Elimination Provision, which we will cover in detail in Chapter 14.

QUICK AND DIRTY—METHOD 2

Understanding these problems with AARP's first way to use its calculator might lead you to say, "Fuhgeddaboudit," and proceed to AARP's second way. But the second way to use the calculator assumes you won't work at all in the future. It also takes you to one of Social Security's online calculators, which will provide a PIA estimate that is guaranteed, if you're under 60, to come back with the wrong estimate of your PIA (as we just explained).

Since the AARP calculator is taking in, in this case, a Social

Security–produced PIA estimate that is likely to be wrong, the question is whether the calculator's underlying code is fixing the problem with the PIA so entered. Setzfand said there is no adjustment to the number received from Social Security. This might not be a material problem. But it could be and, of course, you won't know.

The AARP calculator pays a lot of attention to combined benefits of married couples, and this is a good thing. It also gets a gold star from us for comparing benefit estimates with spending trends among retired persons, providing a useful view of budgeting realities tied to Social Security income. However, for married spouses where one partner's optimal strategy depends on what the other does and vice versa, starting off with off-base PIAs can easily undermine the calculation of what's best for the couple to do jointly.

If you ask for your retirement benefit, the good folks at Social Security may quote your benefit in dollars of the year you will reach full retirement. That could screw up the AARP calculator. Or they may quote you not your full retirement benefit, but your *reduced* retirement benefit if you start talking to them about taking benefits early. This too will screw up the AARP calculator, since it's looking for the full retirement benefit. Then there's the issue of your Medicare Part B premiums and automatic federal income tax withholdings. You may be given a "benefit amount" that's net of one or both of these things. Finally, if you are eligible for an excess spousal or an excess survivor benefit, it's possible you'll be quoted a benefit amount that's inclusive of these auxiliary benefits, which will also cause AARP's calculator to produce misleading benefit estimates.

FINANCIAL ENGINES REVS
UP ITS CALCULATOR

Financial Engines is a 401(k) advisory firm founded by Nobel laureate economist William Sharpe. Its clients provided retirement services to about 9 million employees in mid-2014, which is also when it began to offer a free Social Security calculator. Many of the assumptions in its calculator reflect limitations similar to those noted in the AARP and other quick-and-easy calculators. However, in explaining the rationale behind Financial Engines' work, the company's chief investment officer, Christopher Jones, covered some crucial realities about Social Security that we'd like to share.

First off, Jones said, the need for a quick calculator that can be used in five minutes or less is a necessity, not a marketing gimmick. Otherwise, people will hit what he called a behavioral "blocking condition" and simply will not proceed. There is some sacrifice to accuracy in this calculator, perhaps, but it's not large. And he said the calculator is particularly accurate for those people nearing retirement and thus facing Social Security claiming decisions.

Second, Jones said, the fate of surviving spouses is key to making optimal claiming decisions. Yet many people—and many calculators—fail to consider spousal benefits or consider them accurately. Financial Engines uses longevity odds that include the probabilities for both spouses. On average, he said, the surviving spouse will live another 11 years after losing their mate. This is a much bigger gap than indicated by mortality tables. But this figure is built into the company's calculator when it spits out claiming advice.

Financial Engines also interviewed hundreds of people near retirement before launching its calculator. What it found is that people dread burning though their nest eggs, particularly during their early retirement years. In terms of Social Security, then, they would tend to favor taking benefits earlier to avoid spending down their savings.

So, where the lifetime values of different Social Security claiming options are similar (and Jones said this is often the case), Financial Engines will "tilt" toward recommending that people take benefits earlier. This will, incidentally, give them more money to manage.

Jones himself acknowledged the irony of this approach. For, while there is some risk that people who do not take benefits might die early, deferring Social Security benefits is, in his view, the best financial option available today. Delayed Retirement Credits allow Social Security benefits to rise by 8 percent a year, plus the rate of inflation. And the payments are guaranteed by the federal government. "That's a screamingly good deal," he said, while agreeing that "in general, the population is very poorly informed with respect to the benefits of delaying Social Security."

"The deferral strategies do better 90 to 95 percent of the time," he said. "The only situation where starting early makes sense is where you *and* your spouse both die early."

DECODING "YOUR SOCIAL SECURITY STATEMENT"

Your Social Security Statement is the agency's annually updated record of your actual earnings and projected benefits. Typically, the latest one would arrive in the mail annually and include a year-by-year record of what is called your covered wage employment—each year's earnings, ever since you began working, up to the amount of that year's wage ceiling for payroll taxes. (The statement never explained the wage ceiling, so when some people reviewed their "earnings record," they couldn't figure out why their yearly amounts were lower than what they had actually been paid.)

Despite its idiosyncrasies, Your Social Security Statement was long the single most authoritative look at your Social Security benefits. Besides reflecting your earnings history and, thus, your projected retirement benefits (with the flaws we've already noted), Your Social Security Statement was (and remains) the only easily accessible record of how much money you earned every year. After 30 or 40 years in the workforce, try rounding up this information on your own. With an average of 10,000 baby boomers turning 66 every day from 2011 to about 2030, more and more people need this information. But a couple of years ago, the SSA, its budget pressed, announced that it would stop sending out printed statements. The agency later said it would create the ability to provide the statements online. Still later, it said anyone who asked for an old-fashioned printed statement could get one in the mail. And, more recently, it developed plans to automatically send paper statements to people once every five years—at 25, 30, 35, 40, 45, 50, 55, and 60, as well as annually to those older than 60.

The number of people who have signed up for the online version of their annual statement is, by now, in the millions. But this big number remains a small percentage of the number of people who used to be mailed the annual statement. (The cost of this mailing, by the way, was something like 80 cents apiece.)

One problem, of course, is that if you don't see your statement, you won't be able to take a look at your official earnings record and related benefits projections. More to our point here, you also won't be able to see if the agency has made any mistakes in calculating your earnings record. And, guess what? Mistakes are made all the time. The most frequent cause of errors involves people who over-pay their Social Security taxes because they are working at multiple jobs that take out payroll taxes from both salaries. Not often, but often enough, the agency fails to receive the correct information or to properly track these multiple jobs and, as a result, undercounts your payroll taxes and future Social Security benefits.

You can fix these mistakes. But only if you see them, and then go through an SSA dispute resolution process.

THE PRIVACY PROBLEM: HOW TO UNCOVER YOUR EX-SPOUSAL AND SURVIVORSHIP BENEFITS

Spousal benefits are hugely important in many people's Social Security claiming decisions. So are benefits for divorced spouses and benefits for surviving spouses. Here, our beef is not only with the agency's confusing rules and often inconsistent advice. We're also perplexed by the agency's privacy rules, which won't permit the divorced person access to their ex-spouses' earnings records or automatically let widows and widowers have access to their late spouses' earnings records. Optimal claiming decisions are hard enough even when you know all the numbers. They become impossible when you can't get the information you need.

Given Social Security's benefit formulas, ex-spouses have a legal claim to benefits based on their former spouses' earnings records. But if they can't get access to these records, they can't properly decide when to retire, or how much to save for retirement, or in which order or when to take their spousal, retirement, and survivor benefits, or when to start taking one or more benefit.

Yes, once ex-spouses are close to the time they can collect benefits on their ex- or deceased husbands or wives, they can find out from Social Security what these benefits will be. But that's *very late* in the day. And yes, if they are really knowledgeable about the system, they can roughly infer what their spouses must have made and then run through the potentially thousands of combinations of benefit collection dates to figure out which one is optimal. But this is not something we recommend anyone try on their own.

As for learning whether your ex is collecting benefits, don't expect Social Security to notify you. The Social Security Administration doesn't know who is or was married to whom. You need to establish that you are or were married by providing a copy of your marriage certificate or your final divorce decree. But to collect divorced spousal benefits, you need to have been married at least 10 years, have an ex who is at least age 62, and have been divorced for 2 or more years *or have an ex who has filed for his or her retirement benefit.* Because of those requirements, knowing whether your ex has filed matters a great deal if you were divorced less than two years ago. But the only way to know if your ex has filed is to ask him or her. We think people deserve a better way to get access to benefits to which they are legally entitled.

SOCIAL SECURITY HORROR STORIES

Since writing the first edition we've come across a number of Social Security horror stories that Larry wrote about in his *PBS NewsHour* column, but we thought we should include some of them here. If they were simply rare mistakes by potential claimants or Social Security staff, we wouldn't waste your time. But each horror story provides a lesson about Social Security's help and advice or lack thereof. We have a long list, but we'll limit ourselves to four.

Horror Story 1—Not Claiming Available Benefits

One 73-year old, we'll call him Joe, emailed Larry that he was still working and had just realized he could have started collecting his Social Security retirement benefit at age 70. He said he wanted to sue Social Security for not informing him at age 70 that he was able to collect his benefit and would gain no higher benefit from waiting to collect it. He also felt Social Security should have automatically initiated his benefit payment when he turned 70.

Larry responded that suing Social Security would be very tough and likely produce no favorable result. Social Security is under no obligation to give benefits to people unless they ask for them. The one exception appears to involve people who suspend their retirement benefits. At 70, Social Security is supposed to restart their retirement benefit automatically. Larry told Joe he could ask for his retirement benefit retroactive to 6 months, but that's it.

The lesson here is about non-advice. Social Security would never have told Paul he was about to leave $50,000 on the table. Social Security leaves it up to us to figure out what we're owed and to request it.

Horror Story 2—When Social Security Knows Less About Social Security than You Do

Even if you ask Social Security to do things that are perfectly legal, you may run into a brick wall. One lady, whom we'll call Johanna, took her retirement benefit at 63. When Johanna, who never married, turned 66 in 2015, she called Social Security's 800 number five times and spoke to five different staffers. Each time she told them that she wanted to suspend her retirement benefit and restart it at 70. Each time she was told that she wasn't allowed to do so. A couple of the staffers told her she would have been able to do so had she requested a suspension at 66 back when she filed for her early retirement benefit at 63.

Johanna was perfectly within her rights to request a retirement benefit suspension upon reaching FRA. The law could not be plainer on this point. Nor is there anything in the law remotely suggesting one needs to request benefit suspension before reaching FRA.

And now for the rest of the story.

Johanna contacted Larry, who asked her to go to her local office. (He also let a very senior official at Social Security know they should send a notice to all staff about her right to suspend. He has no idea if that happened.) In any case, Johanna went to her local office and the staffer (we'll call him Ed) with whom she met told her she couldn't suspend. She showed Ed our book, pointing out the section that discussed suspending your retirement benefit. Ed looked at the book, handed it back, and said, no, she couldn't suspend. Johanna asked Ed how long he'd worked at Social Security. Six months was the answer. Was Ed sure about his information? Yes, he was sure.

Johanna insisted Ed check with his supervisor. Ed went to the back of the office, spent a few minutes, returned, and told Johanna that he, Ed, was right. She couldn't suspend. Johanna asked to speak to the supervisor. The supervisor, whom we'll call Gloria, came over and also told Johanna, this time very firmly, that she could not suspend. Johanna asked for her name and phone number, left the office, and then reconnected with Larry.

Larry was aghast. "This is seven people in a row who didn't know about suspending retirement benefits. Unbelievable!"

It was Friday evening, but Larry called the number and left a message on Gloria's answering machine that he'd like to talk with her before his column appeared on Monday—a column that was going to recount Johanna's experience at their office. Lo and behold, Larry received a call Saturday morning from the office's director, whom we'll call Stan. They had a nice chat. Stan said he'd worked for Social Security for 30 years and had never heard about suspending benefits. But, he said, he'd check and call Larry back. Larry said great, but asked why he was working on Saturday. Stan said they were under-staffed and swamped.

Two hours later, Stan called back, and said his office had made a mistake. Johanna could, indeed, suspend and they had called her and were going to do the paperwork with her on Monday. Larry thanked Stan. But Stan was the eighth person in a row who had known nothing—or the wrong thing—about suspending benefits. The lesson here is that you need to *tell* Social Security what to do, not *ask* them. And if they deny you your legal rights, shop around for a Social Security staffer who knows her stuff.

Horror Story 3—Put It in Writing

Larry visited with a doctor, we'll call him Steve, a few months after the book's release. Steve was in his early 70s, but Larry didn't know his age. So Larry asked Steve what he was doing about Social Security. Steve replied that he'd taken Social Security at 70. Larry said that was the right move. Then Steve said the people at the Social Security office had been incredibly nice. They'd even given him free retroactive benefits—an extra check had come in the mail.

Larry's face fell. "Steve, when, exactly, did you go to the office?"

"Oh, three months before I turned 70."

Larry then delivered the bad news.

"Steve, I don't think you got what you were after. I think they gave you your retirement benefit as of age 69 and three months. I think they filed you for your retirement benefit as of the day you went in, but then moved that date back another 6 months. Consequently, you are receiving a check that's short nine months' worth of Delayed Retirement Credits."

Larry checked with our longtime Social Security technical expert Jerry Lutz, who explained that retroactivity is automatically applied to benefit applications filed after FRA unless the claimant expressly rejects or restricts it. In practice, this means that Steve had lost nine months of Delayed Retirement Credits and was receiving—as he would continue to receive for the rest of his life—a check that was fully 6 percent lower than it should have been. Larry was also nearly knocked off his chair by Jerry's explanation of the agency's retroactivity policy, which is: The only way to guarantee they don't do this is to put your precise request down in writing and make sure you get a copy of this signed and dated application, which the agency is always supposed to provide you.

Larry's takeaway from this and from so many emails from people who think they asked for X and got Y and didn't discover it until years later: make sure you receive a dated copy of your application, and confirm right then that it contains exactly what you thought it did. This will provide proof that Social Security received your request when you made it and, if a mistake arises, it will provide you a basis for requesting they fix the problem. Paul and Phil, who, truth be told, are older than Larry and have successfully transacted with Social Security over the phone, feel Larry is being paranoid in insisting on face-to-face meetings with a Social Security representative. And they point out that actually doing this can be a huge hassle, particularly if more and more people take this advice. But then again, Paul and Phil don't get the emails about clear mistakes that Larry receives virtually every day.

Filing online for retirement benefits may be your safest option. This application lets you specify what you want and when you want it. You can also file online for spousal and divorced spousal benefits, but not for widow(er) or child benefits.

Horror Story 4—Has Social Security Effectively Stolen Tons of Money from Widows?

John McAdams, a Social Security claims authorizer in Philadelphia, wrote Larry in the summer of 2015 to blow the whistle on what he felt were mistakes Social Security had made that were costing certain widows a huge amount of money. He wrote Larry because he had been pressing Social Security internally, to no avail, to correct their mistakes and give these widow(er)s what they were owed.

We'll give you an example to make John's concern clear. Take a hypothetical 62-year-old widow. Let's call her Sarah. Sarah comes to Social Security to file for a survivor benefit on her deceased husband or ex-husband's work record. Let's assume Sarah's widow benefit is $2,001 per month and her own age-62 early retirement benefit is $2,000 per month.

Sarah is under no requirement to file for her retirement benefit at age 62. Yes, deeming applies in the case of spousal or divorced spousal benefits for everyone not grandparented under the new law, as explained in Chapter 4. But there is no deeming when it comes to widow(er)s benefits. Indeed, Sarah can wait until age 70 to file for her retirement benefit. At 70, it will start at a 76 percent higher level than at 62.

But, presumably by mistake, the Social Security staffer, with whom Sarah meets, files Sarah for both benefits. In doing so, he leaves Sarah with just her $2,001 widow's benefit, because Sarah can only collect the larger of the two benefits and the widow's benefit is a dollar larger than Sarah's retirement benefit.

In filing for her retirement benefit, the Social Security staffer produces not a single penny more in benefits for Sarah than she otherwise would receive. But in so doing, he prevents Sarah from waiting until 70 to file for her retirement benefit. Had she not been incorrectly filed by the staffer, she would collect, ignoring inflation adjustments, $2,001 a month from 62 through 70 and $3,520 from 70 till the end of her life. But thanks to the "help" from the staffer, her total monthly payment remains fixed forever at $2,001.

"Hold on!" you might say. Sarah never received her retirement benefit so why, at 70, can't she take it? The answer is that when you file for your retirement benefit early your benefit is permanently reduced even if you don't receive it. So at 70, as at 62, Sarah can receive only $2,000 in retirement benefits thanks to the mistake of the staffer. In Social Security's interpretation, Sarah is receiving and will continue to receive her $2,000 in retirement benefits *plus $1 in an excess widow's benefit.* So Social Security's response is that, in filing, Sarah opted to take her retirement benefit early. But, as John McAdams would point out, Sarah would never opt for something that cost her money, indeed a massive amount of money—$18,240 per year upon turning 70. Will Social Security find and compensate all such widow(er)s?

John has petitioned Social Security through internal channels to notify widows in Sarah's situation that their filing was mishandled and that the error will be corrected. This would, of course, cost Social Security a vast sum because if they did it for one widow, they'd have to do it for all. John writes and gets no response. Then he writes to Larry, who quotes John's email in his column and suddenly the particular widow that John seeks to help is notified that she has been underpaid.

This is the power of the press. But it's also a statement about the agency. Social Security makes mistakes, which can, of course, happen in any institution. But it won't necessarily correct its mistakes unless the agency is publicly called out and embarrassed.

7

THE BENEFITS OF
NOT RETIRING

If you're sick and tired of your job, you can't stand your boss, and you can't wait to retire, please stop and think it over. This is a huge financial decision. You need to get it right.

Idyllic retirements are more the stuff of movies than real life. Your golf game may be lousy; your bowling, worse. You may already go to as many book clubs and yoga sessions as you can stand. You could drive your partner nuts hanging around 24/7, and you could live, well, forever. There are mice who now live three times as long as they are meant to thanks to scientists injecting them with special gene therapies. Yes, they are mice and you are men (or women). But don't forget that Jeanne Calment made it to 122 without any PEDs (performance-enhancing drugs). Do you really want to be retired and living on peanuts for more than half a century?

Beyond the issues raised by greater longevity, the Great Recession made retirement impossible for millions. The need to continue earning money for current needs, not to mention rebuilding nest eggs, replaced notions of beachfront cabanas.

The very concept of retirement has gotten a makeover in recent years. The aforementioned recession created a cottage industry of advice about whether retirement was an outmoded concept. It also highlighted our widespread financial unpreparedness for retirement. As we told you in the beginning of *Get What's Yours*, the amount of money that most Americans—even those in middle age—have saved for their later years falls far short of anything resembling a sufficient retirement nest egg. The lesson for millions of us has been to settle for a meager existence in our later years. Or to keep working.

WORKING CAN BE GOOD
FOR YOUR HEALTH

But the point of this chapter is to demonstrate that the financial benefits of staying on the job can be enormous in terms of the Social Security benefits for you and even for others who may be at least somewhat dependent on them.

First of all, each year of continued work means a year of not having to tap retirement savings. Those savings can actually grow, both from a year of investment gains on one's savings and, if the job includes an employer-supported 401(k) or other retirement benefits, a year of new plan contributions. Last, but hardly least, the length of your actual retirement will have been shortened by a year. You will, in sum, wind up with more money to fund a shorter retirement. And, to once again pound the drum we've been incessantly (if not headache-inducingly) beating, should this extra year of work allow you to also delay taking Social Security for a year, your benefit will grow by about 8 percent plus the rate of inflation (although not compounded) until age 70.

Beyond dollars, it turns out that continuing to work also may bring you better health and even a longer life—not bad for whatever passes these days for punching a time clock. Retirement, it turns out, may be hazardous to your health. Studies have found that being in a workplace setting can provide social connections, a sense of accomplishment, and other forms of mental and physical stimulation. Not working can lead to isolation, boredom, and stress.

A French study released in 2013 even found a solid link between continued work and avoidance of dementia. That government study of nearly 430,000 retirees found their risk of being diagnosed with dementia declined by more than 3 percent for each extra year they worked before retiring. Thus, someone who retired at, say, 65, had nearly a 15 percent lower risk of getting dementia than someone who retired at age 60.

Generalizations can be misleading. For example, people with dementia may tend to retire earlier. But there is certainly evidence that work is good for us on many fronts. One of those fronts, as we said at the outset, is Social Security, and the roles it plays in shaping retirement plans.

WORKING CAN BE GOOD FOR YOUR WALLET, TOO

Back in Chapter 3, we talked about Average Indexed Monthly Earnings (AIME) and explained how they were used to calculate your Primary Insurance Amount (PIA). This is the amount of money you would receive in retirement benefits if you filed for them at your Full Retirement Age (FRA). We also emphasized that the PIA is a key figure in determining many other Social Security benefits.

As it turns out, the decision to continue working in later life also may have an impact on your AIME and thus on your PIA and . . . the thighbone's connected to the hipbone, and so on. In short, this is another potentially big deal, and we hope that explaining it in detail will be time well spent.

Every year that you work at jobs where you pay Social Security taxes, your earnings can become one of the years used to calculate your AIME. Recall that there are up to 35 earnings years included in the AIME. If you have more than 35 years, then Social Security uses the *highest* 35 years to compute your AIME. You need to keep this in mind because it could play a role in your decision about continuing to work.

Social Security calculates your AIME by "indexing" your past earnings—adjusting them for subsequent economic growth, just as you'd adjust amounts from the past—wages, prices, and so on—to put them in terms of today's dollars. Social Security does this by multiplying your past earnings by an index that reflects the annual changes in average national earnings for every year since you began making money until you turn 60. It includes what it calls net compensation—wages, tips, and other compensation subject to federal income taxes and reported on your annual W-2. Since 1991, it also has included contributions to deferred compensation plans, excluding certain distributions from plans that are reported as taxable compensation.

(If you're interested in a tangent—and *we* were—in 2014, net compensation in the United States totaled $7.05 trillion—$6.8 trillion in compensation and $253 billion in net deferred compensation. There were more than 158.2 million wage earners that year. Dividing $7.05 trillion by 158.2 million produced an average wage of $44,569.20. But of course the average includes your favorite hedge fund manager and that CEO whose compensation is soaring even as his company's stock is tanking. So, the *average* wage was much higher than the median or midpoint of wages, where half the people made more and half less. The national median wage was $28,851 in 2014. If this were a book about the startling and, in our mind, menacing increase in wage inequality in this country, we would point out that in 1991, the median national wage was nearly 72.1 percent of the average, but that it has fallen steadily since then and was only 63.4 percent of the average in 2014.)

Tangents aside, wage indexing stops at age 60. By the time a person qualifies for early retirement benefits at age 62, their earnings history through age 60 would have been calculated, and the Social Security system would have the information it needs to calculate their PIA and any early retirement reductions that would apply to their benefit should they begin claiming before FRA.

However, for purposes of evaluating the appeal of continuing to work in your 60s and even 70s, *the failure to wage-index back to age 60 (i.e., deflate post-60 wages) could be a very, very big deal.* Remember when we said that your AIME is based on your 35 years of *highest* indexed earnings? Well, not deflating post age-60 earnings means that each subsequent year's earnings have a good chance of *becoming* one of your new top 35 earnings years. And if this happens, this new top-35 year will replace the lowest year of the 35, and Social Security will *automatically recompute* your AIME and all the retirement benefits tied to it.

The reason a new top-35 year is likely past age 60 is that your covered earnings in the year you turn 61—and every subsequent year no matter how old you are—are counted at their actual or nominal value. What might this mean?

Here are three scenarios:

1. Say your earnings rise by about 3 percent in your 61st year and that this is in line with the national wage base. Your nominal earnings will be 3 percent greater than the previous year. Your previous top 35 years of indexed earnings, by contrast, won't change at all. They've already been locked in place—indexed as of age 60 and fixed forever. So, if your compensation at 61 is even only 3 percent higher than at 60, the odds are pretty good it will become a new top-35 year.[1]

2. If you earn above the annual ceiling for payroll taxes, the benefits of continuing to work past 60 are guaranteed. That's because any increase in the Average Wage Index will also increase the ceiling on covered earnings. So, earning above the covered ceiling after 60 will definitely represent a new top-35 earnings year for you. Could an exception occur if the national wage index declined? Since 1951, this has happened only once. But when it did, the tax ceiling did not decline in accordance with the law.

3. The rate of inflation kicks up and your unindexed wages jump
    from the prior year. No matter how virulent the inflation, you
    get full credit for that higher wage in terms of your Social
    Security benefit. In fact, a horrible bout of inflation just might
    put you on Social Security easy street. The agency's Recom-
    putation of Benefits will be very kind to you, and Social Secu-
    rity's annual Cost of Living Adjustment (COLA) will ensure
    that inflation does not erode the purchasing power of your
    benefit.

CASE STUDY: A HIGHER EARNER
WORKS MORE AND COLLECTS MORE

Now let's consider a higher earner whose record we know with absolute certainty: Larry.

Larry did the math for his own benefits. He calculated the present value of all his lifetime benefits using his company's software.
Larry was 62 when these calculations were made. If he had stopped
working at that age and waited 8 years to collect Social Security, his
lifetime benefits to age 100 would have been $774,210.

But here's the epiphany relevant to this chapter: Given that
he has a tenured professorship at an august institution—Boston
University—and various other interests of note, Larry has every
incentive to work until 70 as well. And were he to do so—health
permitting—his lifetime benefits, assuming he makes it to 100 and
future inflation is 3 percent a year, would rise *another* $80,312 to
$854,522. And, if still of sound mind and body, why stop at 70? If he
worked till 80, his benefit would rise another $88,154 to $942,676.

In other words, working to age 80 would raise Larry's lifetime Social Security benefits by 22 percent ($942,676 divided by
$774,210 equals 1.22). And this only has to do with the Recomputa-
tion of Benefits because in each scenario, he is waiting to collect his

retirement benefit until 70 and taking full advantage of the Delayed Retirement Credit (DRC) that increases your benefits if you wait to collect until 70.

Much of the bump in Larry's case comes from the fact that he didn't really start contributing much to Social Security until he was 29. He was in grad school before then and on a postdoctoral fellowship after grad school. So he has low-earning years among the 35 Social Security uses as his base. Given that he now earns well above the covered earnings ceiling, his base will rise every year in which he earns more, in nominal dollars, than he did in a low-earning year of his youth, even though it's been adjusted through age 60 for U.S. wage growth.

In Larry's case, working *up to* age 70 will kick out all the low-earnings ages from his Social Security record. But what seems remarkable is that working from 70 to 80 would generate an even larger increase in lifetime benefits.

The reason is that he's above Social Security's earnings ceiling and thus will enjoy the benefits we noted above in Scenario #2. What's going on here is that the AIME formula, which is centered at 60, doesn't properly deflate for economy-wide wage growth after age 60. This failure confers a Social Security benefit advantage to people continuing to work, especially those earning at or above the payroll tax ceiling. But even people earning below the ceiling can benefit, especially if their current earnings are relatively high and grow relatively rapidly in the future.

WORKING AFTER AGE 60 ALSO CAN RAISE BENEFITS FOR CURRENT AND FORMER FAMILY MEMBERS

But that's not all. There's another kicker, namely spousal benefits. Let's suppose Larry were married to someone his age who had never worked. In this case, her lifetime spousal benefits would rise from $345,586 to $413,570 were he to work till 80. So, in addition to picking up $168,466 for himself by working through age 80, he earns an extra $67,984 for his spouse.

There is a downside here or, at least, something that we know strikes many people as unfair. All covered wages are subject to payroll taxes (that FICA deduction) whether you retire at 62 or continue working until you're 92. So, even after you've begun receiving benefits, any subsequent wage earnings will be subject to payroll taxes. And while we've been emphasizing how additional earnings once you've retired can increase your benefits, this is not *always* the case. Many retirees pick up part-time jobs to augment their Social Security payments. These wages are not likely to be among their top 35 earnings years. Yet they will fork over payroll taxes anyway, even though doing so will not add a penny to their benefits. Many people believe they've already paid for their benefits when they've retired. So it's not surprising that they can't understand or accept the logic of continuing to pay taxes when they're not getting anything in return.

Now, this story changes for high earners. Few people know about the way post-60 work can raise their Social Security benefits. So, they may only look at how continued work could raise their tax bills, and for that reason they may be less inclined to continue working. It is true, in most cases, that these high-income earners will receive higher Social Security benefits. But they should be aware that the extra benefits may not be enough to offset their higher federal income taxes.

Imagine Beatrice, who never married, is now 63, started working at 22 earning $30,000 and received a 3.5 percent raise every year, so she is now earning $123,000. Beatrice is doing what we suggest and waiting till 70 to take her retirement benefit. If she works for one more year, her lifetime benefits would rise by roughly only $4,000, but her extra Social Security taxes would be more than $7,000. So this is not a net win for Beatrice. On the other hand, had Beatrice started working at age 40, earning the same amount between 40 and now, her lifetime benefits would rise by $14,000, which would cover her extra taxes by 7 grand!

THE EARNINGS TEST DOESN'T MEAN WHAT YOU THINK

But all this raises a serious empirical question: Why in the world do roughly two-thirds of claimants not only take Social Security before their FRA but, in many instances, consider it a justification, if not a mandate, to *stop working*? Or, at least, to stop working full-time?

We understand their desire to take Social Security benefits right away for fear that deferring them would cause retirees to lose benefits if they die early, presumably causing them to run short of money in heaven or because they need the money. But we're concerned that something else may be holding them back—holding *you* back—as with many people we've interviewed. We're concerned, that is, that you may feel that if you take your benefits early, you'll have to give them back to the system via its *Earnings Test* unless you stop working. Or you may be tired of paying more Social Security taxes each year and getting nothing back on your contributions. For you, then, here are the facts.

For now let's assume that you are collecting Social Security benefits and continuing to earn wage income. You may have heard that if you earn more than a certain amount, your Social Security benefits will be reduced. This is true. But *it is only true in the short run*. In the longer run, those reductions will, except for some important exceptions, be *paid back to you*. Here's how.

SOCIAL SECURITY ADJUSTMENT
OF THE REDUCTION FACTOR

Social Security applies what it calls a "retirement Earnings Test" to the benefits of recipients who are younger than their normal retirement ages (remember, this is 66 for most people now near retirement age). So, if you are taking benefits and are younger than your FRA in, say, 2016, Social Security will withhold $1 in benefits for every $2 in wages that you earn above a threshold amount of $15,720 in 2016. If you are celebrating your 66th birthday in 2016—and thus reaching your FRA—the agency uses a much higher threshold of $41,880 of wage income, and then withholds only $1 in benefits for each $3 you earn above this higher threshold, and only for those months in 2016 before you turn 66.

This higher threshold is, in a sense, the agency's way of being fair to people receiving benefits who are near their FRA. That's because there is no retirement Earnings Test once you have reached your 66th birthday. None of Warren Buffett's wage income will reduce his Social Security benefits. So, in this respect at least, when you hit your FRA, you and Warren will be in the same boat.

Up to this point, having your benefits reduced for wage income seems like a bad deal and certainly not an incentive to continue working. But wait. As is nearly always the case with Social Security, there is more. And the agency emphasizes this prominently in its explanatory consumer publications and on its website: "It is important to note, though, that these benefit reductions are not truly lost. Your benefit will be increased at your FRA to account for benefits withheld due to earlier earnings. (Spouses and survivors who receive benefits because they have minor or disabled children in their care do not receive increased benefits at FRA if benefits were withheld because of work.)"

Once you reach FRA, Social Security will repay you, in the form of permanently higher benefits from this age on, any dollars it earlier withheld from you. The way it reduces your benefits and, later, restores them, is important and can have a big impact on your cash flow. Let's take a year when a person aged 62 through 65 is receiving his or her retirement benefits. During this year, the person expects to earn $8,400 more than the threshold amount and will therefore have their benefits reduced by $4,200.

If the person was getting $1,000 in monthly benefits, the agency would eliminate all benefit payments for 5 months and then restore the $1,000 monthly payment in the 6th month and thereafter. It uses round numbers in calculating the number of forgone monthly benefits. In this case, it is cutting $5,000 even though the reduction is only $4,200. The $800 difference, Social Security says, will be paid back to you the following year.

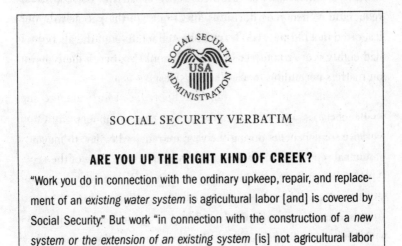

SOCIAL SECURITY VERBATIM

ARE YOU UP THE RIGHT KIND OF CREEK?

"Work you do in connection with the ordinary upkeep, repair, and replacement of an *existing water system* is agricultural labor [and] is covered by Social Security." But work "in connection with the construction of a *new system or the extension of an existing system* [is] not agricultural labor [and] not covered."

ALL QUOTES FROM OFFICIAL SOCIAL SECURITY RULES

AGENCY EXPLAINS EARNINGS
TEST RULES, OR DOES IT?

Does this sound confusing? You bet. What's worse is that Social
Security expects you to estimate your annual earnings at the beginning of the earnings year, tell the agency what you expect them to
be, and begin any benefit reductions right away. We're sorry, but the
world doesn't work that way. Most people probably have no clue that
the Earnings Test even exists or that they might have their benefits
reduced. Almost certainly, they would be surprised to learn that the
benefit reductions would mean they would get no benefits at all until
all reductions had occurred. For a household counting on regular
Social Security payments, losing them for an extended period is a
hardship.

We posed all these questions to Social Security. To be fair, Social
Security's official answers are necessarily broad and incredibly bu-
reaucratic. When your decisions affect most of the people in America, often in a big way, you learn to be deliberate. And the agency has
had eighty years to perfect its goobledygook. So, here's their answer
on matters pertaining to the Earnings Test:

> Beneficiaries who earn over the annual exempt amount and re-
> ceive some benefits during the year are required by law to file an
> annual report with Social Security (SSA) after the close of the tax
> year. Beginning with reporting year 1996 and each year thereaf-
> ter, SSA considers the W-2 filed by the employer and the SE tax
> return information by the beneficiary to be the report required
> by law. Social Security (SSA) will use that information along with
> other pertinent information in our records to reduce a benefi-
> ciary's monthly benefits by the amount of his or her earnings that
> exceed the annual exempt amount if the beneficiary is under or in
> the year of Full Retirement Age (FRA).

To administer the Earnings Test (ET), SSA will:

- identify working beneficiaries during the initial claims process, explain the Social Security ET and code our records with the work and earnings information;
- ask beneficiaries to report any change in their work activity that will result in significant changes in their earnings level;
- send a mid-year mailer letter to certain beneficiaries asking them to update their estimate for the current year and give us an estimate of their next year's earnings;
- ask certain beneficiaries to report their earnings to us at the end of the year;
- use the earnings posted to our records along with other pertinent information in our records to adjust benefits under the ET and ensure proper payment of benefits.

Got all that?

YOU GET THE MONEY BACK
EXCEPT WHEN YOU DON'T

The Earnings Test repayments (with the exceptions we noted) begin when you reach your FRA. They take the form of a monthly benefit that is higher than what you otherwise would receive. The size of the bump-up in your benefit depends on the amount of your earlier benefit reductions.

Here is an illustration provided by the agency:

As an example, let us say you claim retirement benefits upon turning 62 in 2013 and your payment is $750 per month. Then, you return to work and have 12 months of benefits withheld. We would recalculate your benefit at your Full Retirement Age of 66 and pay you $800 a month (in today's dollars). Or, maybe you earn so much between the ages of 62 and 66 that all benefits in those years are withheld. In that case, we would pay you $1,000 a month starting at age 66.

But, and this is a very big but, someone who switches from one Social Security benefit to another will never be able to enjoy the restoration of benefits lost to the Earnings Test. Imagine if you take your retirement benefit starting now, lose some retirement benefits due to the Earnings Test, and then switch to, say, a higher widow's benefit at FRA. What you get is the greater of the two—the retirement benefit and the amount of the widow benefit that is greater than your retirement benefit. So, even though Social Security will say your retirement benefit is larger, and it is, the excess portion of your widow's benefit will be declining, so your overall benefit will not be increased, and you will not be getting any money back from the Earnings Test adjustment.

Our message here, to sum up, is that you shouldn't always stop working because you think you won't get back the money taken by the Earnings Test. You *will* get it back in many cases.

8

PLAYING SOCIAL SECURITY'S
MARITAL STATUS GAME

Social Security provides incentives, sometimes very strong incentives, to change your marital status. There are, depending on your circumstances, reasons to get married, reasons to *stay* married, and incentives to divorce, to remarry, and *not* to remarry. These decisions hinge on many factors, of course. But play your Social Security marital status cards right and it can mean making or keeping more money, and, in some cases, a lot more money. Play them wrong and you can get seriously singed for the rest of your life.

This is particularly important for gay couples who, thanks to the Supreme Court's historic 2015 decision, are now free to marry in any state in the country and collect the same Social Security benefits as heterosexual married couples.

As mentioned in Chapter 1, thanks to the grandparenting clauses of the new law, there is a particularly strong short-run incentive for a select set of married couples to get divorced in the very near term. But for most people not grandparented, the new law reduces one of the payoffs from playing Social Security's marital status game: the ability to pursue the file-and-suspend strategy used by Paul.

We'll consider those who are grandparented at the end of this chapter. For now, we're going to discuss the game from the perspective of those not grandparented under the new Social Security law.

We'll start by cataloging the incentives to change or not change marital status, then try to make them memorable with the titillating tale of one William H. Gigolo (the *H* stands for Hypothetical), who spends his life playing Social Security's marital status game to great personal gain.

FIRST INCENTIVE: THE POSSIBLE PAYOFFS TO GETTING MARRIED

To help celebrate your marriage, Social Security provides you with four special wedding gifts. The first two come within one minute of getting married. The third arrives after you have been married for 9 months. The fourth arrives on your first wedding anniversary.

The first gift isn't a Cuisinart that got lost in the mail, of course, or a Ginsu knife set. It's a special sort of life insurance policy that kicks in if your new mate dies within a minute or second or even a nanosecond of marrying you. (We all know that love kills, but there turn out to be financial advantages if it kills in a hurry.)

Okay, what's the first gift?

The first gift is pretty small. If your spouse drops dead, even the instant they say "I do!" you can hit up Social Security for a $255 lump-sum death benefit. Unless you were temporarily separated due to military service or something similar, the death benefit comes with a catch. You had to be living with your deceased to get the $255. Average cremation costs these days exceed $1,000, so this isn't going to handle disposing of your beloved. But it will buy some very nice flowers.

The second gift is more meaningful. It's your ability to collect mother or father survivor benefits as long as you have your deceased spouse's young or disabled child or children in your care. ("Young" as in under 16; "disabled" so long as the child was disabled before age 22.) These benefits are pretty hefty—75 percent of your late spouse's Primary Insurance Amount, or PIA. (See Chapter 3 if you need a refresher on PIA.) Furthermore, they aren't reduced if you take them at a young age. And they don't trigger the dreaded deeming problem even if you are between ages 62 and 70.

But how can you have children within a nanosecond of getting married? You can't. So we're talking here about children that are premarital, adopted, or from your deceased spouse's previous relationships.

Social Security's third gift is equally morbid, but potentially quite valuable. It's a pair of, in effect, life insurance policies for you and your spouse, based on your two earnings records. The policies go into effect once you've been married 9 months, assuming that each spouse has enough covered earnings to qualify for Social Security benefits.

From 9 months on, either spouse can pass away and the other will be potentially eligible for widow(er) benefits. In addition, you can be taking mother or father benefits, and the children themselves—whether premarital, newborn, adopted, or from previous relationships—will also potentially be eligible for child survivor benefits.

The third gift is especially valuable if your spouse was a much higher earner than you. In this case, you could, when the time comes, take your reduced retirement benefit for a while and then flip to your higher widow(er) benefit, thanking yourself for the rest of your days for having married well.

If *you* were the higher earner, taking your widow(er) benefit early and waiting until, say, 70, to collect your own retirement benefit will generate maximum lifetime benefits. But either way, there can be a decent payoff to either of you as compensation for the death of your spouse.

Things are different if you are already taking your own retirement benefit when your spouse heads to heaven. You'll be in excess benefit world because you are trying to collect two benefits—your retirement benefit and your widow(er) benefit—at once. In this case, you'll get the larger of the two benefits. If it's your own retirement benefit, your spouse will have died in vain, at least insofar as his or her death won't raise your total Social Security payment. In a word, your excess survivor benefit will be zero. However, if your survivor's benefit exceeds your own retirement benefit, you will receive the survivor benefit. But it will be described as the sum of your own retirement benefit plus your excess survivor benefit.

The fourth wedding present, which kicks in one year after the vow exchange, is the ability of one spouse to collect a full spousal benefit (if you were properly grandparented by the gods, as explained in Chapter 4) or an excess spousal benefit on the other spouse's work record. And there is even the possibility of becoming eligible for a full child-in-care spousal benefit before reaching FRA but after 12 months of marriage. For example, if a person receiving disability or retirement benefits marries a spouse under Full Retirement Age with a minor child from another marriage, both spouse and child could be eligible for benefits on the new spouse's account after just 1 year.

SECOND INCENTIVE: THE PAYOFF TO STAYING MARRIED FOR AT LEAST 10 YEARS

Somewhere between 40 percent and half of all American first marriages end in divorce. Second marriages? 50–67 percent of *them* untie the knot. And a discouraging 75 percent of *third* marriages dissolve, despite having been entered into with the benefit of combat experience, firm conviction, we assume, and eternal optimism.

It turns out that, for Americans who get divorced, the median length of first marriages—the length of time by which 50 percent of them end—is 8 years. That means more than half of the divorced may be making a big, if not huge, financial mistake with regard to future Social Security benefits, especially our female readers. Women currently file roughly two-thirds of divorce cases in the United States, but women are the prime beneficiaries of sticking out a marriage for 10 years.

The simple fact is that you need to stay married 10 years and not a day less to be able to collect *divorced spousal* and *divorced survivor* benefits as an ex. So, we caution you not to officially unhitch before a decade's up without at least considering these costs. Social Security has no requirement that you consort with, or for that matter even *live* with, your spouse. You two can move to the opposite ends of the earth and still qualify for spousal and survivor benefits based on the other's work record. Once you have qualified, you can potentially collect on your ex, and your ex can potentially collect on you.

Yes, this would be an example of gaming the system, and we have no intention of corrupting those of you who feel that is inappropriate. But we're addressing everyone, including those of you who have been married for 9 years and 11 months, are now about to get divorced, and only shortly after having done so, learn of the 10-year rule—to their everlasting regret. Are you less entitled to benefits than the Social Security–savvy people who knew to wait a full decade before formally divorcing?

THE THIRD INCENTIVE IS A PERVERSE ONE: TO GET REMARRIED EVERY DECADE

Having been married for a decade, once you get divorced, you retain the right to potentially collect divorced spousal and divorced survivor benefits from your ex's work record. After being married for a decade, staying married won't increase what you can receive based on your spouse's earnings, whether dead or alive. So, the gold diggers out there might consider shopping for a second spouse, preferably a high-earning one, to marry for a decade and then divorce.

Social Security generally won't let you collect more than one benefit at a time. But if you have multiple exes on whom you can collect, you can collect on the one who provides the highest benefit available at any given time.

Will getting remarried and staying remarried wipe out your ability to collect spousal and survivor benefits on your prior spouse's work record? *Yes*, when it comes to divorced spousal benefits; *no*, when it comes to survivor benefits, provided you remarry after 60. And if you remarry before 60 and an ex dies, you can get divorced if it pays to receive a survivor benefit from that first ex. Then you remarry after turning 60.

SOCIAL SECURITY VERBATIM

OF COURSE, I'LL REPORT THAT INCOME RIGHT AWAY

"The illegality of an activity does not prevent it from being a trade or business. For example, professional gamblers, bookies, etc. may be engaged in a trade or business. If you are in this category, you are considered self-employed and are required to report your income and pay self-employment taxes."

ALL QUOTES FROM OFFICIAL SOCIAL SECURITY RULES

And one of the best parts of spouse-hopping is this: when you start collecting early on a different former spouse's work record, Early Retirement Reductions from taking benefits on another spouse at an earlier date don't carry over, as we will illustrate shortly.

FOURTH INCENTIVE: THE PAYOFF
FOR NOT REMARRYING

Why would anyone not want to remarry?

Because remarrying wipes out your ticket to divorced spousal benefits on any ex's work record to whom you were married for at least a decade.

Remarrying before age 60 also wipes out your eligibility for survivor benefits on any deceased *former* spouse's work record for as long as you stay remarried.

So be careful before you strategically remarry. Unless, that is, you are a real pro. Like William H.

PLAYING THE SOCIAL SECURITY
MARITAL STATUS GAME TO THE HILT

It is time at last for the story of William H. Gigolo, our hypothetical master of Social Security's marital status game. He worked not a day in his life (so any excess spousal benefit will also be a full spousal benefit), but instead lived off the relatively high earnings of three lovely ex-wives—call them Sarah, Sally, and Suzie. In each case, William waited until their 10th anniversary, chose a romantic restaurant, and over dessert, announced he was filing for divorce.

Positing William as a sociopath, we picture him pleased to have lived off successive exes and helped himself to half their assets thereafter. Now 62 and single for 2 years, he remains attractive to women, a sad testament to the gender imbalance between eligible baby boomers because women still tend to marry older men, though it was never true, as *Newsweek* famously misreported in 1986, that "a woman over age 40 has a better chance of being killed by a terrorist than to get married." (That mythical single girl would be past 70 today.)

Since a wife has to be at least 62 for the husband to collect spousal benefits, William was careful to marry at least one ex older than himself. This ex, Sarah, is 64 and the lowest earner. The next-highest earner is Sally, 60. Suzie is only 56, but she's earned more than the others.

To maximize his lifetime Social Security benefits, William files for a divorced spousal benefit at 62 and starts to collect half of Sarah's full retirement benefit, although reduced by 30 percent because he takes it early. Then, after 2 years, when *Sally* turns 62, William files for a divorced spousal benefit based on *her* earnings record.

And why not? Since he's now eligible to collect on two exes, he can file for benefits on both. He won't get two divorced spousal benefits—just the larger of the two. But since Sally's full retirement benefit is larger than Sarah's, he gets hers. And here's another advantage from William's perspective: he'll be able to collect half of Sally's full retirement benefit, but it will be reduced by only 13.3 percent, not 30 percent! Why? Because William is now 64 and his early claiming reduction is smaller; that is, the reduction in a spousal benefit from claiming early does not carry over from one ex to another. Yes, he claimed 4 years early (before his FRA) on the divorced spousal benefit provided by Sarah, but he is doing so only 2 years early on the divorced spousal benefit provided by Sally.

So far, so good, as long as you have no scruples. We have already stipulated that William doesn't. So his cash-out plan is working. And here's a yet more perverse part three. When Suzie reaches 62 and William hits 68, he can start collecting a completely unreduced divorced spousal benefit on Suzie's heftier earnings record since he doesn't start collecting this particular benefit (which exceeds the other two) until or after he reaches his FRA. (In William's case it's after.)

Is William done with his optimization? Not necessarily. Let's fast-forward to his 70th birthday and suppose that Sally, who waited until FRA to start collecting her benefit, dies. Sally's full retirement benefit, while lower than Suzie's, exceeds the half of Suzie's on which William has most recently been collecting. So William can now file for and begin collecting a completely *unreduced* divorced widower benefit on Sally's record. That benefit would be equal to 100 percent of Sally's full retirement benefit.

Fast-forward again. William is now 76 and Suzie dies, having also waited until FRA to collect her retirement benefit. What might William do? He files for an unreduced survivor benefit based on *Suzie's* earnings record.

Fast-forward one last time. William is now 88. He's met a very lovely 94-year-old named Sandra, who earned more than any of the exes and is on her last legs. William realizes that he can marry Sandra and, after 9 months, qualify for survivor benefits on Sandra's earnings record. He whisks Sandra off to Las Vegas for a quickie marriage and, 9 months to the day after their nuptials, Sandra falls and breaks her hip. Her last leg gives out. So does the rest of her.

William leaves the funeral early in order to get to the local Social Security office before it closes and file for a full (unreduced) widower benefit on Sandra's account.

This appears to be William's last Social Security play, but who knows? He's still got his looks and, as you read this, he's on Match .com checking out his options. Considering that there were 3.2 million women aged 85 and older in 2012, and only 1.8 million men of those ages, William's pickings are far from slim.

IF YOU'RE SINGLE, IT MAY
PAY TO GET HITCHED

If you receive very low Social Security benefits—or expect to—you might take a deep breath and consider the following secret strategy (though it is one we do not endorse): Find an attractive, single 80-year-old who is receiving a higher Social Security benefit and propose marriage. What might once have been scorned "a marriage of convenience" could very well be a marriage of necessity if you are in danger of outliving your savings. After one year of mutual nuptial accommodation, assuming you and your spouse are at least age 62, you'll be able to collect an excess spousal benefit on your new mate's work record. (This assumes you were not grandfathered against post-FRA deeming.) If, like William H., your own PIA is very small, this excess benefit could matter.

Better yet—from a strictly pecuniary point of view—marry someone on their last legs who receives a much larger benefit than you currently do or can ever hope to. Once you've been married for just 9 months, you'll be eligible to receive a *survivor* benefit, which, depending on when you take it, can equal as much as your unbeloved was collecting before his or her expiration date.

PLAYING THE MARTIAL STATUS GAME
IF YOU WERE GRANDPARENTED
UNDER THE NEW LAW

As explained in Chapter 4, you and your spouse can no longer pursue the file-and-suspend strategy unless you can meet two grandparenting conditions. First, one of you (say, the wife) has to have reached FRA and already filed for and suspended her retirement benefit before April 30, 2016, and the other (in this case, the husband) has to have turned 62 before January 2, 2016. If these conditions are met, the husband can file just for his spousal benefit at Full Retirement Age and wait until 70 to collect his retirement benefit when, as you have learned by now, it will start at its highest value.

Now, what if both spouses met the second condition—they turned 62 in time—but neither is old enough to have filed and suspended? To make things concrete and simple, suppose the spouses shared the same birthday and both were 62 before January 2, 2016. In this case, if they wait till 70 to go for their retirement benefits, neither will be able to collect a full spousal benefit between age 66 (their FRA) and 70. The reason is that to do so, their partner would need to be receiving retirement benefits, which won't happen until they are both 70. And if one files and suspends at FRA, it will be after April 29, 2016, and will preclude all auxiliary benefits during the suspension.

What to do? Full spousal benefits for up to 4 years can be a lot of money. *The answer is that the couple's only option (in financial terms) is to play the marital status game and get divorced (assuming they have been married for 10-plus years) before reaching age 64!* Is getting divorced in order to collect higher Social Security benefits legal? We don't know for sure. Nor, as we said, are we advising anyone to follow this strategy.

Why would divorce help? Because for qualified divorced individuals meeting the age-62 deadline, their ex will be presumed to have filed for his or her retirement benefit (even if he or she hasn't). And why do they need to divorce before turning 64? Because this partially grandparented couple has to be divorced for at least 2 years prior to collecting on their ex's work record.

How much money is at stake? At the extreme, for a couple that earned at least the maximum covered amount throughout their working careers and will continue to earn at or above the ceiling through age 70, we're talking roughly $20,000 in full divorced spousal benefits per year per spouse for 4 years. This comes to $160,000. That's a lot of money to leave on the table, even for a high-earning couple. For lower-earning couples, we're still talking big bucks, especially relative to their income. A couple whose full divorced spousal benefit comes to about $10,000 per year would get $80,000.

Are there other marital status games that the grandparented can play and still score a full spousal benefit? Well, someone who is single and met the age-62 deadline of January 2, 2016, could marry someone who is already collecting their retirement benefit, preferably someone with a very high retirement benefit. After a year and starting at 66, they will be able to file just for a full spousal benefit while letting their own retirement benefit grow through 70.

In closing, we would ask (as might you) why Social Security continues to endorse a retirement saving system with such potentially large impacts on whether we get married or divorced.

MARRIED OR DIVORCED
WITH BENEFITS

Tarzan and Jane were exhausted from the Big Apple's ticker-tape parade for them. It was 1940 and they had just returned from their latest adventure in the wild. The twentieth century's version of Adam and Eve had once again captured the world's attention. Now they were in their suite at the Plaza, trying with their son, Korak, to coax Cheeta down from the drapes. After resting up for a few days, it would be on to visit Jane's family in Maryland.

Life had been good to the tree-swinger and his resourceful partner (Jane, not Cheeta). For the better part of two decades they had been alternating African expeditions with increasingly lucrative visits to the States. Tarzan wasn't keen on being a loincloth-clad pitchman, but it sure beat hunting for a living. And the money was good, so good that after they presented a beaming Cheeta with a large bunch of bananas and slipped Korak a sawbuck, they were on their way to a meeting with their financial adviser.

The topic for the day was Social Security, a still-new program begun in 1935 that was just beginning to pay out benefits five years later.

We hope you will have figured out by now that we've taken some liberties with the story of Tarzan and Jane, who of course never really existed and, even within their fabricated tales, never set foot in a Social Security office as far as we can tell. Also, many current provisions of Social Security did not exist in 1940. But we're assuming they did so that Tarzan's and Jane's decisions make sense to you and your very real Social Security needs.

As a top earner, Tarzan paid the maximum amount of payroll taxes. Jane did not earn an income, but based on the rules of the program she stood to collect a substantial spousal benefit in her later years based on Tarzan's work history. Of course, Tarzan had been born in Great Britain, Jane pointed out, maintained dual citizenship and had worked there. This, too, might affect his and her Social Security benefits thanks to the Windfall Elimination Provision (see Glossary). So many coconuts to juggle!

Furthermore, while longevity tables were not common in 1940, their financial adviser had read, in *Tarzan's Quest*, about the ape man having received an immortality drug and explained that he ought therefore to wait until 70 to start his benefits, for obvious reasons. Moreover, he diplomatically pointed out, if the life span of the jungle man turned out to be brief, due to accident, the longer that Tarzan waited to claim retirement benefits, the greater would be Jane's widow benefit should he wind up on the wrong end of a poison-tipped spear. And then there was Korak to think about. He might also qualify for Social Security benefits.

We'd like to say that wives and husbands—real as well as fictional—have been having similarly fruitful discussions with each other and/or their financial advisers about Social Security over the ensuing 75 years. But they haven't.

Every year, married and divorced couples make uninformed claiming decisions that deny them and their family members access, in the aggregate, to billions of benefit dollars. With retirement prospects dimmer than expected for tens of millions of baby boomers, claiming every possible dollar in Social Security should be a national pastime. Instead, it's an American afterthought. The Home Shopping Network teaches people far more about cubic zirconia than they ever learn about the nation's most basic and important retirement benefit.

If you are married, this chapter is for you. It's also for those divorced after 10 years of marriage. It's for those thinking about getting married and for those thinking about getting divorced. And, unlike the first edition of *Get What's Yours*, all these groups now fully include gay couples who, prior to a 2015 Supreme Court decision, were unable to legally marry in all fifty states. Nor could they necessarily collect spousal or widow(er) benefits if they were married in one state where gay marriage was legal and then moved to another state where it wasn't.

We're going to recap and elaborate on some messages about married couples and the qualified divorced conveyed in prior chapters. Some of these messages pertain to those who were "grandfathered" under the new Social Security law—allowed to act as if the old law still applies, though we have been using the term "grandparented" because we're not just talking about men—and some of our messages pertain to those who weren't. There are also couples in which one spouse was grandparented based on one or both of the grandparenting provisions and the other was not grandparented under either. So the main lesson here is that there is no one rule for all. Every household's situation is different, even more so than before the new law was so hastily enacted. Unfortunately, we don't have enough space, nor you enough time, to consider the whole universe of possibilities. The best we can do is provide enough examples to let you, or some couple you know, see the range of possibilities you or they may face.

What is clear is that, for all but the superrich, a core part of a couple's retirement strategy should be an informed approach to their Social Security spousal benefits. *An obvious fact that we nonetheless feel obliged to note*: it's essential that *both* spouses understand their estimated benefits, especially how they are affected by waiting or not waiting to claim benefits. Moreover, *each* spouse ought to be aware of how their claiming decision will affect that of their partner.

So allow us to review the options for those of you who are married. And please forgive us for yet again repeating ourselves. As we say, the worst that can happen is that you'll skim and skip ahead. Much worse would be your forgetting a key option and thus nullifying, at least for yourself, the whole point of this book. And for those of you who might be cursing yourselves for forgetting what we've already tried to hammer home, know that we ourselves still check our notes on these items when we hit the key age milestones, despite having swung on Social Security's convoluted vines for years.

SPOUSAL BENEFIT STEPPING-STONES

Step One: Create an account on the Social Security website that provides each spouse access to an individualized Your Social Security Statement. We explained how to do this in Chapter 3. To begin, go to "my Social Security" at http://socialsecurity.gov/myaccount/.

Step Two: Revisit the crucial role played in spousal benefits (and lots of other Social Security claiming situations) by Social Security's rules about what it calls full or normal retirement age. Remember: Full Retirement Age is 66 for anyone born between 1943 and 1954. It then rises in two-month steps for those born from 1955 to 1959, and hits 67 for anyone born in 1960 or later years. (Many current reform proposals would increase this age to 68 or even older, but as of this writing, the official FRA is as we've described it.)

Step Three: Understand how spousal benefits actually work. If a couple is married for at least a year, both spouses qualify for spousal benefits. But for one spouse to claim a spousal benefit, the other spouse has to have first filed for their own retirement benefit. As we explained in Chapter 4, it is still possible for some married couples to have one spouse file and suspend their own retirement benefit while the other claims a spousal benefit. However, under the new Social Security rules, this is no longer possible for people who were younger than 62 as of January 1, 2016. For them, one spouse will need to actually file for retirement benefits for the second spouse to claim a spousal benefit.

Step Four: Review the basic options, which will be some variant of what you and your partner do between the ages of 62 (earliest claiming age) and 70 (the latest).[1] You might model them using either Larry's software (http://www.maximizemysocialsecurity.com/) or someone else's.

Step Five: Build your optimal plan and then stay the course and follow it.

Message 1: Do not assume that Social Security has, or will readily provide, an accurate record of your earnings, your marital status, or even your very existence.

Liz and Jane are two very lovely ladies who have been together for 35 years. Both are flower children, so neither was interested in anything conventional like marriage. Liz is 67 and has much higher earnings than Jane, who is 65. They contacted Larry in the spring of 2015 about whether it paid to get married. He explained about the file-and-suspend strategy—that if they married, then Jane could collect a full spousal benefit on Liz's work record while having her own retirement benefit grow through age 70. He also said that Jane would inherit Liz's retirement benefit as a widow's benefit were Liz to pass away. It took repeated cajoling (including the suggestion that more money wasn't such a bad thing and marriage wasn't going to end their relationship), but at last, Jane and Liz agreed to tie the knot—in August 2015.

Jane and Liz invited Larry and his wife to their wedding. Would it be in a big fancy-schmancy country club or expensive restaurant or in a venerable house of worship? Not for these two. It was going to be on the beach, rain or shine. Unfortunately, as wedding plans were being made, Liz found out that Social Security had determined that she was dead. Now, we've already told you at length in Chapter 6 about some of the truly egregious mistakes that Social Security makes. But we just couldn't pass up the opportunity to tell you about Liz's "death." We'll let her tell the story.

I tried to activate a new American Express card online. But there was a problem with the activation. When I called, they advised me that Social Security had notified them that I was deceased. Needless to say, I was a bit taken aback by the news. Despite the fact that I was on the line with American Express, they said they needed verification from Social Security. When I contacted Social Security, who indeed had me in their files as alive, they said they were unable to provide documentation supporting that over the phone. With dread in my heart, I went to Social Security with my passport, birth certificate, and original Social Security card. When I was finally seen, they said they were unable to provide me with any documentation certifying that I was not deceased. I spoke with the head person at the office, who again confirmed that this request was not possible to fulfill, given that they are "not allowed" to originate any correspondence and could only fulfill my request if it was possible to do by form letter, which it was not. This was in spite of my in-person presence with all the appropriate verification in hand! In the meantime, I continued to receive cancellation notices of all my American Express cards and several condolence notices to my estate.

At my wits' end, I called my representative's office, Joe

Kennedy III, given that I was having difficulty with a federal agency. When I spoke with the liaison to Social Security, he was sympathetic, but concerned that there was nothing that could be done. He agreed to connect with his contact at Social Security. After a bit of back-and-forth, he was able to arrange a process where I would pay $38 in-person for them to compose "original correspondence" documenting my viability. The process worked, but it took several months and caused much angst.

And if she *hadn't* called her congressman? And if he hadn't had a contact at Social Security? We'll never know if this was a mistake initially made by Social Security or American Express. But the moral of the story is that the Social Security bureaucracy cannot be relied upon to quickly straighten out snafus in your record.

Message 2: As in comedy, timing can make all the difference.

Jane and Liz got married on Larry's advice. But in mid-December 2015 they learned about the new law and became very concerned that they had gotten married for nothing. They contacted Larry again, who explained that they had been—well, in their case, grand*mothered*—but needed to act a bit faster than previously planned. Liz needed to file and suspend before April 30, 2016. But when Jane reached Full Retirement Age, she could still file just for her spousal benefit and wait until 70 to collect. Jane and Liz had made it in just under the wire.

But now let's change things around and suppose that Jane and Liz both turned 64 in November 2015. They should both wait until 70 to collect. Admittedly, both would be able to escape the dastardly deeming trap at 66, thanks to one of the two main grandparenting provisions. But for Jane to collect a spousal benefit starting at 66, Liz would have to file for her retirement benefit at 66. That would have cost far more to the couple than simply forgoing the spousal benefit, at least until Liz had gotten closer to 70 and accumulated at least some Delayed Retirement Credits.

What should they do?

SOCIAL SECURITY VERBATIM

AND SOCIAL SECURITY WOULD KNOW THIS HOW?

"Third parties may assist a claimant when completing the iClaim [online] application, but the claimant must be present to select the 'Submit Now' button."

ALL QUOTES FROM OFFICIAL SOCIAL SECURITY RULES

The answer depends. If Jane makes enough money and both can live to age 100, the best thing is for both of them to wait until 70 to collect their retirement benefits. For example, we ran a case in Larry's Maximize My Social Security software in which Jane retires in 2014 from a job that initially paid $10,000 per year and gradually rose to $35,000 per year. That's a high enough covered earnings history to make Jane's excess spousal benefit zero. Yes, Liz makes more money than Jane. Indeed, in this example we have Liz making 4 times more, putting Liz's annual earnings above the maximum taxable amount. But earnings over this taxable ceiling don't enter into the AIME calculation, which determines Liz's PIA or full retirement benefit. Also, recall that the PIA formula is highly progressive, so having even a 4-times-higher AIME does not imply a 4-times-higher PIA. In fact, Liz's PIA is less than twice as large as Jane's. But it has to be more than twice as large for Jane's excess spousal benefit to be zero.

But what if we changed the software assumptions so that Jane earned half as much over her working years? Then Liz's PIA will be twice Jane's, meaning Jane's excess spousal benefit will be both positive and significant. As a result, the couple's optimal benefit collection strategy changes radically. Jane should take her retirement benefit at 66 and let Liz collect a full spousal benefit on Jane's work record. This produces almost $24,000 in spousal benefits for Liz between 66 and 70.

When the couple reaches 70, the optimal strategy would have Liz file for her retirement benefit and Jane file for her spousal benefit. Since Jane's earnings are so low, in this case, compared to Liz's, Jane would be able to collect an excess spousal benefit of over $3,000 per year on top of her age-66, full retirement benefit of $12,525.

And consider a third example involving Jane and Liz. Let's assume Jane earned what she originally had, but lower Liz's longevity to 80 from 100. Now the best thing is for Jane to take her retirement benefit immediately at her current age, 65. Liz waits until 66 to take her spousal benefit because she would be deemed if she takes it before 66. (Recall, the grandparenting stops deeming after, but not before full retirement age.) At 70, Liz takes her retirement benefit.

Why the change in strategy? The reason is that Jane would collect for many more years as a widow since Liz would be dead by 80. When Liz died, Jane would collect just her widow benefit (even though it will be described as the receipt of her retirement benefit plus her excess widow benefit). So starting her retirement benefit early doesn't come at much of a future cost.

Even readers anesthetized by case studies may have noted an obvious problem with these last two hypotheticals: how can *anyone* know that they will die by age 80 as opposed to 100? Or even tonight? That's a conundrum for all retirement planning and we're afraid you just have to live with it (if you'll pardon the expression). You can use gross estimates, like Social Security's own life expectancy table, which you'll find in the notes, or more nuanced estimates from software available online that modifies your expected longevity by health factors, family history, whether or not you skydive or bungee-jump. But no matter what technology you employ, the best you'll come up with is an estimate. On the other hand, that's more prudent, if not more pleasant, than avoiding the issue entirely. And we urge you to distinguish between life expectancy and your maximum possible life span—it's this latter number that must shape your retirement planning.

Since there are so many different possibilities, and each can have such different strategic consequences, let's try out a few more permutations, in the hopes that one of them applies to you or someone you know. If they don't apply, feel free to skip ahead.

WHAT IF JANE AND LIZ HAD MARRIED A DECADE EARLIER?

If Jane and Liz were both 64 and had been married for at least a decade, their best option would be to get divorced immediately rather than stay married. Doing so, perhaps via another joyous celebration on the beach, would permit the double divorced to collect full spousal benefits on each other's work record. (This is because, being grandparented, they would not be subject to deeming when they reached Full Retirement Age.) Under our initial assumptions about their earnings, this strategy would have produced $38,320 in full spousal benefits for Liz. The corresponding amount for Jane would have been $63,818. Add these two numbers together and you have a $102,138 incentive to get divorced. After age 70, they could even remarry if they wished. (Note that doing so would not affect Jane's widow benefit were Liz to die first.)

Again, we're not counseling this, because we're not sure if there are laws restricting this behavior. Social Security is used to handling couples that get divorced and remarry, but we note that its rules do not require checking on the grounds for divorce.

WHAT IF LIZ WAS GRANDPARENTED AGAINST DEEMING, BUT JANE WAS NOT?

We've considered cases based on Jane's and Liz's actual ages. Alternatively, we've pretended they were both 64. But what to do if Jane was, say, 60 and Liz was, say, 64 at the end of 2015? Should they both wait until 70 to collect their retirement benefits, as was the case when we assumed they were both 64? Maybe, maybe not. There is still a very big payoff from waiting till 70, but when they were both 64, age 70 was only 6 years off for each spouse. Now age 70 is 6 years off for Liz, but 10 years off for Jane.

Waiting, recall, has a real cost. Receiving a dollar in twenty years is less valuable than receiving it today because a dollar received today could be safely invested and yield more over time. The more time, the more the total return. If Jane files for her retirement benefit early—at 62—Liz will be able to take just her spousal benefit at 66, while letting her own retirement benefit grow. So the two would get some money sooner. But is it worth it?

We checked via software. It was still worth it for both to wait until 70. But then we tweaked some of the inputs. Rather than assuming Jane was a low earner and Liz a very high one, we had both earn the same moderate amount: final earnings of around $63,000. Doing this would give Jane a larger spousal benefit to provide Liz, again at the cost of Jane taking her own retirement benefit early and, thereby, permanently reducing it.

Did that change the optimal plan? The answer was still no.

But with one additional tweak, their best strategy did change and it changed *dramatically*. It turned into what we call the *start, stop, start* strategy.

And here's why. If Liz estimates that 90, not 100, is much more likely to be her maximum age of life, having the couple wait till 70 to start taking Social Security is more costly, for the simple reason that she doesn't figure to be alive as long to collect it. The old strategy had Jane and Liz take two actions—wait till 70 and file for retirement benefits. The new strategy has them take six actions. Bear with us or you can skip ahead to a less thorny hypothetical.

Step 1: Jane takes her retirement benefit at 62.

Step 2: Liz, who is four years older and at FRA when Jane turns 62, files just for her full spousal benefit at 66. (Again, Liz was grandparented against post-FRA deeming because she was 62 before the January 1, 2016, deadline.)

Step 3: Liz files for her retirement benefit at 70.

Step 4: Jane suspends her retirement benefit when she reaches 66 because from that point on it's no longer helping Liz. But by suspending it, Jane can start accumulating Delayed Retirement Credits that at age 70 will bump up her age-62 early retirement benefit.

Step 5: Jane restarts her retirement benefit at 70 at a 32 percent larger value than when she suspended it. From age 70 on, she'll receive 25 percent less in retirement benefits compared to having just waited till 70 to file, but she helped Liz and that raised their household's total lifetime benefits.

Step 6: When Liz dies, Jane takes her widow's benefit, which consists of Liz's age-70 retirement benefit, which is larger than Jane's because Jane took her own retirement benefit early.

WE TAKE LEAVE OF LIZ AND JANE TO MAKE TWO FINAL SUGGESTIONS

We're going to close this chapter by discussing two other issues.

The first is how couples approaching retirement, even qualified divorced couples, should handle their Social Security collection if they have a child who can collect disabled child benefits. This discussion also pertains to an older couple with young children they've adopted.

Our second and final topic is the size of excess spousal and excess divorced spousal benefits. We've discussed above the importance of excess spousal benefits even for those who were, supposedly, grandparented under the new law. And for all married spouses and qualified divorced who were not grandparented, excess spousal benefits is the only spousal benefit left (besides child-in-care spousal benefits). So it's important to know whether you are able to receive a positive, let alone a significant, excess spousal benefit.

OLDER MARRIED OR QUALIFIED DIVORCED COUPLES WITH DISABLED CHILDREN—A TELLING EXAMPLE

Meet John, age 62, Jill, age 46, and Jimmy, who at age 15 is severely disabled. The names have been changed, but the case is based on an actual family that contacted Larry. John retired after a career of moderate earnings. Jill had been a much higher earner, but wanted to stop working and take care of Jimmy on a full-time basis.

Here's the question: Should John start his retirement benefit early, indeed immediately, in order to activate child benefits for Jimmy, which will continue until John or Jill passes away? (At that point Jimmy can switch to a higher child survivor benefit.) Or should John simply wait till 70 to collect his retirement benefit, at which point Jimmy could finally start collecting his disabled child benefit and Jill could finally start collecting her child-in-care spousal benefit?

The good news is that since Jill is no longer going to be working, she won't lose the child-in-care benefit due to the earnings test. Unlike losing spousal, excess spousal, survivor, or excess survivor benefits (and their counterparts for the qualified divorced), losses of child-in-care spousal benefits aren't recouped in the form of higher future benefit levels once you reach Full Retirement Age.

The bad news is that the combined benefits going to Jimmy and Jill will be subject to the Family Maximum Benefit, as explained in Chapter 3.

Yet another big question, given the new law, is what John should do when he reaches full retirement age. Should he, at that point, suspend his retirement benefit and restart it at 70? Under the old law, he could do this and not cut off benefits to Jimmy and Jill. Under the new law, remember, John wasn't grandparented in, because he was too young. He *is* still free to suspend his benefit and restart it later at a higher level. *But if he does, he can't provide benefits to anyone while his retirement benefit is in suspension.* So taking his retirement benefit early comes at a much bigger cost than was previously the case. This loss in benefits to Jimmy and Jill while John's retirement benefit is suspended is an extra cost on top of the fact that, although suspending will raise his retirement benefit significantly, once he re-starts it at 70, it will from that point on always be lower—25 percent lower—than had he never taken benefits early to begin with.

Okay, so what's the best strategy? Well, John takes his retirement benefit early, indeed immediately. And, based on Jimmy's disability, Jill and Jimmy should immediately file in order to collect benefits on John's work record. (Recall that these benefits are based on John's full retirement benefit, not his reduced retirement benefit.) But what does John do at FRA? Does he suspend and cut off Jimmy and Jill for four years? He does not. His optimal strategy is to stick with his reduced retirement benefit for the rest of his life. This is a big cut to his own lifetime benefits, but it maximizes the family's total benefits.

But the story does not end there. Jane is just 46, remember. When *she* reaches 70, she files for her own retirement benefit, which starts at its highest possible value. John's own full retirement benefit is too large compared to Jill's for him to collect an excess spousal benefit. But son Jimmy would now be able to collect a larger disabled child's benefit on Jane's work record, if it were larger than John's. Indeed, that was the case in the actual example we ran. True, Jane had a fairly short career, but she made very good money.

And yet, though we're talking about only three people here, their optimal Social Security strategy has yet another twist. When John dies, Jimmy gets to collect a child survivor benefit on John's work record. Why? Because the child's survivor benefit is 75 percent of John's full retirement benefit, whereas the disabled child benefit Jimmy would be collecting on Jill's work record is only 50 percent of Jill's full retirement benefit. And though Jill was the much higher earner, when we ran the numbers, it turned out that 75 percent of John's benefit was more than 50 percent of Jill's—not surprising, really, since Jill had stopped working at age 46.

The final decision would come when Jill dies. Think for a moment: What should Jimmy do then? He should compare Jill's benefit with John's and switch if it's larger, stay with John's if not.

In total, getting this family all of what's theirs involves eight different moves. So at this point you might ask (assuming you're still reading): Is it worth it to optimize? Most emphatically *yes*, because under the optimized plan, the family's lifetime benefits are $1.2 million, providing them an extra $105,000 compared to doing what most retired couples do, which is simply to take their retirement benefits at age 62.

The broader message here is that the new law has changed optimal strategies, in some cases dramatically. But it hasn't made figuring out what's best to do any simpler. Or any less important.

WHO CAN COLLECT EXCESS
SPOUSAL BENEFITS?

Remember that brain-numbing formula for your excess spousal benefit? To keep it simple, we'll assume you try to collect spousal benefits at Full Retirement Age, but in so doing are deemed under the new law to be also filing for your own retirement benefits. (That is, you are not grandparented under the new rules.) The formula is 50 percent of your spouse's PIA (full retirement benefit) less 100 percent of your own PIA. If this difference is negative, the excess spousal benefit is set to zero.

If you stare at this formula for a while, you'll realize that your spouse's PIA has to be at least twice your own PIA for the excess spousal benefit to be worth anything at all. But, given the significant progressivity of the benefit formula, your spouse's AIME has to be *more* than twice your own AIME for your excess spousal benefit to be positive.[2]

THE BRAVE NEW, AND EXPANDED,
WORLD OF EXCESS SPOUSAL BENEFITS

As we've noted before, the world of excess spousal benefits has gotten much more important since enactment of the new Social Security rules. The table on page 174 shows the excess spousal benefits for a wife based on different monthly incomes (AIME) for herself and her spouse or ex. We could substitute the word "husband" for "wife" and "wife" for "husband" with no change in the table. And, for qualified divorced spouses, we could substitute the words "ex-husband" and "ex-wife." So this table pertains to the qualified divorced just as much as it pertains to the married.

In 2016, the largest possible AIME a high-wage worker could have was just under $10,000 ($120,000 a year), since the ceiling on taxable annual wages in 2016 was $118,500. Let's call an AIME between $1,250 and $2,500 "low-wage," and an AIME of roughly $5,000 "middle-income."

The table shows that middle- and upper-income workers can forget about receiving an excess spousal benefit. Only low- or very low-wage workers can collect this benefit and then if, and only if, they meet the other conditions necessary to receive excess spousal or excess divorced spousal benefits. But the table also raises some troubling questions about basic fairness. High earners whose spouses don't work or who earn relatively little stand to receive the largest amount of excess spousal benefits. Compare, for example, two workers with AIMEs each of $2,500. Their combined AIMEs come to $5,000, but their excess spousal benefit is zero. By contrast, a single-earner couple with an AIME of $5,000 can provide his or her nonworking spouse $1,048 in excess spousal benefits.

What about the total annual benefits of these two couples? The single-earner, $5,000 AIME couple, where both spouses are the same age and take their benefits at FRA, receives $3,144 per month or $37,728 per year in total benefits. The two-earner couple with $2,500 each in AIME collects $2,592 per month or $31,104 per year. This 21.3 percent difference strikes us as a significant tax on dual-earner couples.

Social Security expert Eugene Steuerle of the Urban Institute, a former deputy assistant secretary of the U.S. Treasury for tax analysis and author of the book *Dead Men Ruling*, put it plainly in a column for Paul's *PBS NewsHour* website just after the bipartisan budget bill "reformed" spousal benefits in late 2015: none of the changes get at what he calls the root issue, "that spousal and survivor benefits are unfair. . . . As far as the benefits are meant to adequately support spouses and dependents in retirement, they are badly and regressively targeted. . . . Imagine you and I earn the same salary and have the same life expectancy, but I have a non-working spouse and you are unmarried. We pay the same Social Security taxes, but while I am alive and retired, my family's annual benefits will be 50 percent higher than yours because of my non-working spouse's benefits. If I die first, she'll get years of my full worker benefit as survivor benefits."

Who fashioned Social Security's rules to allow someone to play God here? Who decided that the couple in which both spouses worked year in and year out is less deserving than the couple in which only one spouse worked, even though the two couples have the same wage income as measured by their combined AIMEs?

We don't know and we don't know if anyone does. But if there was a gross injustice in the spousal benefit system, it was in favor of the married over singles, and married couples with one main earner over working couples.

EXCESS SPOUSAL BENEFIT OF WIFE

AIME of Husband	AIME of Wife: $0	$1,250	$2,500	$5,000	$7,500	$10,000
$0	$0	$0	$0	$0	$0	$0
$1,250	$448	$0	$0	$0	$0	$0
$2,500	$648	$0	$0	$0	$0	$0
$5,000	$1,048	$152	$0	$0	$0	$0
$7,500	$1,249	$353	$0	$0	$0	$0
$10,000	$1,436	$540	$140	$0	$0	$0

PATIENCE, NOT FULL SPOUSAL OR EXCESS SPOUSAL BENEFITS, IS THE BIG GAME

We stressed at the outset of the book that the vast majority of benefits associated with maximizing your family's lifetime Social Security benefits arise from taking much higher benefits later in life. Yes, as the table above shows, Congress and the president have wiped out spousal benefits of any kind for millions of working married couples, as well as divorced couples who stuck it out for 10-plus years before legally calling it quits.

Yes, high earners whose spouses play golf their entire lives will still be able to provide spousal benefits to their better halves. But for most of you, when it comes to spousal benefits, it's time to forget about it. Unfortunately, the lure of the file-and-suspend strategy has been key to Social Security optimization in recent years.

Across the country, financial planners and insurance agents have been holding evening meetings, accompanied by free pizza, to tell the public how to use file-and-suspend to collect supposedly "free" spousal benefits, though the term "free" is a curious one, since Social Security benefits, including retirement benefits, are provided in exchange for the substantial tax levied on, for most of us, every dollar we earn. These presentations have been used to engage new clients and help them with their own specific Social Security optimization as well as other financial issues. The spousal benefit pitch was an effective come-on.

And it certainly worked as a come-on for us. The first edition of *Get What's Yours* started with the story of Larry getting Paul an extra $50,000 or so in spousal benefits and the story getting our book plenty of attention. But our bait-and-switch strategy, in sharp contrast, was to bait readers with the spousal benefits, and then switch them to our big messages—how to think properly about longevity risk, how to value Social Security benefits in light of this risk, and how to choose the optimal collection strategies based on valuing Social Security benefits correctly.

10

WIDOWED? WHY SOCIAL SECURITY IS A MAJOR WOMEN'S ISSUE

About 10 million widows and widowers aged 65 and older were receiving monthly survivor benefits in 2013. Of these, 80 percent were awarded to women. So, while we have been taking great pains throughout to discuss Social Security in gender-neutral terms, we won't do so here, even though we realize that with the increase in house husbands and the legalization of gay marriage, the survivor-awards gender ratio will probably shift in the future.

In short, this chapter's specifics apply mainly to women. But husbands ought to read the chapter, too, and read it closely, because their decisions about how long to work and when to begin claiming their own Social Security retirement benefits could have a substantial impact on the quality of their wives' later years. And, to be honest here, the odds suggest that many of those years will be spent as widows. Adult children should read it as well and think about their mothers' unmet financial needs in later life—needs that may fall on them to fund. Then they should talk to both their parents and make sure the claiming decisions of their moms and dads are made with the likely longevity of their moms in mind.

One more point before moving forward. A book of strategies for dealing with a bureaucracy and its rules invites little in the way of empathic emotions, save for frustration. But as all three of us have answered many benefit questions from "survivors," we first want to express our sincere condolences to every reader who has lost a spouse, an overwhelmingly significant other, an irreplaceable parent, or a child. Losing a child, partner, or parent is surely life's heaviest burden, and we have often felt inadequate to the task of providing advice in such circumstances. But we're of sadly little use with regard to soothing your pain, so from here on, we'll stick to pointers for dealing with what is cruelly inevitable.

Back to the hard realities:

1. Widowhood is primarily a woman's issue.
2. The benefits paid to widows, particularly older ones, could be crucial to avoiding years of poverty or something close to it.
3. Changing patterns of male-female earnings, marriage, and divorce make it unclear whether a larger or smaller share of women will be collecting survivor or divorce benefits in the future.
4. Rising labor force participation rates for women, however, and generally rising wages as well mean that women increasingly will be better able to fend for themselves in retirement, including receiving growing benefits as compared with those received by men.
5. And yet, ironically, despite their rising earnings profiles, married women face increasingly raw deals when their husbands die.

Here's a specific example that came in the form of a question to Larry on Paul's PBS Money Sen$e website from "Helen" of Eureka, California:

I am twice divorced and began taking my own Social Security benefit at age 66. My first husband died last year. We were married over 10 years. Am I eligible to collect his Social Security benefit?

Our answer: Yes, Helen—and everyone in her position—would be *eligible* to collect on a deceased former husband's earnings record, even if long divorced from him, even if she remarried (so long as she did so on or after her 60th birthday), all assuming that she was married to the deceased ex-husband for at least a decade, as she says she was.

To be clear as well as comprehensive, Helen, like everyone in such a position, would be in line to receive a widow's benefit based on her husband's earnings record *or* she could continue to get her own retirement benefit, the one she already started taking at age 66. She would be eligible to receive the larger of the two benefits.

We weren't able to reach Helen to quiz her on the specifics, but since the average American man earns something like 25 percent more than the average woman does, let's assume that's the case here, and that Helen is able to collect a widow benefit that exceeds her retirement benefit (and that she is not already doing so without realizing it).

Now, if Helen were just taking a spousal benefit, the most she could collect would be half of his PIA. The math is simple. His PIA is only 25 percent higher than hers, so half of his would be only 62.5 percent of her PIA.

However, she's not going to take a spousal benefit but a widow's benefit. The math here may be much, much trickier. Helen is eligible to collect the greater of her retirement benefit or, depending on when he began taking benefits and the age at which he died, *all* of her late former husband's benefit. We don't know these facts in Helen's case. But if her late former husband didn't begin taking retirement benefits until he was 70, for example, they would be 132 percent of a PIA that already was 25 percent larger than Helen's. So her widow's benefit would be much larger than her own retirement benefit. Remember, she started taking that benefit at her Full Retirement Age, so it would be only equal to her PIA (plus subsequent Cost of Living Adjustments). Again, an easy decision for her.

But if, like most men, he claimed retirement benefits early (before FRA), the benefits would be reduced and so would her widow's benefit. The only way to know for sure is to review the numbers carefully. A visit to her Social Security office *should* do the trick here. But we hope Helen brushes up on the portions of *Get What's Yours* that explain the benefit cuts caused by these RIB-LIM rules. (See Chapter 3 or Glossary for the RIB-LIM definition.)

But wait. Helen's situation suggests another possibility. Suppose Helen had filed for her widow's benefit and also had suspended her retirement benefit and requested the suspension before April 30, 2016. (As we said, we haven't been in touch with her.) Then she is now collecting her excess widow's benefit. Remember from earlier discussions that the excess widow's benefit is the difference between her widow's benefit and her own suspended retirement benefit. We're assuming here it will be positive.

If Helen did this, her own retirement benefit will be growing at 8 percent a year until age 70, inflation adjusted, due to those Delayed Retirement Credits we keep touting. In other words, as long as her survivor benefit is *greater* than her own current benefit, she will be getting *something* while waiting for her maximum possible benefit, which she can get by restarting her own retirement benefit at 70. Of course, this might not represent a lot of dollars, so problems in being able to afford to delay her own retirement benefits might be an issue.

Moreover, if the extra money showing up at 70 isn't big bucks, this entire strategy would be misguided. She'd be giving up four (or so) years of large benefits of, say, size X in order to collect what might be a small excess widow's benefit and then start collecting at 70 total benefits of size X plus something that may be very small. The costs of pursuing this strategy could clearly exceed the gains.

The moral? It's a *tricky business* to figure out when to take widow's benefits and when to take retirement benefits and whether to suspend retirement benefits if you can collect excess widow's benefits only because you took your retirement benefit before your spouse died.

Furthermore, you can be the smartest person in the country and still make terrible collection mistakes. Before going through some of the nitty-gritty details of widow(er) benefits, let us tell you about how Larry collected yet another dinner, this time from his friend Glenn.

LARRY EATS SUSHI FOR FREE

Glenn Loury is one of the world's premier economists and has constructed incisive mathematical models covering topics as diverse as the intergenerational transmission of inequality, the process of technological innovation, and the creation and propagation of racial stereotypes. But Glenn, a chaired professor at Brown University, knew very little about Social Security's survivor benefits. Well, nothing really.

And, tragically, survivor benefits were relevant to Glenn. His wife, Linda, had passed away about a year before Larry and Glenn's dinner. Linda was also an esteemed economist, with a long and well-paid career at Tufts University. Glenn and Larry had just finished eating when Glenn mentioned he was thinking about selling his house and moving into a smaller place. Age 65, he said that he (like Paul) expected to keep working until at least 70 and take his Social Security then.

"Glenn," said Larry, "have you thought about taking survivor benefits?"

"You mean from Linda?"

"Yes."

"No. I earned a lot more than Linda."

"And so you're sure that disqualifies you from survivor benefits?"

"Yes."

"Are you really sure?"

Glenn laughed. "No, I'm not *really* sure. Am I missing something?"

"How does this sound? I make you, let me see, about $120,000 in the next two minutes and you pay for dinner." (Larry was getting used to the gravy train after dining out on his earlier advice to Paul.)

"I'm in," said Glenn.

Larry then explained to Glenn that in a year, when he turned 66 and reached FRA, he could apply just for a survivor benefit based on Linda's earnings record. Linda had passed away at age 58, but the survivor benefit is equal to what her full retirement benefit *would have been* had she lived until 66—$30,000 per year.

"But," Glenn asked, "how can I collect benefits if I'm the higher earner?"

"Good question," said Larry. "Even though you're the higher earner, you're not going to take your own retirement benefit until 70. Yes, once you start taking your own retirement benefit, you'll get only the larger of the two benefits—your retirement and survivor benefits. But between 66 and 70, that won't happen.

"And the beauty of this is the part that you already knew—by waiting four years until age 70 to collect *your* retirement benefit, it will rise a lot." Then Larry repeated the familiar 32 percent increase refrain. "So you get a lot more money in retirement benefits by waiting, and you also get the survivor benefits for four years, well, for *free!*"

"But," objected Glenn, "I'll still be working. Isn't there an Earnings Test whereby I lose benefits if I earn too much money?"

"Yes, but it ends when you reach 66, which is your Full Retirement Age."

Yet another friend was picking up the tab for Larry's dinner.

Let's expand on this case study just a bit, because of course most people aren't going to be in Glenn's shoes.

Glenn wasn't able to benefit from taking a survivor benefit before FRA because he was still working, and at his relatively lofty income, the Earnings Test would have wiped out any benefits (survivor or retirement) that he could have taken before FRA.

Yes, he'd get the money back later. But the Earnings Test money is returned to you in incrementally higher benefits over the years of your actuarial life expectancy. Since Glenn would be taking the survivor benefit only until age 70, however, he wouldn't recoup most of the deferred money.

But if there was another person in this situation who was at least 60 and not working, taking his survivor benefit right away, followed by his retirement benefit at 70, would be his best option.

Yes, taking a survivor benefit as early as age 60 (the earliest age at which you can do so) means a big early survivor benefit reduction, specifically, 28.5 percent. The choice was whether to begin taking the reduced survivor benefit at age 60 or wait until a later year, when he'd get a higher benefit. We calculated all possible scenarios—wait until age 61, until age 62, etc.—and it turned out that even with the steep reduction, waiting past age 60 to collect a survivor benefit never made sense. This, again, is the case with a survivor whose age-70 retirement benefit exceeds his or her unreduced survivor benefit.

A SHORT (AND ADMITTEDLY DRY)
PRIMER ON THE BASICS FOR
WIDOWS AND WIDOWERS

Any widow or widower married for more than 9 months is eligible to receive survivor benefits keyed to the Social Security earnings record of their late spouse. Survivor benefits based on the work record of a deceased and divorced spouse are also possible if you have not remarried before the age of 60, but you must have been married for at least 10 years.

Survivor benefits begin as early as age 60, unlike retirement benefits, where 62 is the earliest age for filing. If you are disabled, you may elect to begin receiving survivor benefits at the age of 50.

Spousal survivor benefits can amount to as much as the deceased spouse's age-70 retirement benefit—the spouse's full retirement benefit at FRA plus all Delayed Retirement Credits. They can also amount to a lot less. The total depends on a number of factors, including the age of death of the deceased spouse and the timing of his retirement benefit, assuming he already took it. It also depends on whether the survivor takes the widow benefit before her own full retirement age. Finally, it depends on whether the survivor is disabled and, if disabled, whether she became disabled before the ex-spouse died.

There is a penalty for early survivor filing, beginning at age 60 and ending when you reach FRA, which is 66 for anyone born between 1945 and 1956. During this 72-month period, survivor benefits are reduced by just under four-tenths of a percent (0.396, to be precise) for each month prior to turning 66. This works out to 4.75 percent a year, or a 28.5 percent early filing penalty for the full 6-year period between ages 60 and 66.

A final "basic," in the form of a mild warning: if you file for survivor benefits early—before 66—you could also be affected by the *Earnings Test*, the same one that temporarily reduces retirement benefits for early filers. But, as with those benefits, any survivor benefits reduced by this test will be restored once you've reached FRA.

TIME FOR ANOTHER EXAMPLE

To return from the abstract to the concrete, here's a seemingly straightforward email from a Texas woman:

My husband died yesterday. I live in Houston, Texas. Am I entitled
to his Social Security paycheck?

Well, the easy answer is "no, you're entitled to *your own* Social Security paycheck, in the form of your *survivor's* benefit." But if the
emailer means "Am I entitled to the *amount* of my late husband's
paycheck?" the answer, unfortunately, is that, as with Helen's situation, there's no way to say without knowing exactly how much the
husband was receiving, based on his earnings record, *when* he starting taking his benefits, and when the surviving widow decides to take
her survivor's benefit.

The point of this case study is that Social Security does not make
the process of finding such information easy. Here is what a widow
like this woman in Houston would have to go through when trying
to determine when to take her survivor benefit.

First thing first. If she is 60 or over (or 50 or older and disabled), she
can collect widow's benefits starting immediately, subject to the Earnings Test and early claiming reductions if she is younger than her FRA.
That's the easy part of the answer. But how much will her widow's
benefit be? It hinges on who takes (or in this case, *took*) their benefits
when. There are four different situations to consider, and each one
yields a different answer: (1) both wait (waited) until full eligibility age;
(2) husband waited (until FRA) but *wife* now takes early; (3) husband
took early, wife now waits; (4) both take (or took) early. Because there
are bound to be readers facing the situation sketched in the email, we'll
consider the answers one painstaking permutation at a time.

1. If the husband took his retirement benefit after FRA and the
    widow takes the widow's benefit at or after her own FRA, she
    will, indeed, receive his actual retirement benefit—his full re-
    tirement benefit inclusive of his Delayed Retirement Credits.
    As it happens, this may be even *more* than the check he was

receiving each month. Why? Because his monthly Medicare Part B premium may have been withheld from his monthly Social Security check and of course those premiums no longer need to be paid. His check may also have been less than his retirement benefit for another reason: Social Security may have been withholding some of his retirement benefit for income taxes and the amount of this withholding could decline if his widow is in a lower federal income tax bracket after he dies.

2. Even if the husband took his retirement benefit at FRA, if the widow took her widow's benefit *before* FRA, her survivor benefit will be reduced. For example, it will be reduced by 28.5 percent if she took it at 60.

3. Now suppose the opposite: the husband took his retirement benefit early and the widow waits to take her widow's benefit until her full retirement age. In that case, the survivor's benefit would equal the larger of two payments: (1) the early retirement benefit he was receiving, or (2) 82.5 percent of his full retirement benefit. So, by way of example, let's say he took his retirement benefit at age 62. It would then have been smaller than 82.5 percent of his full retirement benefit. So, by waiting until her FRA, her widow's benefit would exceed what her husband had been receiving. However, the widow in this case could receive just as much if she filed at a certain point prior to FRA, due to the RIB-LIM formula.

4. If the husband took his retirement benefit early and the widow also takes her widow's benefit early, the reduced widow's benefit could be less than what he was receiving, depending on how early she starts taking. In this case, her widow's benefit will equal either 82.5 percent of her late spouse's full retirement benefit, or her late spouse's reduced retirement benefit, or her late spouse's full retirement benefit reduced by her widow's benefit reduction factor.

THE WIDOW'S LIMIT (RIB-LIM)

When Social Security's foundational laws were enacted in the 1930s, the rules regarding women were shaped by men, thinking about what would happen to their predominantly nonworking wives when the men died. Here's what one of the program's primary oversight groups said back then, as cited in a 2010 SSA research paper on widows:

> A haunting fear in the minds of many older men is the possibility, and frequently, the probability, that their widow will be in need after their death. The day of large families and of the farm economy, when aged parents were thereby assured comfort in their declining years, has passed for a large proportion of our population. This change has had particularly devastating effect on the sense of security of the aged women of our country.

Survivor benefits weren't even included in the law as originally enacted. In later years, debates on the level of widow benefits included discussions that concluded that widows could live more cheaply than widowers because they knew how to take care of their domestic needs. Men, by contrast, were assumed to need more money. Among other reasons, it was assumed they could not cook and would thus have to buy their meals at a restaurant. We kid you not.

Even today, more than seventy-five years later, Social Security planners say that poverty rates of older widows are one of their greatest concerns. And one of the major causes of low widow benefits, besides having earned less and therefore saved less than men, is that their husbands overwhelmingly took their retirement benefits early, thus locking in lower widow's benefits for their wives for the rest of their lives.

This is reflected in what's called the Retirement Income Benefit Limit, or, like some abbreviation out of the old Soviet Union, RIB-LIM. It is also called the widow's limit in some Social Security discussions. We discussed RIB-LIM at some length in Chapter 3 and will spare you an encore here. But it affects lots of women: roughly 3 million, or about 3 out of every 8 widows, according to a 2010 research paper. In cases involving the retirement benefits of non-disabled husbands who died, nearly 60 percent of their widows saw their survivor benefits reduced by RIB-LIM.[1]

Okay, here's another survivor's question that came in over the electronic transom:

> My 70-year-old husband passed away and he was collecting Social
> Security at 62. I am 64 and still working. Will I receive a portion
> of my husband's Social Security?

Our answer: Yes, but your timing here is crucial. Remember that if someone tries to take her own retirement benefit and her survivor benefit at the same time, she'll get only the larger of the two benefits. (You might remember from an earlier discussion that deeming does not affect survivor benefits.)

Normally, we'd recommend that a widow in this position take the smaller of the two benefits earlier, allowing the second benefit to rise in value, and then switch to it after it no longer rises with age.

But in this case, because the husband took his retirement benefit early, the survivor benefit is calculated based on the RIB-LIM referred to above, which means the survivor benefit will be 82.5 percent of the husband's full retirement benefit, regardless of whether it is taken immediately or not until FRA.

In other words, for the widow in this situation, there is no advantage to waiting to collect her survivor benefit. There is, however, a possible advantage—and a large one—from waiting to collect her own retirement benefit. If she waits, for example, until age 70, when it's as large as possible, it may exceed her survivor benefit, in which case she'll collect *it* rather than her survivor benefit.

But it's also possible that her retirement benefit may exceed her survivor benefit even *before* age 70. So we think she and people in her situation should apply right now for their survivor benefit and then apply for their own retirement benefit at or after the point that their retirement benefit exceeds the survivor benefit, which, again, may never happen. There's some homework to do here, but by this point in *Get What's Yours*, we are confident you'll be up to it!

A last caveat: the annual Earnings Test may prevent this widow from receiving all or part of her potential survivor benefit before FRA. But, as we've often pointed out, she'll get the money back via higher monthly benefits starting at FRA.

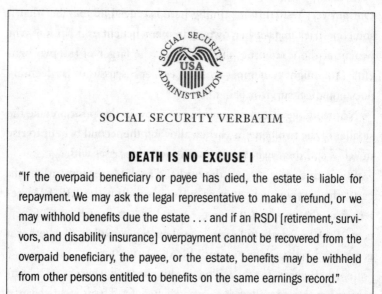

SOCIAL SECURITY VERBATIM

DEATH IS NO EXCUSE I

"If the overpaid beneficiary or payee has died, the estate is liable for repayment. We may ask the legal representative to make a refund, or we may withhold benefits due the estate . . . and if an RSDI [retirement, survivors, and disability insurance] overpayment cannot be recovered from the overpaid beneficiary, the payee, or the estate, benefits may be withheld from other persons entitled to benefits on the same earnings record."

ALL QUOTES FROM OFFICIAL SOCIAL SECURITY RULES

MIXED SOCIAL SECURITY
BLESSING FOR WIDOWS: MORE
WOMEN IN THE WORKFORCE

In the "olden days," of course, many wives *never* worked outside the home. Without survivor benefits, they would have been destitute. Thus it is that a woman whose husband died at age 70, after deferring his retirement benefit and enjoying 4 years of Delayed Retirement Credits, may be eligible to receive his entire benefit for the rest of her life, including annual increases to adjust for the effect of inflation. And she may receive this without ever having worked for Social Security–covered wages a day in her life.

More likely in this era, however, wives will have worked but will still have earned less than their husbands. This means that their benefits as surviving spouses may be higher than their own retirement benefits, for which they have paid taxes their entire working lives. As an agency 2010 research paper observed, "The auxiliary benefit provisions, including spousal and widow's benefits, mean that many women do not receive higher benefits in return for their contributions than they would have received had they never worked or contributed to the program."

On the other hand, as more women have entered the workforce and as more of them have begun to earn higher salaries, a growing percentage of women has begun to earn Social Security retirement benefits on a par with men in general and their husbands in particular.

The problem is, it will be decades before this trend takes full effect. (Recall, if you will, that benefits are tied to a person's top 35 years of covered earnings.) Moreover, fewer women are getting married. And to compound the problem, a rising percentage is getting divorced, more and more of them after fewer than 10 years of marriage, the minimum needed to qualify for survivor divorced spousal benefits.

The net effect of these trends is that despite women's slow and steady entry into the workforce, there's been a slow and steady countereffect on what surviving female spouses can expect from Social Security. Just look at the so-called income replacement rate: the percentage of a person's pre-retirement income represented by their Social Security benefits. This rate is a key measure of the impact and adequacy of Social Security benefits, and it has been declining in a big way. Without getting into the minutiae of demographic shifts, women's changing role in the workforce, and other statistical details, the bottom line here is that everyone—but particularly women—will be depending on Social Security for an ever-shrinking share of their retirement income needs, and therefore had better get as much as they possibly can. Women (and men, for that matter) need to save more for retirement.

Everyone—aging wives and their husbands, as well as their grown children—needs to think carefully about women's relatively greater needs for retirement security. And the sooner such recognition is incorporated into a family's financial plans, the more likely widows are to live the kinds of lives their husbands and children want for them.

A LAST (AND TOUCHING) CASE STUDY

I am 67 and married and have been diagnosed with terminal cancer. I have another five years at most to live. The people at my local Social Security office said I should file to begin taking my retirement benefits right away so I'd at least get something back before I die for all my years of contributions. What do you think?

This question was posed to Larry in person and so we let him narrate the rest of the story, and his answer:

You could not meet a nicer or better man, and he's facing his situation with joy for all the good he's done and experienced and with determination to live out his remaining days helping others, all while living life to the fullest.

In between telling me about his recent and pending fly-fishing expeditions, which he can partake in thanks to oral chemotherapy, he asked if he should follow the Social Security office's strong advice.

I told him this probably was bad advice for the following reason: Each year between FRA and 70 that he waits to collect will increase by 8 percent (not compounded) the real (inflation-adjusted) amount of Social Security survivor benefits his wife, who hadn't worked much, will receive for the rest of her life after he passes away. For example, if he survives to 70, his wife will receive a 24 percent higher survivor benefit check every month than she would receive if he took Social Security benefits now.

The reason the wife's work history matters, I told him, is that she'll get a check equal to the larger of her own retirement benefit or her survivor benefit. If she had earned more than her husband and waited, say, to age 70 to collect her retirement benefit, the survivor benefit wouldn't matter because she'd never collect it.

One moral to this story is to be very careful taking Social Security's advice. Another is to bear in mind that your decision about when to take your own retirement benefit will impact what your spouse and, indeed, any ex-spouses to whom you were married for 10 or more years will receive in survivor benefits.

Social Security Administration employees are specifically trained not to advise people what to do but instead to explain their options and let them decide what is best for them. Some employees hesitate to mention what will happen in the event of a person's death simply because it's an uncomfortable subject. But we sometimes have the worst of both worlds: they give advice when they shouldn't and then don't do a very good job of it.

11

NEVER MARRIED OR
DIVORCED TOO SOON

Social Security provides a host of incentives to strategically tie the knot, as we explained in Chapter 8. But what about those of you who never marry? What strategies and tactics are available to *you*?

This is not an idle question because the ranks of the unmarried have swelled in recent years and decades, perhaps because the stigma against what used to be scornfully called *cohabitation*—or even *out-of-wedlock* child rearing—has faded. It's true that less than 10 percent of people in the United States aged 55 to 64 have never been married. But the Census Bureau reports that this figure is higher for younger age brackets and has steadily been increasing in recent decades. The percentages of never-married persons is about 12.5 percent for those 50 to 54; 14 percent for people aged 45 to 49; 17.5 percent for the 40–44 age group; and more than 23 percent for persons aged 35 to 39.

Let's say you're between 50 and 64 and you never married. There were *6.5 million* of you as of 2014[1]—6.5 million people who should both be stressing about—and *doing* something about—their Social Security and retirement needs, even if the "doing" has involved nothing more to date than getting this book as a gift.

Another 10.3 million Americans between 50 and 64 were divorced. And these days, more than 50 percent of people who married don't stay hitched for the 10 years needed to qualify for Social

Security divorce benefits. In short, lots of people may have benefit pressures and choices similar, if not identical, to the never-hitched.

So let's get down to cases. Say you're single with neither kids nor ex, or you were married for fewer than 10 years and thus have no basis for receiving divorced spousal or widow(er) benefits. In this case, your Social Security choices hinge on these questions:

1. When do you want to begin receiving benefits?
2. If you're already getting benefits, might it be worth your while to change your mind?
3. If you do change your mind, what do you do?

MEET PATRICIA D., SINGLE AND 66

Patricia D. of Connecticut turned 66 at the end of 2013, when the old law prevailed. We interviewed her in the spring of 2014. She had sent us an email. Should you ever have thought—before reading this book—that the benefit elections of a single person were simple, or that the advice of Social Security was always clear or accurate, Patricia would have begged to differ. She learned firsthand that her decisions and those of millions of other single persons include challenging issues about not only Social Security but their broader finances, their health, and the type of lives they hope to live.

Here is part of her email to Phil.

I will be 66 at the end of this month. I will receive my first Social Security check in January. I'm single, never married. When I went to Social Security to sign up, I asked if I could suspend my payment in the next year. I was told that I could but that I would have to pay back all payments that I have received. This is never mentioned in your articles.

The folks at Social Security were mixing up *suspending* and *withdrawing* retirement benefits. When you have reached your Full Retirement Age and *suspend* benefits, you put them on hold and let them accumulate Delayed Retirement Credits. You have no obligation to repay anything. (You will, however, have an obligation to pay Medicare premiums yourself, because they can no longer be deducted from your now-suspended Social Security payment.)

If Patricia had wanted, instead, to *withdraw* her benefit, then Social Security would have been correct, though she would have had to make this request within one year of beginning to receive payments from Social Security. (Waiting even one day beyond this deadline would have canceled her ability to withdraw her benefit.) So, if she did "withdraw," she would, indeed, need to repay the Social Security benefits she had so far received. Withdrawing and repaying her past received retirement benefits would effectively reset her Social Security status to that of someone who had never filed for retirement benefits at all. Also, this would ensure that she received all her Delayed Retirement Credits when she finally did begin to collect her retirement benefit.

As we suggested in Chapter 3, *withdrawing* is a do-over option after having made a decision that you wish to change within a year. *Suspending*, by contrast, is a strategy to be adopted at Full Retirement Age that can be reversed at any time. As we explained in Chapter 4, the new Social Security rules can also have a big impact on suspending.

Very few people, single or otherwise, withdraw their benefits. First, it can cost a lot of money to repay up to a year's benefits. Second, few people know this right even exists. Third, the reasons that more than 98 percent of people begin claiming Social Security retirement benefits before age 70 are not likely to go away, so most people simply will never consider withdrawing their benefits.

SOCIAL SECURITY VERBATIM

DEATH IS NO EXCUSE II

If someone formally requests that Social Security reconsider an adverse benefit decision: "In the event of claimant death, process the death termination. If there are no other parties, dismiss the request for reconsideration unless there is an overpayment on the record with no waiver request. A reconsidered determination should be rendered since recovery from the estate is possible."

ALL QUOTES FROM OFFICIAL SOCIAL SECURITY RULES

DOCUMENT YOUR INTERACTIONS
WITH SOCIAL SECURITY

It's always possible that Patricia and the Social Security representative with whom she spoke misunderstood one another. This is one reason we urge you to take notes and keep solid records of your communications with Social Security. Sadly, the art of letter writing may be dead. But the benefits of having a written record of your dealings with Social Security could be enormous. If the agency did make a mistake or misunderstood your claiming preferences, putting a time stamp on when you logged your request can lock in a claiming date. To be sure communications are properly logged, go to any Social Security office and formally document your intentions. Or send a certified letter to the agency, requiring a signed acknowledgment of its receipt.

We spoke with Patricia to make sure we understood her situation. It was clear she had no intention to withdraw benefits, which, after all, hadn't even begun yet. She had been living for decades on a very tight budget. She had continued to work well into her 60s and, in fact, would have continued to work past age 66 had she been able to find a job that paid her enough to allow her to defer collecting her Social Security and watch her Delayed Retirement Credits add 8 percent a year—in today's dollars—to her monthly benefit.

Last decade's Great Recession cost Patricia her last full-time job in 2009, and she spent the next four years working part-time whenever she could. A close reader of Larry's blog, Patricia knew that once she reached Full Retirement Age at 66 she would enjoy two aspects of that milestone: (1) none of her outside earnings would reduce her Social Security benefits, even temporarily, and (2) if she got a job that paid well enough, she could suspend her benefits once she reached FRA and restart them at any time until she turned 70 (when Social Security would automatically restart them for her).

PLAYING THE BENEFITS WAITING GAME

"What I was doing was waiting to claim until 66," Patricia said. "So, I would begin claiming at 66 and then keep looking for a job. And if I found one, I would then suspend"—her benefit, that is. That was the question that she posed to Social Security.

Patricia decided not to claim benefits early. Had she begun claiming at age 62, Patricia said, her monthly Social Security benefit would have been substantially reduced to $740. When she finally began claiming after she turned 66, her benefit was $1,052 a month.

"And I'm still looking for work but I'm not necessarily focused on getting a full-time position," she explained. "I am looking for something that I would like to do. I am not trying to make the round ball fit into the square box."

Realistically, the idea of suspending is not feasible for her unless she gets a high wage, she added. In fact, Patricia's income is so low that she qualifies for reduced Medicare premiums and also gets food stamps. Fortunately, she is in good health and her only prescription drug costs $10 for a three-month supply. "From what I get from Social Security I can pay my bills, but I can't buy food."

Because a new job could end her eligibility for food stamps and other forms of government assistance, Patricia figures any new job would have to pay her at least 25 percent more than her Social Security benefit for her to consider suspending and reapplying later.

HOW TO SUSPEND BENEFITS

If Patricia *had* decided to suspend her benefit, however, she would only have had to call, visit, or write her local Social Security office. Here's what the agency has to say, officially:

You do not have to sign your request to suspend benefit payments. You may ask us orally or in writing. [Remember, we prefer writing because it establishes the time of your request. And while the agency doesn't specify sending a certified letter, we think this is prudent.] If your benefit payments are suspended, they will start automatically the month you reach age 70. If you change your mind and want the payments to start before age 70, just tell us when you want your benefits reinstated (orally or in writing). Your request may include benefits for any months when your payments were suspended.

UNDERSTANDING LUMP-SUM PAYMENTS

Anyone who suspended their benefits before April 30, 2016, should be aware that they can decide later to collect the cumulative value of these suspended benefits in a lump-sum payment should an emergency or the siren song of that bucket-list trip to Bali beckon. This payment would include any cost-of-living adjustments that affected benefits during the period. It takes time to process this request, so don't expect the funds right away. Also, if you request a lump-sum payment of suspended benefits, Social Security will treat this as if you had filed for retirement benefits back at the date you had originally suspended benefits.

For those grandparented under the new law who un-suspend their benefits, here's the rub—their lump-sum payment will be based on the benefits that would have been due them at age 66, not the age when they requested the payment. And their regular monthly payments thereafter also would be based on a claiming age of 66. In other words, they would *lose* any and all Delayed Retirement Credits she had accumulated.

But what if someone didn't need *all* that money but, instead, say, just one year's worth? At age 69, she could tell the agency she wanted to resume her benefits as of the age of 68 (remember, they have been suspended since age 66). She would get a lump sum equal to just one year's worth of those payments. But when she started her regular monthly benefits at age 69, she would enjoy two years of Delayed Retirement Credits. That is, her monthly benefit would be 16 percent higher than at age 66. And it's this higher payment that she would receive each month for the rest of her life.

Let us summarize. Those never married whose options have *not* been affected by the new law should *always* file for their retirement benefit at FRA. If you can wait and want to wait to take advantage of the Delayed Retirement Credit, then suspend your retirement benefit. This will put you in the same boat as not filing-and-suspending when it comes to collecting these credits. But it will also give you the option of collecting all suspended benefits in a lump sum should an emergency arise. But if you failed to suspend by April 30, 2016, forget about un-suspending your benefits. The new law won't let you do so even if you come down with a terminal disease.

HOW TO WITHDRAW BENEFITS

If Patricia instead gets a terrific job and can afford to withdraw the benefits she began at age 66, she has until the day before her 67th birthday to do so. A *withdrawal* does require a form—SSA-521. Call Social Security to have one mailed to you or enter SSA-521 in an Internet search engine and you can print out your own. Compared to other SSA forms, this one is a snap.

The only open-ended information required on the form is its request that you provide a reason for your decision. There are only two boxes—the first says you are withdrawing because you intend to keep working. It also has what we'll call a "heads-up" notice: "I have been advised of the alternatives to withdrawal for applicants under FRA and still wish to withdraw my application." This is bewildering, as the only alternative we know of is to continue receiving benefits. Remember that the only other choice—*suspending* benefits—is not available to a claimant until FRA.

If Patricia *does* withdraw, she needs to repay all her benefits, including any withheld taxes and Medicare premiums deducted from her Social Security benefits. If she was or had been married, or had qualifying children, any benefits any of these folks received on her record would also need to be repaid.

And finally, if she does withdraw, she must reapply for benefits when she wants them to resume. Social Security will *not* automatically restart them, even when she turns 70.

12

HIDDEN BENEFITS FOR
THE DISABLED

Just as Social Security has become the dominant source of income for most older Americans, so has it become the nation's default welfare program. Neither role was part of the agency's founding mission, which envisioned Social Security as a modest source of income to augment people's savings and pensions. Yet here the program finds itself, some 80 years later, paying out benefits under two programs to more than 20 million disabled Americans. That's a huge number in its own right and even more so considering how many additional lives and livelihoods are affected by the $200 billion in annual benefits the disabled receive.

It used to be otherwise. More than 14 million Americans were dependent on federal welfare as recently as 1993, when President Bill Clinton took office. But with his vow "to end welfare as we know it" and the advent of welfare-to-work reform, welfare now provides benefits to barely *4 million* Americans, though the U.S. population has increased by 60 million since 1993. The tax code has helped a lot here. Refundable tax credits totaled about $150 billion in 2013, nearly all to low-income households. And then there is "disability."

Supplemental Security Income (SSI) and Social Security Disability Insurance (SSDI) compensate for the disappearance of traditional welfare. SSI is for disabled adults, older Americans, and disabled children with limited incomes and resources. SSDI is hardly welfare in the classic sense but is nonetheless a huge support program, available to workers who are certified as disabled and who have logged the requisite "covered" work under Social Security rules, which we'll relegate to a note, quoting the official language.[1] (Even if it's not relevant to you or yours, you might take a look to reassure yourself that you'd rather be reading our prose than that of the Social Security Administration.)

There were 8.3 million SSI recipients as of November 2015, including 1.3 million under the age of 18; 4.9 million aged 18 to 64; and 2.2 million who were 65 or older.[2]

Total SSI payments are approaching $60 billion a year, and the average monthly payment is about $540. The number of SSI recipients has doubled since 1985 and began a sustained rise in the 1990s. Even the end of the Great Recession has not ended the annual increases.

SSDI is a distinct program that is available to all disabled persons who qualify. Its ranks have swelled as well. The agency projects it will pay out between $150 billion and $160 billion in annual SSDI benefits, more than 90 percent to disabled workers and the rest to their children and spouses.

There were nearly 11 million SSDI recipients as of November 2015. As with SSI, the numbers of SSDI beneficiaries have been steadily climbing, mostly due to the general aging of the population. The recession also drove more people to seek disability payments because of job losses and family economic pressures.

It should be noted that when it comes to qualifying for the programs, neither SSI nor SSDI is a slam dunk. Barely a third of disability claimants who initially apply are accepted into the programs. Many of those turned down hire lawyers to appeal their denials. But though the success rate for "reconsideration" varies drastically by state, the national average was barely 13 percent as of a few years ago. Fraud remains a serious problem, although some claim it is not as acute as in the past.

Are recipients scamming the system? It depends what you mean by *scamming*. More than a few seem to exaggerate or even feign symptoms in order to qualify, as the sharply differing rates in percentage of "disabled" by state suggest. Theoretically, it could be the case that inhabitants of the so-called disability belt (Appalachia, the Mid-South, and the Mississippi Delta) become physically or mentally unable to work at double the rate of a state like Utah, for example, or that back problems have become far more disabling than in the past, as the data now indicate. A simpler explanation is that in poor states with difficult job markets, more people are functionally unable to find work that pays the bills, for *whatever* reason. And remember, less than half of applicants actually wind up getting benefits, so for those "scamming" the system, it's not an easy con.

But regardless of whether or not you think *you* might be less generous were you doling out disability money for the Social Security system itself, as things stand, disability programs are a big and growing expense. And while a dedicated part of Social Security payroll taxes goes to SSDI programs, it is scheduled to run short of money in 2016. Even our divided Congress cannot continue to ignore this funding shortfall.

On the assumption that this chapter will be read primarily by those who might qualify for SSDI, because of their work record, and are not among the indigent disabled who have rarely or ever been able to work (SSI recipients), the rest of this chapter concerns SSDI strategies. SSI deserves a book of its own. Understanding Social Security's treatment of the disabled matters to more than 20 percent of households. Indeed, it may eventually matter to many of today's 140 million nondisabled workers, given the considerable odds that they or their spouses someday will become disabled.

Those receiving Social Security disability benefits enjoy seven advantages relative to other covered workers, but they are also subject to some bad-news provisions. First the good news.

ADVANTAGE 1—EFFECTIVELY
TAKING RETIREMENT BENEFITS
EARLY WITH NO REDUCTION

Workers who qualify for disability benefits are able to receive them through Full Retirement Age. At that point they formally convert to the worker's full retirement benefit. The conversion doesn't change the amount of the benefit, just its name.

If the same-size benefit is being called a full retirement benefit after FRA and a disability benefit before FRA, we can just as well say that disabled workers are able to receive their full retirement benefit throughout all the years of their retirement benefit eligibility, that is, from age 62 onward.

This fact, that disabled workers can receive retirement benefits (even if they are called disability benefits) early (between 62 and FRA), *but subject to no reduction*, is a big advantage. Indeed, for disabled workers now reaching 62, their benefits from age 62 through the ends of their lives are one-third larger than would be the case for a nondisabled worker with the same full retirement benefit who takes retirement benefits starting at age 62.[3]

ADVANTAGE 2—THE DISABLED
AREN'T SUBJECT TO DEEMING

Disabled workers collecting their benefits before their FRA aren't deemed to be filing for their spousal benefit even if their spouse has already filed for retirement benefits. This exemption carries over to divorced disabled workers. Disabled workers thus aren't forced to take the larger of their disability and spousal (or divorced spousal) benefits prior to reaching full retirement.

Once they do reach full retirement, disabled workers can and should file for their spousal benefit, if married, or divorced spousal benefit, if they are qualified (were in a marriage that lasted 10 or more years). If their spousal benefit exceeds their full retirement benefit (which until FRA was called their disability benefit), they'll collect a higher total payment by waiting to collect it. Technically speaking, Social Security will consider they are collecting their full retirement benefit *plus* their "excess" spousal benefit. *But their excess spousal benefit won't have been reduced* because they didn't take it early. Ignoring any reductions for taking it early and any Delayed Retirement Credits, the excess spousal benefit formula is the same, by the way, for the disabled and the nondisabled: the formula at FRA is half of the disabled worker's spouse's PIA less 100 percent of the disabled worker's PIA.

ADVANTAGE 3—OLDER SPOUSES (AND EXES) CAN COLLECT SPOUSAL BENEFITS EARLIER

The conditions under which spouses, ex-spouses, and children of disabled workers can collect auxiliary benefits based on the work record of the disabled worker are the same as in the case of retired workers, with one exception: the spouse or ex-spouse who is at least 62 can collect a spousal or divorced spousal benefit regardless of the age of the disabled worker.

ADVANTAGE 4—THE DISABLED CAN TAKE REDUCED WIDOW(ER) BENEFITS STARTING AT AGE 50

If you're disabled and your spouse (or ex-spouse of 10 or more years) has passed away, you can collect reduced widow(er) or divorced widow(er) benefits 10 years earlier—at age 50, not 60—than if you aren't disabled. Furthermore, there is no additional reduction for taking the widow(er) survivor benefit starting at age 50 or at any other age before age 60.

There is a condition attached to this advantage, however. You have to become disabled within 7 years of your spouse's death to take your disabled widow(er)'s benefit between ages 50 and 60. But—surprise!—there's a condition to that condition: if you were entitled to collect a mother's benefit after your spouse died (because you had a child under 16 or a disabled child of your deceased spouse in your care), the 7-year clock won't start ticking until you stop collecting that benefit.

ADVANTAGE 5—ONCE SOME DISABLED WIDOW(ER)S REACH FULL RETIREMENT, THE EARLY SURVIVOR BENEFIT REDUCTION GOES AWAY

Let's assume you become disabled before your spouse dies and take your disabled widow(er) benefit starting early, indeed as early as age 50. If so, when you reach FRA, this benefit no longer will be reduced even though you began taking it early. However, if your deceased spouse began taking *their* retirement benefit early, the amount you receive will be affected by the RIB-LIM provision we explained in Chapter 3.

There is one important gotcha here. If you take your survivor benefit early, the restoration of your reduced survivor benefit to its full retirement level will occur only if you started taking disability benefits on your own account before or at the same time as your survivor benefits. If you took your reduced survivor benefit, say, at 60 and began taking disability benefits later at, say, 62, you'd receive no restoration (that is, there would be no elimination of the reduction).

ADVANTAGE 6—SPECIAL RIB-LIM
FORMULA FOR DISABLED WIDOW(ER)S

Survivor benefits for a disabled widow(er) whose spouse took benefits early are calculated using a special formula that can be more generous than if the widow(er) was not disabled. The formula includes complex RIB-LIM calculations that should be discussed with a Social Security technical expert. The special RIB-LIM formula can make a decent difference in what a disabled widow(er) can collect. Jerry Lutz, the former Social Security technical expert who has kindly reviewed both editions of this book, provided us an example in which the widow(er) benefit is 15 percent larger thanks to the special formula. That's a healthy increment to receive every month for the rest of one's life. As is the case with Advantage 5, however, this special formula applies only if the widow(er) was entitled to disability benefits on his or her own record at the same time or before becoming entitled to widow(er)'s benefits.

ADVANTAGE 7—YOU DON'T HAVE
TO WORK SUPER-LONG OR EARN
LOTS OF MONEY TO QUALIFY
FOR DISABILITY BENEFITS

The rules for disability benefit eligibility are quite demanding. They are less strict if you are younger, however. For example, someone who is disabled prior to age 25 can collect disability benefits with only 6 quarters of covered earnings. For middle-aged workers, the requirement is 20 quarters of covered work out of the prior 40 quarters (ending with the quarter in which you become disabled) and having accumulated sufficient overall quarters of coverage to obtain fully insured status. Obtaining fully insured status doesn't require the 40 quarters that would apply to nondisabled workers. Another key point (which applies to the non-disabled as well): you can obtain up to 4 quarters of coverage in a given quarter simply by earning enough money in that quarter.

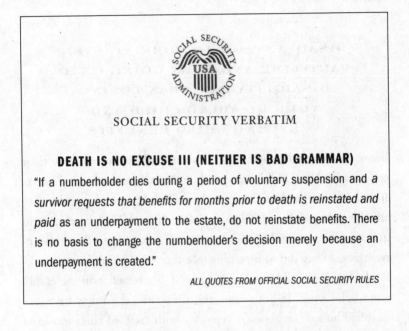

SOCIAL SECURITY VERBATIM

DEATH IS NO EXCUSE III (NEITHER IS BAD GRAMMAR)

"If a numberholder dies during a period of voluntary suspension and *a survivor requests that benefits for months prior to death is reinstated and paid* as an underpayment to the estate, do not reinstate benefits. There is no basis to change the numberholder's decision merely because an underpayment is created."

ALL QUOTES FROM OFFICIAL SOCIAL SECURITY RULES

BUT, AS ALWAYS WITH SOCIAL SECURITY, DANGER LURKS

So much for the advantages. Let's now talk about some disadvantages of being disabled when it comes to Social Security.

DISADVANTAGE 1—YOU CAN LOSE OTHER BENEFITS IF YOU COLLECT DISABILITY BENEFITS

SSDI benefits are often reduced because of worker's compensation payments and public disability benefits. So, if you've received them, be aware that they might reduce your SSDI payments. If you are collecting SSI (Supplemental Security Income), you may also be forced to kiss all or most of that money goodbye if you go onto disability benefits.

DISADVANTAGE 2—WORKING EVEN PART-TIME AND THEN GOING ONTO DISABILITY CAN MEAN LOSING YOUR DISABLED CHILD AND SURVIVING CHILD BENEFITS

We've had several people with disabled children ask us how their child could collect child benefits while they themselves are still alive, and child survivor benefits after they die. Just as we were about to tell them they only needed to apply for their child to receive them if that child was disabled prior to age 22, they stopped us dead in our tracks. They did so by telling us either (1) their child was working or (2) their child was receiving disability benefits on the child's *own* work record. In both cases, this meant the child may have disqualified himself or herself, *forever*, for both disabled child and child survivor benefits.

The reason is that for disabled children to collect on their parents' work records, they not only have to have been disabled before age 22, but they have to stay disabled. And if your child earns too much money in even one year, Social Security will view the child as not having remained disabled. For 2016, the limit was $13,560, with some adjustment for work expenses. That's not a lot of money.

In one case, a parent told us they had employed their disabled child themselves for one year to make the child feel he played a meaningful role in society. (In fact, the child had not earned his pay and had not been able to continue coming to work.) When we asked how much the child had been paid, we winced. It was about $1,000 more than the annual limit, meaning the parent may well have disqualified the child for the rest of the child's life from collecting benefits on the parent's work record.

DISADVANTAGE 3—THE DISABLED CAN'T PURSUE THE FILE-AND-SUSPEND STRATEGY EVEN IF THEY WOULD OTHERWISE BE GRANDPARENTED UNDER THE NEW LAW

In this book's first edition, we provided the disabled with a strategy for pursuing the file-and-suspend strategy. Admittedly, they'd have had to jump through an extra hoop, namely, withdraw their retirement benefit when they reached Full Retirement Age. But then they'd be able to file just for their spousal benefit and restart their retirement benefit at 70.

This strategy was permitted when we wrote the first edition. But on December 23, 2014, Social Security gave a very nasty Christmas lump of coal to millions of disabled workers, naughty *or* nice. Some or several bureaucrats rewrote a few sentences of the agency's official Program Operating Manual System, known as POMS, to prevent the disabled from exercising the file-and-suspend strategy. And, poof! The disabled could no longer do what the nondisabled could do.

We checked with the good folks at Social Security, who claimed they were just clarifying existing policy. But we view this as a clear act of discrimination. At the time, Larry was actively helping a disabled divorced woman convince the Social Security authorities that she could withdraw her retirement benefit and just file for her divorced spousal benefit. Her request conceivably could have prompted the Christmas attack.

DISADVANTAGE 4—A TRULY
NASTY FAMILY MAXIMUM BENEFIT
FOR DISABLED WORKERS

Disabled workers face a different and potentially far more restrictive formula for the Family Maximum Benefits (FMB) available to themselves and their qualifying children and spouses. For nondisabled workers, as we told you in Chapter 3, the FMB ranges from 1.5 to 1.87 times the worker's Primary Insurance Amount.

But for disabled workers it's the smaller of 1.5 times the disabled worker's PIA and a second amount. This second amount is itself the larger of two numbers, namely, 85 percent of the disabled worker's Average Indexed Monthly Earnings (AIME) and the disabled worker's PIA.

The real problem, however, is that for many disabled workers who were low earners, the FMB will end up equaling just the worker's PIA and not a penny more. This means that the child and child-in-care spousal benefits available to children and spouses will be *zero*! This seems unfair and heartless to our disabled citizens and their families.

Now, disabled workers between ages 62 and FRA who are in this situation could opt to take their reduced retirement rather than disability benefits. This would raise their FMB during those years. But doing so would come at the cost of a reduction in the disabled worker's own benefit since their reduced retirement benefit is lower than their disability benefit, as explained above. So this is a tricky comparison, but one that sophisticated Social Security software like Larry's should be able to handle.

13

SOCIAL SECURITY
AND MEDICARE

Medicare rules can have a big impact on your Social Security, affecting the size of your monthly income payments and sucking up a lot of Social Security's annual Cost of Living Adjustments to pay for rising Medicare expenses. Social Security oversees rules, in turn, that can have a big effect on your Medicare, including how much you pay in premiums, tacking on high-income surcharges to those premiums, and very complicated enrollment rules that can leave you with late-enrollment penalties or, in some potentially catastrophic situations, no insurance protection at all.

Understanding these actual and potential pitfalls requires a brief Medicare primer. After spending so many chapters talking about Social Security, we hope you don't mind a healthful diversion into Medicare. And if you'd like to make that diversion a longer outing, Phil has written an entire book about Medicare that will be published soon. Designed as a companion to this book, it is called *Get What's Yours for Medicare: Maximize Your Coverage; Minimize Your Costs.*

THE ABCS—AND D—OF MEDICARE

There are four parts to the federal Medicare program, plus what's known as Medigap or Medicare supplement insurance, a complementary set of state-regulated insurance policies for Medicare beneficiaries. Created in 1965, Medicare is now used by roughly 55 million people, including about 45 million persons aged 65 or older and nearly 10 million disabled persons who may be of any age.

Parts A and B of Medicare are usually referred to as "original" or "basic" Medicare. Part A covers care provided by hospitals, skilled nursing facilities, home-health agencies, and hospice programs. Part B covers costs for doctors, outpatient expenses, and durable medical equipment.

These programs aren't free. Individuals pay a 7.65 percent payroll tax and their employers pay the same; self-employed persons are on the hook for both shares. Of that 7.65 percent, 6.2 percentage points go to Social Security and 1.45 percentage points go into a Medicare trust fund that covers Part A expenses. While there is an annual wage ceiling on Social Security payroll taxes ($118,500 in 2016), there is no wage ceiling on the 1.45 percent Medicare tax. So that means any earned income above $118,500 will incur an additional Medicare tax. Furthermore, the Affordable Care Act socks earners with incomes of more than $200,000 ($250,000 for joint filers) with an added 0.9 percent Medicare tax. Because these taxes fund Part A costs, Part A usually charges no premiums to Medicare beneficiaries.

Part B, however, *does* charge premiums—to nearly everyone. Medicare has support programs to subsidize premiums for low-income people, mainly drawn from the roughly 10 million Americans who are dually eligible for both Medicare and Medicaid. Nearly everyone else who owes a Part B premium pays the lowest, or basic amount, which is $104.90 a month. Where Social Security comes into the picture is that by law, anyone who owes this basic Part B premium who is also receiving Social Security must have this premium deducted from their monthly Social Security payment. About 5 percent of Medicare beneficiaries—those who make more than

$85,000 ($170,000 for joint returns)—pay high-income surcharges for Part B. Usually these sums are also subtracted from monthly Social Security payments.

Part C of Medicare is the formal name for Medicare Advantage plans—increasingly popular private Medicare insurance policies that more than 30 percent of all Medicare beneficiaries now choose instead of original Medicare. Medicare Advantage plans must cover at least what original Medicare covers, and policyholders usually must have, and must pay any premiums required for, Parts A and B of Medicare before they can purchase a Medicare Advantage plan.

Part D of Medicare covers prescription drugs. These policies, also from private insurers, have been around since 2006. More than 40 million Americans have either stand-alone Part D plans or get their drug coverage bundled in with their Medicare Advantage plans. There also are high-income surcharges for Part D, which may or may not be deducted from Social Security payments, depending on how people get their Part D coverage.

Medigap. Original Medicare doesn't cover all expenses and has no out-of-pocket ceiling on how much a beneficiary has to pay for insured health care. Its biggest gap is that it pays only 80 percent of most Part B expenses. Medigap plans can pick up these uncovered charges. Medicare Advantage plans also have annual out-of-pocket ceilings, so people with these plans do not need Medigap protection (and are, in fact, legally prevented from having both policies).

In terms of Medicare–Social Security interactions, there is not much else you need to know about Medigap and only a little more about Medicare Advantage. But now at least you know your Medicare letters. And as students of Medigap plans know, these policies have their very own lettering system—Plan A, Plan B, and so forth. We'll save this alphabet for another day or, to humor Phil, another book.

MEDICARE PART A IS FREE EXCEPT
WHEN SOCIAL SECURITY SAYS IT'S NOT

For nearly everyone, there is no annual premium for Part A of Medicare. That 2.9 percent payroll tax (from you and your employer) is certainly payment enough. You need only 40 quarters of "covered" work—jobs where you pay Social Security payroll taxes—to qualify for free Part A. Even if you don't qualify based on your own work record, you still get free Part A if your spouse qualifies.

A "quarter" of coverage probably doesn't mean what you think it does, however. Why should we not be surprised by this when discussing Social Security? For starters, it has little if anything to do with working at a job for three months. Instead, it's a measure of how much money a person makes. During 2016, a quarter of coverage is earned for each $1,260 in covered earnings.[1] You need not earn this much in every quarter of the year to earn your four quarters of Social Security eligibility. As we explained earlier, you could earn $5,040 (4 times $1,260) during a single quarter of the year, or even a single week or day, and still garner the yearly maximum of four quarters.

However, if you don't have the 40 quarters to qualify for free Part A, the premiums are steep: $226 a month for those with between 30 and 40 quarters and $411 every month during 2016 if you have fewer than 30 covered quarters. So, if you are coming up on your Medicare eligibility in this or any other year and are short on covered earnings, it might pay you to take a part-time job that year to reach that 40-quarter limit.

PART B AND THE "HOLD
HARMLESS" DEBACLE

There is a comfort-inducing rule in Social Security that says a person's benefits, as stated in nominal dollars, generally cannot decline from one year to the next. On its face, this "hold harmless" rule, as it's widely known, is good news for Social Security recipients. It means their benefits can never go down, and what more could you ask of a program that makes payments to tens of millions of beneficiaries who are living on fixed incomes? In other words, even if there's *deflation* and prices go *down* from one year to the next, your Social Security payments will remain fixed. In effect, you'll be getting a cost-of-living *raise* in retirement.

Occasionally, however, the hold harmless rule creates problems for Medicare. Following this story may require you to ingest your preferred memory enhancement beverage. It begins with a tale of two types of inflation: (1) the overall measure of consumer prices on which Social Security's annual Cost of Living Adjustment is based, and (2) price increases expected in the health-care expenses covered by Part B of Medicare.

Weirdly, in 2015, these measures of inflation moved in sharply different directions. First, the average of consumer prices actually dropped between the third quarters of 2014 and 2015. This meant Social Security's annual Cost of Living Adjustment, or COLA, was going to be zero in 2016, even though the officially measured average cost of living had dropped slightly.

Now, a zero COLA upsets Social Security recipients, first, because they're used to their benefits rising, and second, because they're older than average Americans and live in a world of health-care inflation. Putting a labor economist or Social Security official in front of a crowd of seniors to defend a zero COLA might make the amphitheater spectacles of ancient Rome seem tame.

What recipients almost surely don't realize, however, is that a zero COLA, combined with the hold harmless rule, is a very good thing, because it means that for most of them, their Social Security checks can't go down, even if the level of Part B premiums increased in 2016. This meant that about 70 percent of all Medicare beneficiaries thus could not be asked to pay more than the same $104.90 a month in Part B premiums in 2016 than they paid in 2015.

This is where the plot thickened, turned ugly, and could stay ugly for a long time. Medicare officials took a look at 2016 projected health-care expenses. They foresaw a resurgence of inflation in Part B expenses. Higher fees for doctors. Big boosts in drug prices, only some of them covered by Part D. More expensive medical equipment.

Medicare is required by law to recover about a quarter of total Part B expenses from beneficiaries, expenses that would surely go up. But with 70 percent of Medicare beneficiaries held harmless in 2016, the agency was forced to get the money from the other 30 percent, a group that includes higher-income Medicare beneficiaries with modified adjusted gross incomes of more than $85,000, or $170,000 for joint returns.

It also includes people who would be new to Medicare in 2016. They are not held harmless because they didn't have Medicare premiums deducted from their Social Security payments in 2015 and, as a result, Social Security was under no obligation to hold their deductions constant.

It also includes this book's favorite group of people (because they agree with us)—those on Medicare who have delayed filing for Social Security in order to receive higher benefits later. Because these folks aren't collecting Social Security yet, they must pay their Part B premiums directly to Medicare. There is no basis for them to be held harmless.

The last group of people not held harmless are low-income beneficiaries whose Part B premiums are subsidized, often by the states as part of their Medicaid programs.

So here's the ugly truth. When Medicare did the math in the summer of 2015, it projected that people who were *not* held harmless would have to pay Part B premiums in 2016 that were *52 percent higher* than in 2015!

Manners prevent us from describing exactly what hit the fan after this projection was made public. But as you can easily visualize, the collision wasn't pretty. Senior groups and consumer advocates went ballistic. The "Ask Phil" column that Phil writes for Paul's Making Sen\$e website at PBS was flooded with questions from anxious Medicare beneficiaries. Already stung by news of a zero COLA, they had now learned they might have to absorb an enormous increase in Part B premiums.

Eventually, even our barely functional Congress came to the rescue. It issued a \$7.5 billion loan to Medicare that allowed the agency to pare back that 52 percent increase to "only" 16 percent. The lowest monthly premium for these folks thus rose from \$104.90 to \$121.80 a month (this includes a \$3 loan charge to help pay off the Treasury loan). The annual Part B deductible—the amount that beneficiaries must pay each year before their Part B insurance coverage kicks in—increased as well, rising 13 percent, from \$147 to \$166.

A STRATEGY FOR A ZERO-COLA WORLD

There are, the late economist John Kenneth Galbraith used to say, two kinds of economists: those who don't know the future and those who don't know they don't know it. Count us among the former. So we don't know what will happen to interest rates going forward. However, low rates of inflation *could be* a regular occurrence. If future COLAs are zero, or close to it, people who have not yet filed for Social Security will in most cases not be held harmless during the year they file. They thus will have to evaluate their exposure to higher Part B premiums.

In limited cases, people who have reached Full Retirement

Age can take advantage of Social Security's retroactivity rules to be treated as being held harmless. That's because people who file for benefits after reaching FRA can elect to receive as many as six months of retroactive benefits when they file.

This is a lump-sum payment to compensate people who filed "late." If you file between zero and six months late, your retroactive payment will cover the actual period you were late in filing. If you file more than six months late, your retroactive payments usually will be capped at no more than six months.

Accepting retroactive payments, however, may also allow a person to qualify as being held harmless, even if they had not filed for benefits during the year in question. Here's how: if you were 66½, for example, and filed for Social Security in April 2017, you would qualify to be held harmless in 2016 because your Social Security filing date would be retroactively set at October 2016. Your "first" Social Security payment would be in November 2016, and your "first" Medicare Part B premium would be deducted from your Social Security payment in December (there is a one-month lag). Voilà! You are held harmless.

However, and you know by now there is nearly always one of these "howevers" lurking nearby, you will have sacrificed up to six months of delayed retirement credits to use this strategy. Because credits accrue at 8 percent annual rates, forgoing six months of them would pare your Social Security benefit by 4 percent a month for the rest of your life. If you had a monthly FRA benefit of, say, $1,500, you would be out $60 a month. That's roughly triple the level of the Part B premium increase faced this year by people who were not held harmless.

We'd thus advise you not to use this strategy, clever though it may be, unless projected hikes in Part B expenses once again cause projected 50 percent hikes in Part B premiums and Congress does not come to the rescue.

SOCIAL SECURITY VERBATIM

THE DEFINITION OF A CIRCULAR DEFINITION

"What does actually paid mean? Actual payment occurs when you are actually paid. . . ."

ALL QUOTES FROM OFFICIAL SOCIAL SECURITY RULES

HOW THE OTHER HALF GETS
TO PAY WHAT'S THEIRS

Roughly 5 percent of higher-income Medicare beneficiaries face further reductions in their net Social Security payments because additional monies are deducted to cover premium surcharges for both Medicare Part B and Part D prescription drug plans. These fees are part of Social Security's income-related monthly adjustment amount. As readers well know by now, all government agencies seem to have an obsession with program acronyms that run-of-the-mill humans don't share. This one is known as IRMAA.[2]

IRMAA surcharges are based on a measure of income known as modified adjusted gross income, or, you guessed it, MAGI for short (no wisecracks, please). It includes your adjusted gross income plus any tax-exempt interest income. Social Security derives this number from your federal tax returns, so you need to calculate it only if you think the agency has made a mistake. And the agency is supposed to send you a letter informing you that it has determined that an IRMAA surcharge is warranted.

Lots of people with "Ask Phil" Medicare questions are surprised when they find out that their IRMAA surcharges are based on tax returns from two or even three years ago. The normal lag is two years, so any 2017 IRMAA surcharges will be based on your 2015 tax return. If you filed your 2015 taxes late, your 2014 return might be used instead. If you've filed an amended return that affects your IRMAA surcharges, tell the agency.

Many people have one-time blips in their income that will cause their MAGI to rise into IRMAA territory two years hence. Usually there is nothing to be done about this. When a person's income returns to "normal" levels, the IRMAA charges will disappear.

However, there are what Social Security and Medicare call "life-changing" events that can provide relief from this one-time hit. The eight listed on the agency's relief application form[3] are marriage, divorce or annulment, death of your spouse, work stoppage, work reduction, loss of income-producing property, loss of pension income, and employer settlement payment. So, for example, if the source of your IRMAA surcharges is simply high wage income from a job from which you're now retired, you can petition Social Security to reduce this charge if your income is now lower simply because you've retired.

While Part B premiums total about 25 percent of program costs for most Social Security recipients, IRMAA brackets require people to pay from 35 to 80 percent of expenses. IRMAA premiums also rose 16 percent from 2015 to 2016. Here's what the 2016 monthly IRMAA levies look like for Parts B and D:

2014 MAGI*	PART B PREMIUM	PART D** SURCHARGE
$85,001–$107,000	$170.50	$12.70
$107,001–$160,000	$243.60	$32.80
$160,001–$214,000	$316.70	$52.80
$214,001+	$389.80	$72.90

There are separate brackets for married folks who file a separate return:

2014 MAGI*	PART B PREMIUM	PART D** SURCHARGE
$85,000-$129,000	$316.70	$52.80
More than $129,000	$389.80	$72.90

Just to wring a bit more from those who have more, a 2015 law (the one that got rid of Medicare's long-standing threat to cut program payments to doctors) will begin in 2018 to apply the higher IRMAA surcharges to more people:

2016 MAGI*	PART B PREMIUM	PART D** SURCHARGE
$85,001-$107,000	$170.50	$12.70
$107,001-$133,500	$243.60	$32.80
$133,501-$160,000	$316.70	$52.80
$160,001+	$389.80	$72.90

* Double for joint tax returns

** Plus your Part D premium

These projections assume no change from this year's Part B premiums. The actual surcharges will be linked to future rates of inflation and thus could be a bit higher. But these four brackets must continue to recover roughly 35, 50, 65, and 80 percent of Medicare expenses. So, if you are in a higher income bracket when 2018 rolls around, just take that year's basic Part B premium (the one that is $121.80 this year) and multiply it by 1.4, 2, 2.6, or 3.2, depending on which of the four brackets applies to you.

For good measure, if any was needed, that 2015 law also froze the IRMAA brackets until 2020. Wage inflation, of course, has not ended, meaning that more and more Medicare beneficiaries will be making IRMAA tithes. Which, of course, presumably was the goal of the law's framers.

People not yet using Medicare, of course, will be spared the joys of Part B premiums and IRMAA surcharges. For now.

WHY MEDICARE IS A HEALTH SAVINGS ACCOUNT BUZZKILL

High-deductible employer health plans are increasingly popular, and often include health savings accounts (HSAs). HSAs are funded with pretax dollars, which may be placed in investment accounts like 401(k)s. Unlike 401(k)s, however, investment gains from HSAs are not taxed when they're withdrawn from the account so long as they're spent on qualifying medical expenses. Employers often chip in part of the annual contribution to these accounts. Further, any unspent funds can be carried over to later years. In short, HSAs can be a great health and retirement tool.

What they can't do, however, is coexist with Medicare. A person who is signed up for Medicare can no longer make tax-free contributions to his employer's HSA. Any funds already in an HSA will not be lost, however, and can be spent at any time. The IRS rules[4] here are clear.

What does this have to do with Social Security? Well, to the surprise of many older employees with HSAs, it turns out that you can't receive Social Security benefits without also getting Part A of Medicare. It's mandatory. It doesn't matter if your Part A is free, as we explained above, or if you don't use the coverage: getting Social Security means you are signed up for Medicare. Even people who have filed and suspended their Social Security benefits (before this strategy was eliminated at the end of April 2016) cannot escape Part A.

The only way to avoid being formally enrolled in Medicare is to withdraw your Social Security benefit, an act that includes having to repay any monies received from Social Security. It is a nuclear option that we only rarely recommend.

This gotcha seems particularly unfair for older workers. We've dwelled on the enormous financial shortfalls facing Americans in their retirement years. Continuing to work is a prudent and perhaps unavoidable necessity. Socking aside more retirement money inside an HSA is icing on the financial preparedness cake. Yet doing so is disallowed for anyone who has filed for Social Security benefits. We need to make it easier for people to do the right thing, not harder. Congress needs to do a better job of recognizing the changing worlds of aging, retirement, and work. Changing this rule would be a fine place to start.

Before we despair too much, however, it turns out that IRS rules for so-called HSA family plans will permit one spouse to continue participating in the plan even if the other has, intentionally or not, filed for Medicare. So, if you and your spouse have a group health insurance plan where you work, you can still use it even if only one of you remains eligible. An IRS spokesman confirmed, in addition, that all of the allowable pretax contributions to the plan can be made in the name of only the eligible spouse (even if it's the ineligible spouse who works for the employer). The only casualty here is the additional $1,000 HSA per-person contribution that participants aged 55 and older are permitted under IRS rules. If one spouse is ineligible for an HSA, that $1,000 contribution is disallowed.

WHEN SOCIAL SECURITY BEGINS DEDUCTING YOUR MEDICARE PREMIUMS

By law, as we noted earlier, people receiving Social Security and Medicare must have their Part B Medicare premiums deducted from their monthly Social Security payments. It's also possible to have your Part D premiums deducted this way, although most people pay these premiums directly to the private insurers who provide their Part D prescription drug coverage.

More and more people are deferring their Social Security benefits to Full Retirement Age and beyond—a decision we generally applaud. Because many of these patient folks are already receiving Medicare, they must pay their Part B premiums directly to Medicare. These payments tend to be made in three-month installments.

This may raise timing issues when Social Security benefits begin. For example, what if you've just forked over three months in premiums to Medicare and now see at least one or even more of those monthly expenses deducted again from the Social Security payment you've just begun receiving?

We often abhor paying for something once, let alone twice, so any double payments are simply unacceptable. Clearly, however, the most compelling objective when you begin receiving Social Security benefits is to make sure you do not miss any Medicare premiums and possibly threaten the continuation of your Medicare coverage. Once you've made sure this goal has been achieved, you can then worry about avoiding or recouping any double premium payments.

For this reason, we advise against trying to time this transition too precisely. You might be tempted to figure out when your direct Medicare payments to Social Security will begin and perhaps pay only one or two months' worth of your current Medicare payment directly to Medicare. We applaud your planning skills but think it best if you just pay the full premium. If you wind up double-paying a month or two, Social Security is supposed to automatically correct this and will make you whole, though it might take up to sixty days.

DON'T FALL INTO A MEDICARE
LATE-ENROLLMENT GOTCHA

Today, signing up for Medicare can cause a major brain freeze. People frequently are confused by the act of just getting this piece right, let alone the kinds of Medicare policies they should sign up for and, God forbid, actually tackling the details of how they can make the best possible use of the health insurance they have used their hard-earned retirement dollars to purchase.

Based on changes to Social Security rules included in the program's major 1983 reforms, the so-called Full Retirement Age—the age at which people get their full retirement benefit—has been steadily rising. As we've noted earlier, it began moving in two-month increments from 65 in 2002, for people born in 1937 or earlier, to 66 in 2009, for those born from 1943 to 1954. It will stay there until 2020 and then begin moving again in two-month units for people born from 1955 to 1959, rising to 67 by 2027, for anyone born in 1960 or later.

In addition, and as we've been shouting from our soapbox throughout this book, people should consider delaying to file for Social Security until age 70, or at least as long as possible if they can't wait until then. Of course, this shift to later claiming ages is a big deal for Social Security. But it's also a big deal for Medicare, because it reduces the linkage between the two programs in terms of when to file for benefits.

This bond has been further weakened if not torn asunder by the historic rise in the percentages of people who keep working well past their 65th birthdays. Roughly a third of people aged 65 to 69 are still in the labor force, and about 20 percent of those aged 70 to 74 are also still working, including two of the three authors of this book. (Larry is still in his sixties.) Toss in the lingering effects of the Great Recession on household wealth and, for sure, retirement is not what it used to be.[5]

This is a big deal when making the Medicare decision because it means you can't simply assume you will need it as soon as you turn 65. Coauthor Paul is 71, still working, and still buying private health insurance through his main workplace. So some people will have to opt for Medicare at 65 and others won't. But the circumstances under which we do or don't need Medicare at any age are often unclear. And Medicare has not done a notably good job of helping mere mortals figure out when and how to claim their Medicare benefits.

The transition into Medicare from employer health insurance or, increasingly, an Affordable Care Act state insurance exchange is already stressful and difficult for many of us. No wonder that some people think they need Medicare when they don't. They may wind up paying premiums for coverage they will never need. Other people think they don't need Medicare when they do. It's potentially catastrophic that failing to sign up for Medicare on a timely basis can leave you with absolutely no health insurance at all for an extended period.

Adding injury to insult, if you will, the government has also created a set of potentially harsh and lifelong financial penalties for people who get this decision wrong and miss one of Medicare's many enrollment deadlines—10 percent tacked onto Part B premiums *each* year; 1 percent added to Part D average premiums each *month*.

No wonder that Medicare seems destined to be a lifetime employment act for the "Ask Phil" column. For those taking the long view, and with memories to match, the title of Phil's new book is, once again, *Get What's Yours for Medicare: Maximizing Your Coverage; Minimizing Your Costs.*

GOVERNMENT PENSIONS AND WINDFALL PENALTIES

Millions of people work or have worked at jobs that are not covered by Social Security laws; many state and local government employees, for example. They don't have to worry every year about those relentlessly rising FICA payments listed on their W-2s or, for the self-employed, the substantial FICA contributions on their tax returns. Lots of these folks, however—at least a million and a half—also work or have worked at different jobs that *are* covered by Social Security. More will do so in the future. And even if they haven't, perhaps their spouses have or will.

From this fact flows a question: where a person's work history involves both non-covered *and* covered employment, how are their Social Security benefits affected? Those of their spouses? Their children?

Not to worry. As we've seen in about every other realm of working life, Social Security has programs and rules for these situations. They are covered in the Windfall Elimination Provision and the Government Pension Offset, which we'll be calling WEP and GPO. These rules are meant to produce a rough degree of fairness in the treatment of people who have earned retirement pensions from work not subject to Social Security payment taxes, as compared with those whose pensions do stem from such covered employment. Like much else, this is another situation where Ricky Ricardo might say,

as he is credited with telling his wife on the *I Love Lucy* show, "Social
Security, you have some 'splaining to do!"

As we've emphasized, the formula used to determine the Primary
Insurance Amount is very progressive. This means that lower-paid
workers get a Social Security retirement benefit that represents a
much higher percentage of their pre-retirement earnings than do
more highly paid persons. The PIA (see Chapter 3 for more details)
is calculated by dividing a worker's lifetime average covered earnings
into three pieces separated by two bend points. It then credits lower
earnings amounts by much higher percentages than higher earnings.
In 2016, the PIA included 90 percent of the earnings below the first
bend point (up to $856 of average monthly earnings), 32 percent
of the amount between $856 and $5,157 (the second bend point),
and 15 percent of any amount higher than this. Thus, the less you
earned, the greater the percentage of your total earnings that are
replaced by Social Security benefits. (See Glossary for further explanation of bend points.)

Fine and dandy, perhaps, but this created the problems that
spawned the WEP. People who earned plenty of *non-covered* income
might have *covered* income as well—but not that much of it. Yet they
would benefit from the progressivity adjustment as if they hadn't
earned much at all. Social Security would, and did, treat them as
poorly compensated earners and rewarded them accordingly with very
progressive PIAs, even if they had a boatload of non-covered income.

An *unfair* windfall, you might say.

GETTING WEP'D OUT

And so, the major Social Security reforms of 1983 included the
Windfall Elimination Provision—the WEP—to cancel out the progressivity adjustment for people it was never aimed to help. It did so

by modifying the formula for calculating the PIAs of such people. For people subject to the WEP, the 90 percent adjustment that had been applied to the first bend point became *40* percent instead.

WEP applies only to the first bend point, since that's where almost all the benefit formula's progressivity lies. Remember, the first bend in 2016 comes at $856 of Average Indexed Monthly Earnings. Before the WEP, beneficiaries would get 90 percent of that: $770. Reducing that to only 40 percent gives you only $342, which is $428 a month less. So, this is the most that *you* can lose due to the WEP. But auxiliary benefits based on your earnings record—for spousal, divorced, child-in-care spousal, and child benefits—are also affected.

Fortunately for those affected, there are other factors limiting the WEP.

First, you can lose at most half of your Social Security pension from non-covered earnings. An example will make this clear. Say your non-covered pension is $600 a month. Under the WEP, your Social Security benefits can't be reduced by more than half this amount, which is $300. So even though the WEP could potentially reduce your benefits by up to $428, they actually will be reduced by only $300.

Next, in its continuing quest for fairness, the agency figured that the more years someone spent in covered employment, the smaller the impact of the WEP should be. So, regardless of how large your pension from non-covered employment might be, you wouldn't be penalized if you made enough Social Security tax payments for a long enough period of time. At a maximum, there's no WEP effect at all if your work record includes a full 30 years of substantial covered employment, and there's a sliding scale for the WEP reduction, in percentage terms, depending on how many years of *substantial* covered earnings (e.g., $22,050 in 2015) you've logged.

Years of Substantial Earnings [1]	Percentage Adjustment
30 or more	90 (no WEP impact)
29	85 percent of WEP applies
28	80
27	75
26	70
25	65
24	60
23	55
22	50
21	45
20 or less	40 (maximum WEP impact)

Source: Social Security Administration.

Using this chart is anything but simple. If the WEP applies to you, you'll need to access your official Social Security earnings record, see whether each year of covered earnings officially qualifies as "substantial," figure out how many years of substantial earnings you have, and then determine what percentage the agency will use in determining your benefits under the WEP. Larry might say this is bedevilingly difficult and a good example of Social Security's extravagant and unnecessary complexity. Paul would chalk it up to the inevitable tangle of a rules-based system trying to be as fair as it can. Phil sees both of their points.

BACK TO THE WEP RULES THEMSELVES

But you're presumably more interested in the particulars than our value judgments about them, and so there's another set of WEP rules that may apply to you and yours. Since the WEP reduces your PIA and thus your retirement benefits, it will, while you are alive, *also* reduce benefits to anyone else who stands to collect benefits based on your record. The good news, if you want to call it that, is that the WEP does not reduce the benefits of your survivors when you die. That first bend point of your earnings base is automatically reset to 90 percent.

We've already explained how much Social Security likes calculators, offering four different ones for figuring out retirement benefits (which don't always agree with one another). You may be excited to learn that the agency also has not one but two calculators to estimate WEP benefits—simple and detailed. The simple one is located online at http://www.socialsecurity.gov/retire2/anyPiaWepjs04.htm. It resembles the Online Calculator for regular Social Security benefits (http://www.ssa.gov/retire2/AnypiaApplet.html) but has added a place to enter the amount of any non-covered pension payments. It then calculates the WEP reduction in determining your Social Security benefits. The detailed WEP calculator actually is the identical calculator used to determine regular benefits (http://www.ssa.gov/OACT /anypia/anypia.html). It includes a non-covered pension choice that is simply left blank for those without a non-covered pension.

All of the things that can affect your retirement benefit—the annual Cost of Living Adjustment, the Early Retirement Reduction, and the Delayed Retirement Credit—are applied to your lower WEP PIA. But be aware that these adjustments are applied to your benefit only after your basic WEP benefit has been determined.

ANOTHER COUNTRY

Here's a situation that may apply to more than a few readers. What if your non-covered pension is from work done in another country— as ambassador to Dristanistan, say? In rare cases like these, WEP reductions to your *Social Security* earnings will still apply. Unless— you'll especially like this wrinkle, we think—you worked in one of the 25 countries with which the United States currently has what is called a totalization agreement. Of course, this being Social Security, these agreements have different rules. In some cases, a non-covered pension based on work outside the United States will WEP you; in other cases, it will not. For example, in Canada, some of your U.S. covered earnings may be credited toward your Canadian pension, and so you may not be WEP'd by that pension. (You can find details and a list of the countries at http://www.ssa.gov/international/agree ments_overview.html.)

How big is the impact of the WEP? Consider a 60-year-old minimum wage worker who works only 10 years in covered employment—just enough to qualify for a retirement benefit. Her full Social Security retirement benefit will be about $7,700 if she doesn't collect a non-covered pension and $3,400 if she collects such a pension equal to $10,000—close to half her final salary. So being WEP'd would reduce her Social Security benefit by 56 percent.

Now suppose she earns four times as much, but, again, doesn't work in non-covered employment. In this case, her full retirement benefit would be close to $13,400. If she does work in non-covered employment, receiving a $40,000 annual non-covered pension, her full retirement benefit would be cut to $8,500, by 37 percent.

These two cases illustrate two things. First, the WEP can lower benefits a lot. Second, the WEP hits low earners disproportionately hard because it reduces covered earnings only in the first bend-point bracket.

The irony here is not lost on us. The WEP was designed so that people with non-covered pensions and relatively low covered earnings would not benefit from the program's progressivity. Yet the effects of the WEP are felt more heavily by lower than higher earners. We would just remind you that we don't make the rules (and, because we can't avoid piling on, that we hope never to make up rules with such unintended, illogical, and unfair impacts as some of the doozies brought to us by the SSA).

SOCIAL SECURITY VERBATIM

DID YOU CATCH THE ADDRESS ON THAT COFFIN?

"The lump-sum death payment cannot be paid on the earnings record of a worker who dies in or after the month we receive notice of deportation or removal."

ALL QUOTES FROM OFFICIAL SOCIAL SECURITY RULES

GETTING GPO'D

Like the WEP, the GPO—the Government Pension Offset—is tied to receiving retirement income from non-covered employment. But it applies to *dependent* benefits, in this case, spousal and child benefits that you and your kids can receive based on the work records of your current or former spouses.

The GPO—enacted in 1977 and amended in 1983—eliminated a perceived windfall benefit that occurred when a person who worked in non-covered employment was receiving a Social Security spousal benefit based on the covered earnings of a current or former spouse. Before the GPO, the non-covered spouse could receive their own pension *and* all of their Social Security spousal benefit. That would be more, by comparison, than had this person been in covered employment, where they could receive only the greater of their own retirement benefit *or* their spousal benefit.

Like the WEP, the GPO is designed to eliminate what the agency perceived as windfalls to non-covered employees. If you get a pension from a government or other non-covered employer, the GPO says that two-thirds of this pension will be deducted from any spousal or widow(er) Social Security benefit linked to your spouse's Social Security earnings record. If your non-covered pension is based on work in foreign countries, it will not trigger the GPO.

Here's an example provided by Social Security: a person is receiving a $600 monthly government pension and is also eligible for a $500 Social Security benefit as a living or surviving spouse. After deducting two-thirds of their government pension from this amount, or $400, Social Security will pay the recipient only $100. Their total monthly retirement benefit from these two sources thus will be $700, not $1,000. The provision works the same way even if the person takes their government pension in a lump sum. In that case, Social Security will determine what the monthly government pension benefits would have been and make the appropriate deduction from any monthly Social Security payments due to the person based on their spouse's covered earnings record.

There are several exemptions from the GPO related to the timing of non-covered employment and pension entitlement, and the conversion of some government jobs from non-covered to covered status. Further, non-covered employment in foreign countries doesn't trigger the GPO. The relevant details can be found at http://www .ssa.gov/retire2/gpo.htm. When mastering them, may the Force be with you.

THE WEP AND GPO: A RECAP

To recap. If you get a non-covered pension:

The WEP reduces your own Social Security retirement benefits and those of your family members collecting on your work record while you are alive. Once you die, the WEP doesn't affect your family members' survivor benefits.

The GPO reduces your Social Security spousal, child-in-care spousal, widow(er) divorced spousal, mother (father), divorced widow(er), and divorced mother (father) benefits based on the work records of your spouse (current or ex, alive or deceased). The reduction is two-thirds of your non-covered pension. Taking your pension in a lump sum? Social Security will calculate an equivalent non-covered pension and reduce your spousal and survivor benefits by two-thirds of this amount. If two-thirds of your non-covered pension exceeds your benefit, you'll get zero benefit until this is no longer the case.

In short, the WEP and the GPO can add disheartening details to your job of getting Social Security right. So we are ending this chapter with a sextet of approaches to cope with these two challenging acronyms.

MAXIMIZING LIFETIME
BENEFITS UNDER WEP/GPO

1. If Possible, Wait to Collect a Larger Non-Covered Pension and Take Social Security Benefits Early

The WEP and GPO don't kick in until you begin collecting your non-covered pension. So consider delaying your pension's start date, *but only if it will rise in value during this deferral period by enough to compensate for the later start date.* In the meantime, you can collect your Social Security benefits without being WEP'd or GPO'd. Adopting this strategy involves taking your retirement benefit early, which will permanently reduce the benefits available to those whose benefits depend on yours. As we note below in item 4, this caveat is *very* important when it comes to your current or former spouses. Their widow(er) benefits won't be WEP'd after you die, but they will be lower if you take your retirement benefit early.

If your spouse, rather than you, takes their retirement benefit early while deferring their non-covered pension (to delay being WEP'd), you may want to take your spousal benefit before your spouse starts taking their non-covered pension. Recall that your spousal benefit is based on your spouse's PIA. If your spouse delays their non-covered pension, the WEP will not kick in and their PIA will not be WEP'd until the non-covered pension begins. If their PIA is not reduced, of course, this means that your spousal benefit will be higher. If this makes your head spin, it did the same to ours. But it is, as they say, a true fact.

2. Once Your Spouse Is WEP'd and GPO'd, Joint Optimizing May Be Less Important

Suppose your husband has a non-covered pension and you don't, and that he's already started taking it. This limits the spousal benefit you can receive from his work record, since his PIA will be WEP'd. It also means that the spousal and widow's benefit he can receive from your work record will be reduced, if not eliminated, since these benefits will be GPO'd. Furthermore, if he dies after you start taking your retirement benefit and your own benefit exceeds your widow's benefit, which is based on his work record, you'll never collect a widow's benefit.

In this case, where there is little he can collect from you and little or nothing you can collect from him, there may be scant reason to coordinate your Social Security decisions.

3. Accumulate More Years of Covered Earnings to Limit or Avoid the WEP

Take a 60-year-old with 10 years of covered earnings who makes four times the minimum wage. If she works 20 years, not 10, her annual full retirement benefit rises from $8,500 to $17,000! In terms of lifetime benefits (measured as a present value as of age 60), this represents almost a $200,000 increase. And if she squeezes in a full 30 years in covered employment, she'll have enough substantial earnings to avoid the WEP entirely and end up collecting $27,000 per year, or more than $420,000 in extra lifetime benefits as of age 60.

4. If You Have a Young Spouse and Are Being WEP'd, Waiting till 70 to Collect Your Retirement Benefit May Beat Approach #1

Roughly 1 in 5 married men are married to women 6 or more years younger. There is also a significant life expectancy difference in favor of women. If, for example, you are a 60-year-old male and your wife is 52, you can expect to die 14 years before she does.

If she's had a low earnings history and you've had a decent amount of covered earnings, waiting till 70 to collect may be the best way to maximize your joint benefits. This is particularly the case if you have a medical condition that makes your early demise relatively certain. By waiting to collect, you'll be able to bequeath the highest possible widow's benefit to your wife.

But, again, this is tricky. If her own retirement benefit exceeds her widow's benefit and you die after she's age 70 and is taking her own retirement benefit, she'll never collect a penny of her widow's benefit. Why not? Because she'll receive the larger of her own retirement benefit and the widow's benefit.

If you can count on dying before your eight-years-younger wife was, say, at your own FRA, she could collect the widow's benefit through age 70 and let her own, larger, retirement benefit keep growing. But while death and taxes are the only sure things in life, you generally can't count on dying young.

This discussion assumes that approach #1—taking Social Security before your non-covered pension begins—is feasible. If your non-covered pension starts, say, at 62 and there is no option to let it grow and take it later, you are going to be WEP'd no matter when you start collecting. In this case, waiting until 70 to maximize your retirement benefit will likely be the best option.

5. Even if You Are Currently Fully GPO'd, Consider Filing for Your Spousal and Widow(er) Benefit

Be aware of whether your non-covered pension has Cost of Living Adjustments each year, as does Social Security. If it doesn't, then the impact of the GPO may decrease over time. This is because the inflation-adjusted value of your pension will decline compared with your Social Security benefit. The GPO, recall, subtracts two-thirds of your non-covered pension from your auxiliary Social Security benefit. But if your non-covered pension is fixed in dollar terms, what's being subtracted will also be fixed in dollar terms. Meanwhile, your auxiliary benefit will, in dollar terms, rise through time thanks to Social Security's annual COLA. Hence, even though you may receive no auxiliary benefit initially, over time you may receive a benefit. Yes, we know it may be time to assume the lotus position again.

6. Taking Your Non-Covered Pension Early May Be Best

Say you are 55 and have the option of taking your non-covered pension now or waiting to take a larger benefit later. Also say you have a decent amount of covered earnings under your belt. In this case, taking your non-covered pension early has some advantages in terms of getting more from Social Security.

Remember that the WEP can't lower your PIA by more than half your non-covered pension. And if your non-covered pension is smaller, this can limit the amount of damage inflicted by the WEP. Also remember that your auxiliary benefits from current and former spouses (alive and dead) will be reduced by two-thirds of your non-covered pension. But if your non-covered pension is smaller because you've decided to take a smaller sum for more years, the impact of the GPO will be smaller and less damaging.

60 GOOD-NEWS SECRETS TO HIGHER LIFETIME BENEFITS

You could say that the first edition of this book was a post Larry submitted several years ago for Paul's *PBS NewsHour* daily blog, Making Sen$e. In it, Larry listed 34 Social Security "secrets" he'd come across in his years of researching the system while designing maximizing-benefits software. The post drew several hundred thousand readers. This response prompted Paul to propose that Making Sen$e solicit questions from the public for Larry to answer. The "Ask Larry" Q&A column has been featured each Monday ever since.

In the first edition, the list of "secrets" swelled to an even 50. In this edition, we're up to 60. We collect them all here, knowing that many people may not have the energy or inclination to read a whole book, but that lots of people will use a good quick list to get their bearings. Also, we figure that pretty much everyone enjoys a treasure hunt. So consider this the optimist's approach to Social Security: an engaging search for the path to maximum lifetime benefits.

It is also a *unique* path, because what's best for any given household critically depends on a host of variables: that household's specific marital status, age(s), covered earnings histories, projected course of future covered earnings, presence and ages of children, disability status of yourself and your children, maximum age(s) of life, pensions from non-covered employment, and other factors.

In fact, there are so many combinations of these factors that it's impossible to consider them separately, even in a book like this one. That's why Larry's weekly "Ask Larry" column, posted at www.pbs .org/newshour/making-sense, continues to draw a flood of questions, years after it began in August 2012.

The best we can do is provide more or less general rules, the most important specific strategies, key clues for finding your unique Social Security Easter (nest) egg, and case studies illustrating specifically how to get what's yours. But part of aiding your treasure hunt is to take you into the weeds and point out some very nitty-gritty but extremely important secrets, many of which you'll likely never learn on your own. So here's our latest and greatest list. For those who have paid close attention up until now, consider it a review, or better, read the title of each secret and see if you now know the answer.

THE SECRETS

1. Don't Assume You Know About All Your Benefits

Social Security has so many different benefits and provisions about these benefits that you may be entitled to benefits you don't even know exist. Or you may be ineligible for benefits you thought would soon be yours.

2. Unless You Ask, You Won't Receive

Social Security doesn't know to whom you are married, whom you've divorced, whom you will divorce, whether your spouse or ex-spouse(s) died, whether you have young or disabled children, whether you are taking care of dependent parents. It knows nothing about your family—absolutely nothing. So if you can collect benefits for yourself based on the work histories of current or former relatives, or if current relatives can collect benefits based on your work record, *you must tell the agency*. Furthermore, if your marital situation changes, or a former or current spouse dies and this can affect your current benefits, *you must tell the agency.* Don't expect your benefits to change unless you *tell the agency.*

3. Patience in Benefit Collection Can Pay Off Big-Time

Social Security provides very strong incentives for you to wait to collect benefits. For example, if you were born between January 2, 1943, and January 1, 1955, your age-70 retirement benefit is 76 percent higher, after inflation, than your age-62 retirement benefit. Taking much higher benefits for somewhat fewer years can maximize lifetime benefits. And don't focus on the break-even date—it is only one of many dates at which you can die. Worry about the broke date— the date you can't pay all your bills because you took benefits that were too low, too early.

4. So Can the Timing of Benefit Collection

If you are able to collect two benefits, you'll want to take one early and the other later. Why? Because you can't collect two benefits at once, just the larger of the two or something very close to that. By timing your benefit collection, you can take one benefit early while letting the other benefit's starting value grow.

5. If You Were 62 before January 2, 2016, You May Be Able to Take a Full Spousal or Full Divorced Spousal Benefit at or After FRA While Letting Your Retirement Benefit Grow Through Age 70

Married spouses who satisfy this grandparenting clause can do this if their partners filed and suspended before April 30, 2016, or if their partners are collecting retirement or disability benefits, regardless of when they started collecting those benefits. The qualified divorced (those married 10 or more years) who satisfy this grandparenting clause can also do this if they (1) have an ex over 62 and have been divorced for 2 or more years, or (2) have an ex who has filed for or is receiving their retirement or disability benefit.

6. Widow(er)s Who Haven't Yet Filed for Their Retirement Benefits Can File First for Their Full Widow(er) Benefit and Later for Their Retirement Benefit, or Vice Versa

The new Social Security law did not alter the treatment of widow(er) benefits or qualified divorced widow(er) benefits. There is no deeming when it comes to taking widow(er) benefits either before or even after Full Retirement Age. But if you take your own retirement benefit, or even just file for it and then suspend it before your spouse or ex-spouse dies, you won't get your full widow(er)'s benefit when you apply for it. You'll get your excess widow(er) benefit.

7. Generally, If the Widow(er) Benefit Is Less than the Age-70 Retirement Benefit, It Will Be Optimal to Take Your Widow(er) Benefit as Early as Possible

"As early as possible" is age 60 for widow(er)s and qualified divorced widow(er)s, and age 50 for disabled widow(er)s and qualified divorced disabled widow(er)s. If the widow(er) or divorced widow(er) benefit exceeds the age-70 retirement benefit, it will generally be best to take your retirement benefit at 62 and your widow(er) or divorced widow(er) benefit at full retirement age or earlier.

8. There Is No Advantage to Waiting Past 70 to Take Your Retirement Benefit or Past Full Retirement Age to Take Spousal or Widow(er) Benefits

If you wait to collect your retirement benefit beyond FRA (66 these days), it will be increased due to the Delayed Retirement Credit. This credit applies only to retirement benefits and ends at 70. There is no incentive to wait beyond FRA to collect either spousal or widow(er) benefits.

9. There May Be No Advantage to Waiting Until FRA to Collect Widow(er) or Divorced Widow(er) Benefits

If you are below FRA and are (1) widowed (or were widowed but remarried after age 60) or (2) qualified, widowed, and divorced (including those who remarried after reaching 60) and your deceased spouse took retirement benefits early, there may be no incentive in waiting to collect survivor benefits even *before* you reach FRA. This is due to the RIB-LIM widow(er) benefit formula, which entails no increase in this benefit past a certain point that comes before FRA, even up to 51 months before FRA.

10. Already Collecting? Consider Suspending and Restarting Your Benefits Later

If you are already collecting your retirement benefit and want to raise it, there may be a way. If you are between FRA and age 70, you have the option to suspend your retirement benefit and restart it at any time up to age 70. Social Security will add its Delayed Retirement Credit—8 percent a year or 32 percent for 4 years—to your existing benefit.

But be *very* careful. Some people suspend their retirement benefits and restart them four or so years later only to find their benefit hasn't gone up. These are folks who are receiving their own retirement benefit plus an excess spousal, an excess divorced spouse, an excess widow(er), or an excess divorced widow(er) benefit. These excess benefits are designed to decline dollar for dollar with the increase in one's own retirement benefit due to accretion of Delayed Retirement Credits. This dollar-for-dollar reduction in excess benefits leaves the total payment when it's taken unchanged *unless* the excess benefit has been reduced to zero before the retirement benefit stops growing. Even then, it may not pay to file and suspend because what's lost in the short run may not be made up in the long run when properly valued.

11. If Your Spouse Was Grandparented Under the No Post-62 Deeming Provision, You Can Let the Spouse Collect Full Spousal Benefits on Your Record by Filing for Your Own Retirement Benefit if You Didn't Suspend Before April 30, 2016

Married couples are connected at the hip when it comes to making collection decisions that can involve full or even excess spousal benefits. What one spouse does affects what the other can collect.

12. If You Suspended Your Retirement Benefit Before April 30, 2016, Family Benefits Can Be Paid on Your Work Record While Your Retirement Benefit Remains Suspended

If you are in this special grandparented group, filing for your retirement benefit, but suspending its collection, can provide benefits to your unmarried children under 18 (under 19 if still in elementary or high school) as well as your unmarried disabled children (if they are older than 18, became disabled before age 22, and don't earn so much that they lose their disability status), regardless of age. The child benefits equal 50 percent of your full retirement benefit, but are subject to the Family Maximum Benefit.

13. Filing Early Can Be a Winning Strategy for Some

If you have a spouse and children who can collect on your record, starting your retirement benefit early can permit your family members and, indeed, your ex-spouse, to collect on your work record sooner than would otherwise be the case. But doing so comes at a cost of permanently reducing your age-70 retirement benefit.

14. Survivor Benefits Are More Generous than Spousal Benefits

Apart from any reduction for taking a widow(er) benefits early, your widow(er) benefit will equal at least what your spouse was collecting as a retirement benefit. Child survivor benefits are also larger than child benefits paid to young or disabled children of retired or disabled workers, that is, 75 percent versus 50 percent of the worker's PIA.

15. Take Your Widow(er) or Retirement Benefit First?

If you haven't taken your retirement benefit when your spouse or ex expires, you can take one benefit early and let the other one grow. Which should you take first? Typically, the smaller of the two.

16. You Can "Repay and Replay," but Only Within One Year

Once you file for your retirement benefit, you have exactly one year—and not a day more—to *repay and replay*, that is, withdraw your benefit and be treated as if you had never yet filed at all. To repay and replay, you must repay all benefits (net of any withholding for Medicare Part B premiums and federal income taxes) paid to you, your spouse, and your children on your earnings record.

17. You May Be Able to Collect Suspended Benefits in a Lump Sum, but at a Cost

If you suspended by April 29, 2016, you can request a lump-sum payment of all your suspended benefits: the benefits you *would have received* had you never suspended. But doing so will reset your monthly retirement benefit to the level it was at the time you suspended. And you will not be credited with any Delayed Retirement Credits—the bonus that prompted you to suspend in the first place. On first reading of the new law, this option appears to have been eliminated for anyone who didn't suspend their benefits prior to April 30, 2016. But closer reading by some lawyers suggests it may not. As we go to press, this issue remains unresolved.

18. Some Filers Can Get Retroactive Benefits

If you are above FRA and you realize that you should have filed in the past for a benefit, you can collect up to 6 months (for most people; see below for exceptions) of that benefit retroactively in a lump sum. Take Sally, a 67-year-old widow who never worked and whose husband died several years ago. Sally just learned she could have started taking widow's benefits at age 66, and that they will not increase if she waits to take them. Sally rushes over to the Social Security office and files. To her partial relief, she learns she lost only half a year's benefits, not a full year's benefits, because she can collect 6 months of benefits retroactively. Taking retroactive widow's or spousal benefits comes at no cost. That's not the case for retirement benefits. If Sally were a never-married worker applying for her retirement benefit retroactively, she'd get a lump-sum payment for 6 months of forgone retirement benefits, but she'd also lose 6 months of her Delayed Retirement Credit. The retroactivity period is up to a year for some but not all claims of disabled persons and their auxiliaries (spouse, ex-spouse, children, etc.). If you think you may qualify for this longer period, make sure you ask Social Security about it.

19. In Most Cases, There's No "Earnings Penalty" for Taking Benefits Early

If you take retirement, spousal, or widow(er) benefits early and lose some or all of them because of Social Security's Earnings Test, Social Security will make up (via its Adjustment of the Reduction Factor) for the loss in benefits starting at your FRA, based on the number of months of benefits you forfeited. This is true whether the benefits lost are based on your earnings record or on your spouse's or whether the loss of benefits reflects you or your spouse being hit by the Earnings Test.

20. But in Some Instances, the Earnings Penalty Is *Never* Recouped

Benefits that aren't reduced, specifically spousal and mother (father) benefits when there is a young or disabled child in care, and that are lost via the Earnings Test, aren't recouped via the Adjustment of the Reduction Factor because there was no reduction factor applied to begin with. Also, if, after reaching FRA, you start taking a different benefit (switching, for example, from a widow(er) benefit to your own retirement benefit), the level of that different benefit will *not* be increased to reflect the prior loss—due to the Earnings Test—in the benefit you were receiving.

21. Earnings Penalty Impacts Are Shared by All Beneficiaries of a Worker's Record

If a worker earns enough to trigger the Earnings Test, the reduction in benefits will be apportioned on a pro rata basis to the benefits of the worker and the benefits of any family members who are collecting from his earnings record.

22. Working Longer May Mean Higher Benefits for You and Your Family

For many of you—and certainly *all* of you who will earn above Social Security's maximum taxable earnings level after age 60—the longer you work, the higher will be your Primary Insurance Amount, which determines your own retirement benefit and the auxiliary benefits available to your spouse, ex-spouses, and children. This reflects Social Security's Recomputation of Benefits provision that replaces one of your previous 35 highest-earnings years with your latest year's earnings if it's higher. Any new top-35 earnings year, even one occurring when you're 90, will raise your earnings record and thus your PIA and all related benefit entitlements.

SOCIAL SECURITY VERBATIM

THE FAT LADY NEVER SINGS I

"We may always make a new initial determination whenever a change occurs in the factual situation despite how much time elapses from the date of that change."

ALL QUOTES FROM OFFICIAL SOCIAL SECURITY RULES

23. There's a Family Maximum Benefit Available on Each Worker's Record

There is a Family Maximum Benefit (FMB) that applies to the total benefits that you, your spouse, and your children can receive on your earnings record. It ranges from 150 percent to 187 percent of your PIA. The exact multiple depends on the level of your PIA. This maximum includes your own full retirement benefit. This leaves only 50–87 percent of your PIA available to be split between your spouse and children regardless of whether you suspend your retirement benefit. But you can raise your Family Maximum Benefit if you earn enough and thereby raise your PIA, which determines your FMB.

24. For Disabled Workers the FMB Is Potentially Much Smaller

One of Social Security's nastiest hidden provisions involves the maximum amount of benefits available to a disabled worker and their family while the worker is receiving disability benefits. Social Security uses a different formula for calculating this maximum than it does in the case of workers who have filed for their retirement benefits. The disabled FMB formula is less generous in general and far less generous in the case of low-earning workers. Indeed, the formula for low-earning disabled workers may keep their children and spouses from collecting any benefits whatsoever.

25. Die Early? Kids and Spouses (Including Exes) May Still Get Survivor Benefits

You could die at any age and still provide Social Security survivor benefits to family members, as well as ex-spouses to whom you were married for 10 or more years, provided that you worked enough to be considered fully insured. If you die in the year you reach age 28 or earlier, you need to earn the minimum of at least 6 quarters of coverage (periods when you paid payroll taxes to Social Security) to die fully insured. For each additional year you live, you need to earn an additional quarter of coverage, up to a maximum of 40 if you die at age 62 or older. So, for example, if you die at age 42, you must have earned at least 20 quarters of coverage to meet the fully-insured requirement. More limited death benefits are available to certain family members if you are not fully insured but you earn at least 6 quarters of coverage during the 13-quarter period that ends with the quarter in which you die.

26. Unreduced Child-in-Care Benefits May Be Available at Any Age

If your spouse has filed for a retirement benefit and you have unmarried children of that spouse who are in your care (either under age 16 or disabled, having become disabled before age 22), you can receive a child-in-care spousal benefit at any age. It will not be reduced even if you collect it before FRA. The benefit is half of your spouse's PIA, but may be less due to the FMB. Father and mother benefits, available to surviving spouses with a child in care, are available at any age and are not reduced based on age.

27. Worker's Death Presents New Benefit Choices for Surviving Spouse

If the worker dies, the child-in-care spousal benefit becomes a mother benefit if she still has a child in care, and rises to 75 percent of the deceased worker's PIA. If the spouse is aged 60 or older, she has the choice of continuing the mother benefit or filing to receive her widow's benefit. If she does file for her widow's benefit, Social Security will pay her the greater of the two. If she is below FRA, her widow's benefit may be reduced. In that case, it might increase if she defers taking it, so she will need to evaluate the difference between the two to decide on her best course of action. She may, for example, decide to continue her mother benefit and let her widow benefit increase before filing for it.

28. Child Survivor Benefits Are Larger than Child Dependent Benefits

The surviving child's benefit for a deceased worker is larger than the child benefit available from a retired worker. This is because the benefit for a qualified child of a retired worker is 50 percent of the worker's PIA. But the child survivor benefit is 75 percent of the deceased worker's PIA. A qualified child—a child eligible to collect a child benefit—is defined as any child who is unmarried, under 18 (or under 19 and still in elementary or high school), or, if disabled, at any age if disabled before the age of 22, as well as thereafter.

29. A Different PIA Formula May Apply to Survivors

Surviving spouses and ex-spouses of workers who die at a relatively young age may benefit from a second PIA formula. This formula was designed to help survivors of workers with short earnings histories. It does so by raising the deceased worker's PIA.

30. Worker's Death Frees Up More of Family Maximum Benefit for Survivors

When a working spouse dies, any benefits received by his or her spouse and qualifying children are likely to increase. This is because the worker's benefits are no longer included in the FMB calculation, leaving more room under the maximum for other family members. Moreover, in the case of the death of a disabled worker, the FMB formula itself changes from the one pertaining to disabled workers to the more generous one pertaining to retired and deceased *workers*.

31. Your Delayed Retirement Credit Doesn't Increase Spousal and Child Benefits

Spousal (including divorced spousal benefits and child-in-care spousal benefits) and child benefits will not rise if you suspend and restart your retirement benefit at a higher level. This is because spousal and child benefits are based on your PIA, not the actual retirement benefit you collect.

32. Your Parents May Be Entitled to Survivor Benefits Called Parent Benefits

Your parents, if age 62 or older and dependent on you for at least half of their financial support, can collect parent benefits on your earnings record after you die. One surviving parent would receive 82.5 percent of your PIA. If both parents qualify and are alive, each would receive 75 percent of your PIA. These benefits would be subject to the FMB.

33. Ex-Spouses May Need to Wait to Collect Divorced Spousal Benefits

If you are divorced, but were married for 10 or more years and are not married, you may be able to collect divorced spousal benefits starting at age 62. However, to do so, your ex-spouse must be at least 62 or receiving disability benefits. Further, you have to have been divorced for 2 years unless they have already filed for their own retirement or disability benefit.

34. Divorce Benefits Are Not Subject to the Family Maximum Benefit

Benefits to divorced ex-spouses are not restricted by the FMB and don't affect what your current spouse and children can receive. This secret means that the spousal benefit for your divorced ex-spouse may be higher than for your current spouse.

35. Divorced? Forget About Child-in-Care Benefits Until Your Ex Dies Unless You've Reached 62

You cannot get child-in-care benefits as a divorced spouse prior to age 62 even if you have your ex-spouse's children in your care. However, once your ex dies, you can receive mother or father divorced surviving spouse benefits based on having a child in care.

36. Divorced? You Can Be Deemed Even if Your Ex Has Not Filed for a Retirement Benefit

Your ex over 62 is treated as having filed for a retirement benefit when Social Security considers whether to deem you when you file for a benefit. So, if you are under FRA, even if your ex has not actually filed for retirement, when you file for either your retirement or your ex-spousal benefit, you will be deemed to be filing for both and will collect only the greater of the two. This also means that both exes can be deemed.

37. Deeming Was Extended Through 70 Under the New Law

This one is easier to understand than to explain! For married spouses, deeming occurs when a spouse files for either retirement or spousal benefits before reaching FRA and after FRA if not grandparented. Deeming automatically triggers the simultaneous filing of the other benefit.[1]

38. Divorced? Think Before Remarrying

If you get divorced and then remarry, you will *not* be able to receive a spousal benefit based on your ex's work history as long as you remain remarried.

39. Remarrying Can Cost You, Big-Time

If your spouse or ex-spouse (of 10 or more years) dies, you won't be able to receive widow(er) benefits if you remarry, unless you remarry after age 60. On the other hand, you can, it seems, get divorced and wait until you are over age 60 to remarry. Or if you are already over 60, you can, apparently, divorce and remarry the next day.

40. Marrying for a Nanosecond Can Pay Off

To get benefits based on your ex's work record, you need to have been married for 10 years. To get spousal benefits from your retired spouse's work record, you need to be married for a year. To get survivor benefits from your deceased spouse's work record, you need to be married for 9 months. But to get mother-father benefits (survivor benefits for spouses with a child in care), you need to be married only for a nanosecond or less. There's also no time requirement for receiving mother-father benefits as a divorced spouse.

41. Multiple Marriages? Multiple Benefit Choices

If you were married more than once, you can apply for spousal benefits or survivor benefits on the earnings record of whichever ex-spouse provides you the largest benefit. And you can switch at any time and apply for benefits from another ex-spouse. This might easily be the case, for example, if one ex-spouse died and your survivor benefit from this ex was higher than your spousal benefit from a different ex. The size of your new benefit will depend on when you claim it, but a reduction factor applied to one former spouse's benefit *does not apply* to a benefit you collect based on a different former spouse's work record.

42. If Your Spouse Dies Before Collecting Retirement Benefits

If your spouse dies before age 62, a specially calculated PIA will determine your widow(er) benefit. If your spouse dies between 62 and FRA, the benefit will be based on their full retirement benefit. If they die later, the benefit will be based on whatever retirement benefit they were entitled to, including any Delayed Retirement Credits.

43. Delaying Retirement Benefits Can Help Your Survivors

If you make it to FRA, delaying taking your retirement benefit—either by not filing for it, or if you have already filed and suspended it—may mean higher survivor benefits for your spouse, as well as ex-spouse(s), whenever you pass away.

44. Taking Retirement Benefits Early Can Hurt Your Survivors

Widow or widower benefits are normally equal to the deceased worker's (assume here he's the husband) benefit at his FRA or, if he dies later than this age, what he was entitled to receive at his death, including any Delayed Retirement Credits. However, if he filed for retirement benefits early, his widow will not receive his full PIA but something smaller based on a complicated formula involving his reduced benefit.[2]

45. Work in Non-Covered Jobs Can Reduce Your Social Security

The Windfall Elimination Provision (WEP) may reduce your Social Security benefit if you receive a pension from work where Social Security taxes were not taken out of your pay, such as a government agency or an employer in another country. The reduction arises through the application of a less generous PIA formula.

The purpose of the WEP is to put high earners who didn't pay SSA payroll taxes on roughly the same footing as high earners who did pay SSA taxes. That is, to not treat them as if they were low lifetime earners. The percentage paid to lower-paid workers is higher than that paid to highly paid workers. For example, workers making $3,000 per month could receive a benefit of $1,439 (48 percent) of their pre-retirement earnings. For a worker making $8,000 per month, the benefit could be $2,666 (33 percent).

46. Spousal and Survivor Benefits You Might Receive May Also Be Affected by Your Non-Covered Work

Thanks to the Government Pension Offset (GPO) provision, if you receive a pension from work where you did not pay Social Security taxes, your Social Security spousal, divorced spousal, widow, and divorced widow benefits based on any spouse's—current and former, living or dead—covered earnings record are reduced by two-thirds of your pension from non-covered employment. There are exceptions for some non-covered pensions, including pensions based on work abroad (foreign pensions).

47. It May Make Sense to Defer Non-Covered Pensions

Neither the Windfall Elimination Provision nor the Government Offset Provision kicks in until you start collecting your non-covered pensions. Hence it may behoove you to wait as long as possible to collect non-covered pensions, while starting as early as possible to collect your Social Security benefits. This would be the case if your non-covered pension compensates you for waiting to collect by providing a higher payment once you do so.

48. WEP Doesn't Affect Survivor Benefits

The Windfall Elimination Provision does not affect the survivor benefits your former spouse, your ex-spouse (if you were married more than 10 years before getting divorced), and your children can receive based on your covered earnings record.

49. Disability Benefits Automatically Convert to Retirement Benefits at FRA

When a disabled worker reaches FRA, her disability benefit becomes her retirement benefit. Like other workers, she can suspend her retirement benefit between FRA and 70 to accumulate Delayed Retirement Credits.

50. Disabled Workers Aren't Subject to Deeming and Receive Special Widow(er) Benefits

Regardless of when they file for disability, workers aren't subject to deeming. They also can collect widow(er) benefits as early as age 50, and receive as much as if they had waited to age 60. There is a reduction if benefits are claimed before FRA, but upon reaching that age, the reduction factor is eliminated for widow(er)s or surviving divorced spouses who were also entitled to disability on their own work records when they began receiving survivor benefits.

51. Social Security Treats You as Having Attained a Given Age on the Day Before Your Birthday

If, for example, you turn 62 on January 1, Social Security says you attained the age of 62 on December 31.

52. You Need to Be 62 for an Entire Month Before You Can Collect Reduced Retirement Benefits

If you are born on the first of the month, say, January 1, Social Security says you actually attained age 62 on the last day of December. Hence, during all of January you will have been 62. This means you are entitled to benefits for January. These benefits, like all Social Security benefits, will be paid one month in arrears. Hence, while your first check would arrive in February, you'd be paid for all 12 months of the year. The same is true if you were born on January 2. In this case, you'd be 62 for all of that January, because Social Security says you attained the age of 62 on January 1 and by the end of January you would have spent a whole month at age 62. On the other hand, if you were born on January 3 through 31, you'd have to spend all of February until you had been 62 for a full month. In this case, you'd be receiving payments for only 11 months and the first payment would arrive in March, not February.

53. If You Have Been Impacted by the RIB-LIM and You File a Bit Later than When Your Benefit Reached Its Maximum Level, You Can Collect up to Six Months of Retroactive Benefits Where Some Months Precede Full Retirement Age

In general, there is a 6-month grace period that Social Security grants you if you don't file for your widow(er) or divorced widow(er) retirement benefit when you should file. But, with the exception of some of those hit by the RIB-LIM formula, Social Security won't given you retroactive benefits before Full Retirement Age.

54. If Both Parents of a Child Are Collecting Their Retirement or Disability Benefits or Are Deceased, Their Family Maximum Benefit Amounts Can Be Combined to Provide a Larger Benefit than Would Otherwise Be the Case

Say for example that both you and your wife are disabled with PIAs of $1,000 and family maximum benefits of $1,500 each. If you had one minor child, that child would receive $500 monthly, or 50 percent of your PIA. Normally, if a second child was added to your record, the children would have to split the $500 available from the family maximum ($1,500, representing, say, the dad's family maximum less the $1,000 paid to the dad) and be limited to $250 each.

But suppose your wife is collecting Social Security too. Say she's collecting her retirement benefit, and her PIA is also $1,000 and her own family benefit maximum (FMB) is $1,500. In this case, each spouse can add the other spouse's FMB to their own FMB. So your FMB becomes $3,000. Subtracting your PIA of $1,000 leaves $2,000 that can be provided to your two kids. So each can collect their full child benefit of $500. This combining of the two spouses' FMBs doesn't mean the children can collect on both parents. They can't. They can only collect on one of the two parents, which will be the one whose FMB and own PIA permit greater benefits payable to the family.

55. If You Time When You Earn Money During the Course of the Year, You Can Receive Almost a Full Month of Free Benefits

For example, say you will reach age 66 in November 2016, and will earn $41,910 in the first 10 months of the year. Instead of waiting until November to apply, you could start benefits one month earlier, that is, in October. Since your earnings will exceed the Social Security Earnings Test exempt amount of $41,880 (that applies in the year you reach FRA) by $30, $1 of your benefits would be withheld for each $3 of the excess, for a total of $10. In other words, Social Security would pay you all but $10 of your October check, and then full benefits from November on. And here's the critical part: since you would not be paid a full check for October, Social Security bumps up your benefit at FRA by a full month's benefit. This gives you almost a month's benefit for October at no long-view cost.

56. Couples Who Have Private Businesses May Be Able to Legally Allocate the Earnings Between the Two Spouses to Raise the Household's Total Benefits

For example, if one spouse is earning more than the other and the other spouse has a spotty earnings record, paying the higher-earning spouse less and the lower-earning spouse more can raise the lower-earning spouse's Social Security benefits with no extra payroll taxes if both are earning below the maximum taxable wage ceiling. We're not sure about the legality of this, but many couples appear to be doing it.

57. Since the Regular Family Maximum Benefit Can Exceed the Disabled Worker Family Maximum Benefit, It Can Somethimes Be Best for Those over 62 and Below FRA Who Are Eligible for Disability Benefits to Also File for Their Early Retirement Benefit

This depends, of course, on how many family members can collect on the worker's record. But there's another sweetener. If you take your retirement benefits early, they will be reduced, but not permanently. At Full Retirement Age, the reduction will be eliminated and you'll be paid your full retirement benefit.

58. There Is a Separate and More Generous RIB-LIM Formula (Actually, a More Generous Application of the Standard Formula) for Disabled Workers

This can make a substantial difference to one's widow(er)'s benefit if one is disabled.

59. Disabled Widow(er)s Can Take Their Widow(er) Benefits as Early as 50 with No Greater Reduction than Were They to Take Them at Age 60

But if they are collecting their disability benefit, they will only receive their excess widow(er)'s benefit.

60. At FRA the Reduction to a Disabled Widow(er) Benefit Goes Away in Some Cases

The requirement is that your widow(er) benefit begins simultaneously to or after your disability benefit. This means there is no disadvantage to taking one's widow(er) benefit as early as possible if one is disabled and already receiving disability benefits on one's own record.

40 BAD-NEWS GOTCHAS THAT CAN REDUCE YOUR BENEFITS FOREVER

Hidden deep within Social Security's Handbook and Program Operations Manual System (POMS) are lots of what Larry calls "gotchas." We've collected the 40 worst. (This is 15 more than we listed in the first edition! Why? Well, you live and learn.) Some will be familiar. Others won't. But we present the whole list here, in one spot, for easy reference. Take a look if you want reassurance that you aren't falling into any of the system's traps.

If your blood pressure rises, bear in mind that the folks at Social Security aren't to blame. They didn't design this maddening system, which despite its many deep flaws has done enormous good over the decades for hundreds of millions of Americans. No one at Social Security is trying to get us to make the wrong decisions and end up with lower benefits than possible. But very few people at Social Security know the rules well enough to guide many of us to the right choices. So, as the old saying goes, forewarned is forearmed.

1. If You Take Two Benefits at Once, You Lose One of the Two

Social Security won't pay you two different benefits at the same time. Instead it will pay you the larger of the two benefits (or something pretty close to this amount).[1] For example, if you are married and take or are forced to take your retirement benefit when you take your spousal benefit, you'll lose your retirement benefit if your spousal benefit is larger. Social Security won't say it has eliminated your retirement benefit. Instead, it will claim it's giving you your retirement benefit plus the difference or *excess* between the two. But, in reality, it has used the spousal benefit to wipe out your retirement benefit. Spouses and qualified divorced spouses who were 62 before January 2, 2016, can take just their spousal/divorced spousal benefits starting at FRA and their retirement benefit at 70. Those spouses who were widowed before taking their retirement benefit can take their widow(er) benefit before or after they take their retirement benefit. The same holds for qualified divorced widow(er)s.

2. Once You File for Your Retirement Benefit, You Can Never Take an Auxiliary Benefit by Itself

The instant you file for your retirement benefit you forfeit *forever* your ability to file for any other benefit just by itself. This is true even if you suspend your retirement benefit.

3. If You Are Forced to Take Your Retirement Benefit at the Same Time as Your Spousal or Divorced Spousal Benefit, Your Retirement Benefit Will Generally Wipe Out Your Spousal or Divorced Spousal Benefit

As we discussed in Chapter 3, the formula that takes your Average Indexed Monthly Earnings and turns it into your Primary Insurance Amount—your full retirement benefit—is highly progressive. Benefits paid to lower-paid workers are a much higher percentage of their pre-retirement incomes than is the case for highly paid workers. Consequently, even if you've earned relatively low covered wages during your working years, taking your retirement benefit will likely mean never receiving a spousal benefit because (1) taking your retirement benefit keeps you from ever taking another benefit by itself (Gotcha #2) and (2) spousal benefits are at best only half of your spouse's PIA, so your retirement benefit will likely exceed your spousal or divorced spousal benefit and, therefore, wipe it out. Stated differently, as shown in Chapter 10, excess spousal benefits or divorced spousal benefits are generally zero or very small if we're talking about two spouses or two ex-spouses who earned even modest wages.

4. Thanks to the New Law, All Those Not 62 Before January 2, 2016, Are Deemed to Be Filing for Their Retirement Benefit Whenever They File for Their Spouse or Divorced Spousal Benefit. And Vice Versa if They File for Their Retirement Benefit and Meet (or as Soon as They Meet) the Conditions to Receive a Spousal or Divorcee Spousal Benefit

When you are forced to file for a spousal or divorced spousal benefit at the same time as you file for your retirement benefit, you get your retirement benefit plus an excess spousal or excess divorced spousal benefit. For most two-earner couples or qualified divorced couples, these excess benefits will be small or zero.

5. Thanks to the New Law, Anyone Who Didn't Suspend Their Retirement Benefit Before April 30, 2016, Cannot Collect an Excess Spousal, an Excess Divorced Spousal, or an Excess Widow(er) Benefit While Their Own Retirement Benefit Is in Suspension

6. Thanks to the New Law, Anyone Who Didn't Suspend Their Retirement Benefit Before April 30, 2016, Cannot Provide Benefits to Anyone—Not Their Spouses, Not Their Qualified Ex-Spouses, Not Their Young Children, and Not Their Disabled Children While Their Retirement Benefit Is in Suspension

7. Thanks to the New Law, Those Who Suspend Their Benefits After April 30, 2016, Are Unable to Ask for Their Suspended Benefits in a Lump Sum

Under the old law you could suspend your own retirement benefit at FRA, but then had the option before or even after age 70 to collect all suspended benefits in a lump-sum payment less any DRCs received.

8. Being Deemed Before Age 70 Leads to Permanently Reduced Retirement Benefits

Apart from those grandfathered against post-FRA deeming, being deemed whether before or after FRA, but before age 70, forces you to take your retirement benefit earlier than 70, which means your retirement benefit will permanently fall below its value were you to start it at age 70. Furthermore, if your excess spousal benefit is zero, you'll receive only your reduced retirement benefit.

Yes, you can undo some of the damage by suspending your retirement benefit at FRA and starting it up again at 70 at a 32 percent higher real (after inflation) level. But this 32 percent kicker coming from the Delayed Retirement Credit will be applied to your reduced retirement benefit, not to your full retirement benefit. So once this gotcha gets you, you are gotten for life.

9. Deeming Dangers for the Disabled

If you are collecting a disability benefit and your spouse tries to collect just her retirement benefit early or even after FRA (if she is not grandparented against post-FRA deeming), she will be deemed to be filing for her spousal benefits as well. In this case, your spouse will get her reduced (if taken early) retirement benefit plus her reduced (if taken early) excess spousal benefit.

10. For Those Grandfathered with Respect to Post-FRA Deeming, Only One Spouse in a Married Couple Can Receive a Full Spousal Benefit by Itself

For married spouses who are grandparented under the new law and can still collect a full spousal benefit (a spousal benefit by itself), collecting the full spousal benefit requires that one's partner either be collecting their retirement benefit or have suspended it before April 30, 2016. If they are collecting their retirement benefit, they can collect only an excess spousal benefit. The same is true if they have suspended their retirement benefit.

11. For Those Not Grandparented with Respect to Post-FRA Deeming, Only One Spouse in a Married Couple or One or More Qualified Ex-Spouses Can Receive an Excess Spousal Benefit by Itself

Your excess spousal benefit is positive only if your partner's PIA is more than twice your own. But if this is true, your PIA can't be more than twice your partner's—the requirement for your spouse to receive an excess spousal benefit. So you both can't collect excess spousal benefits even if you were both also grandparented with respect to providing benefits off a suspended retirement benefit.

The same logic applies to qualified ex-spouses. Only one of the two divorced spouses can have a PIA that's less than half of their ex's.

12. If You Take Your Retirement Benefit Before Age 70, You May Permanently Reduce Your Surviving Spouse's Widow(er) Benefits

Your surviving spouse's widow(er) benefits is based on the actual retirement benefit you were receiving when you passed away, so the earlier you take your benefit, the smaller this surviving benefit will be.

13. You Can Contribute to Social Security Your Entire Working Life and Receive Nothing Whatsoever in Extra Benefits

Suppose you start working at age 16 and continue working through FRA. Every week, week in and week out, you and your employer pay 12.4 percent of every dollar you earn in Social Security payroll (FICA) taxes. Also, suppose you earn relatively little in absolute terms and also relative to your spouse. Then you may do best to wait to collect your spousal benefit starting at FRA (spousal benefits don't increase after FRA) assuming your partner has filed for his or her retirement benefit and you were 62 before January 2, 2016.

At age 70, you file for your own retirement benefit, but now you get hit by Gotcha #1. And if your spousal benefit exceeds your age-70 retirement benefit (that is, inclusive of the Delayed Retirement Credits), your total payment will continue to equal just your spousal benefit. Yes, Social Security will describe your total check as consisting of your own age-70 retirement benefit plus your excess spousal benefit. But the sum of these two components will just equal your spousal benefit. So you'll get nothing in extra benefits for all the years you contributed. Furthermore, when your spouse dies, you'll collect a survivor benefit based on their earnings record, which will be even larger than your spousal benefit, which is larger than your own retirement benefit.

14. If You Suspend Your Retirement Benefits and Don't Directly Pay Your Medicare Part B Premiums, Your Medicare B Will Be Canceled

Say you're a 62-year-old husband and your wife is 66—at her FRA and grandparented under the new law. You'd like her to be able to collect "free" spousal benefits for 4 years and wait until 70 to take the highest retirement benefit possible. So you apply for your retirement benefit. When you hit 66, your wife is 70 and is collecting her retirement benefit. "So now you say, "Gee, if I suspend my benefit I can get 32 percent more at age 70." So you suspend your retirement benefit.

But you're in Medicare Part B and you don't think about paying the Part B premium via a separate payment, since you're used to Social Security deducting the premium from your Social Security payment. Our understanding is that if you don't pay this out of your own pocket, your Medicare Part B will be canceled.

Social Security, as we understand it, used to simply reactivate your retirement benefit if you didn't pay your Medicare Part B premium. But they wouldn't pay you your benefit; they'd simply take the premium and when you reached 70, they'd say, "Sorry, no DRCs for you. You reactivated your benefit in not paying for Part B." This ultimate gotcha is, fortunately, now gone.

15. Get Divorced a Day Too Early and Potentially Lose Tens of Thousands of Dollars in Divorced Spousal and Divorced Widow(er) Benefits

If you get divorced just one day shy of 10 years, neither you nor your ex will collect a dime in divorced spousal or survivor benefits. But if you wait one more day—just stick it out with the hate of your life for 24 more hours—you and your spouse can qualify for these benefits. For those who don't stay married for the full 10 years, but get close, and divorce not realizing the value of waiting it out, this is a real gotcha.

16. Remarry and Potentially Lose Divorced Spousal Benefits Potentially Worth Tens of Thousands of Dollars

Suppose you stick it out for 10 or more years with the hate of your life, who happened to be a high earner (thanks to your raising the kids). You then divorce the SOB, spend years looking for love in all the wrong places, and finally meet your own true love—an impoverished artist. If you marry your own true love, you will lose your spousal benefits from your ex. Depending on your ex's earnings record and your own, getting remarried can cost you big Social Security bucks over your remaining lifetime.

SOCIAL SECURITY VERBATIM

THE FAT LADY NEVER SINGS II

"The fact that we determine that a claimant meets the requirements for entitlement does not preclude us from making another determination that the claimant no longer meets those requirements at some subsequent date."

ALL QUOTES FROM OFFICIAL SOCIAL SECURITY RULES

17. Remarry a Day Too Soon and Lose Divorced Widow(er) Benefits Potentially Worth Tens of Thousands of Dollars

You are a 59-year, 364-day-old divorced woman who was miserably married to Mr. Big Bucks for 10-plus years until he dumped you for a starlet from *Real Stepford Housewives*. You are standing on the altar having just said "I do" to Mr. Perfect. Your mother, who wasn't invited, swings open the church door and screams, "Stop, you idiots! You need to wait till tomorrow to get married." But it's too late. By remarrying before age 60, you just gave up your claim to divorced survivor benefits on Mr. Big Bucks, who has recently been diagnosed with terminal cancer.

18. Working in Non-Covered Employment Can Reduce Your Retirement Benefits from Working in Covered Employment

Jobs on which you fork over payroll taxes to Social Security are known as covered employment. Jobs for which you don't—mostly federal and some state and local jobs—are called non-covered employment. If you don't work 30 or more years in covered employment, the formula determining your full retirement benefit (PIA) from covered employment becomes less and less generous (up to a limit) the longer you work in non-covered employment. As we explained in Chapter 14, this is called the Windfall Elimination Provision (WEP). It was implemented to keep non-covered workers from double dipping, that is, collecting full pensions and Social Security because they worked in non-covered employment. But many non-covered workers may not realize how the WEP works and that you need to work 30 years in covered employment earning at least Social Security's substantial earning level to fully escape its impact.

19. Working in Non-Covered Employment Can Mean Reduced Spousal and Child Benefits for Your Spouse and Child, Even if Your Spouse Never Works in Non-Covered Employment

The WEP, if it reduces your PIA, will mean lower spousal and child benefits because those benefits are pegged to your PIA. The WEP does not, however, affect survivor benefits since the PIA for that calculation does not incorporate the WEP reduction.

20. Working in Jobs Not Covered by Social Security That Provide Pensions Can Cost You All or Most of Your Spousal and Divorced Spousal Widow(er) Benefits

If you receive a pension from uncovered work, Social Security's spousal, divorced spousal, survivor, and divorced survivor benefits for which you may be eligible based on your current spouse, ex-spouse, deceased spouse, or deceased ex-spouse's earnings record will be reduced by two-thirds of the pension you receive from the non-covered employment. This reduction is called the Government Pension Offset, or GPO.

From a fairness perspective, the GPO can lead to some troubling questions. Take Joe, who is married to Sally, who works in covered employment. Suppose Joe is a good-for-nothing lazy bum who hasn't worked a day in his life. Doesn't matter. Joe can collect spousal benefits and survivor benefits on Sally's work record. Now suppose Joe is a good-for-something guy. Indeed, suppose Joe teaches school in a tough district his entire career, but the job isn't covered by Social Security. If Joe gets a decent-size pension from the uncovered job, his spousal and survivor benefits from Sally's work record probably will be wiped out by the GPO.

21. If You Make a Mistake in Your Retirement Benefit Filing Decision and Wait a Day Too Long to Fix It, Too Bad. You're Stuck.

If you file for your retirement benefit, you have one year to withdraw your benefit, that is, to "repay and replay"—pay back every penny of benefits received on your work record (gross of any deductions for Medicare Part B premiums and withholdings for income tax) and start from scratch in making your Social Security collection decisions. If you decided on the 366th day to start over, you're out of luck. Unless it's a leap year such as 2016, of course, in which case we will have to consult our Social Security rule book again and get back to you.

22. Suspending Your Retirement Benefits Can Cost You Big Bucks

This gotcha pertains to those whose auxiliary benefit is larger than their retirement benefit even inclusive of the maximum amount of Delayed Retirement Credits that can be accumulated. For these people, the amount by which their auxiliary benefit exceeds their

retirement benefit is treated by Social Security as their excess auxiliary benefit.

Now suppose you are in this boat and you decide to suspend
your retirement benefit and restart it at 70. Under the new law,
you can't collect any excess benefit of any kind during the period
your benefit is suspended. So you get nothing whatsoever until
you reach 70. At 70 you restart your retirement benefit only to
find that the total payment is no larger than you would have received during the suspension period had you not suspended. Yes,
your retirement benefit is larger thanks to the Delayed Retirement
Credits. But, given our assumption that your excess benefit at 70 is
still positive, this excess benefit is lower by exactly the amount by
which your retirement benefit is larger. Hence, suspending in this
situation is simply a decision not to take benefits for the period of
suspension. It does nothing to raise your total future benefit payment.

In other words, you would have suspended for nothing, losing potentially thousands of dollars in lifetime benefits. If you realize you
made a mistake in suspending your retirement benefit (and seeing no
change in your monthly payment is the clincher), you may be able to
undo the mistake and recover all your suspended payments. But, it
appears, only if you suspended before April 30, 2016.

23. The Family Maximum Benefit (FMB) Means That Applying for Additional Benefits on a Worker's Record May Mean No Extra Total Family Benefits

The FMB—the most benefits available on your earnings record—is
an awful piece of work. It can range from 150 to 187 percent of your
PIA. But in order for family members to collect spousal or child
benefits, you need to file for your retirement benefit. But since you
are tagged for receiving 100 percent of your PIA in retirement benefits, *even if you have suspended your retirement benefit*, this leaves only

50 percent to 87 percent of your PIA available to other household members.

Since the child and spousal benefits available on your work record equal half of your PIA, it can take benefits to only one family member and at most two to hit the FMB. When this happens, the same 50–87 percent of your PIA will be proportionally divided up among your family members. So you may think you are getting an extra benefit for a spouse or a child in having them apply for a spousal or child benefit, but it's coming out of the pockets of your other family members.

24. Depending on Their Level and Your Other Income, 50 to 85 Percent of Your Social Security Benefits May Be Subject to Federal Income Taxation

Receiving less than $25,000 ($32,000 for joint filers) in combined income means that none of your Social Security benefits are subject to federal income taxes. Combined income is defined as your non–Social Security income *plus* tax-exempt interest (on government securities, for example) *plus* half your Social Security benefit. Between $25,000 and $34,000 ($32,000 to $44,000 for joint filers), up to half of your benefits may be taxable. Above these amounts, 85 percent of your Social Security benefits may be taxable but never more than this percentage.

25. Social Security Benefit Taxation Rises with Inflation

The thresholds beyond which the first 50 percent and then 85 percent of your Social Security benefits are subject to federal income taxation are explicitly *not* indexed for inflation. Hence, eventually all Social Security recipients will be taxed on 85 percent of their Social Security benefits, assuming the rules don't change.

26. Disabled Workers Who Appear to be Grandparented Against Post-FRA Deeming Aren't

Social Security staff took it upon themselves to modify the system's program operating manual system on December 23, 2014, when no one was looking. They did so with no public knowledge, let alone debate. Like the writing of the new Social Security legal provisions, this was another eleventh-hour, back-door, dead-of-night act with no public discussion. It has prevented millions of disabled workers from pursuing the file-and-suspend strategy.

27. A Special Family Maximum Benefit Formula Can Hurt the Disabled

If you're disabled, Social Security has a special formula for calculating your FMB. It's less generous than the standard formula for many if not most disabled workers. And for those with very low earnings, it's draconian, permitting no benefits whatsoever to spouses over 62, spouses with children in care, or young or disabled children. If you are disabled or have a disabled family member, please read Chapter 12 to find out how to navigate Social Security's rules affecting benefits for disabled persons.

28. Social Security Can Change Its Rules

This is the gotcha of all gotchas! Social Security's existing rules give it broad leeway to change its mind. Even if it doesn't, Congress might change the rules. See, for example, Gotcha #26. Or the major changes in rules we wrote about in Chapter 4, which also were introduced and approved with no public discussion or congressional hearings.

29. Social Security Staff Will Often Tell You with 100 Percent Certainty Things That Are 100 Percent Untrue

We routinely hear from people who are told they can't collect a benefit when in fact they can or can't suspend their retirement benefit when it's their right: This behavior peaked in early 2016 when Social Security sent its staff misleading statements about the new law.

30. Social Security Can Deny You Some of Your Delayed Retirement Credits Unless You Put Your Requested Start Date in Writing

According to our esteemed mentor, former Social Security technical expert Jerry Lutz, Social Security staff must provide you all retroactive benefits to which you are eligible if you file for your retirement benefit after FRA, unless you specify that you do not want them. As happened to Larry's dentist, this means you could go into Social Security's office or talk to them over the phone, say, three months before reaching 70, and tell them you don't want your retirement benefit to start until age 70. You would think this would entitle you to all possible Delayed Retirement Credits. But after you have left the office or hung up the phone, unless it is specified on your application that you wish to refuse retroactive benefits, the staff person with whom you dealt is required to start your retirement benefit 6 months early—and not six months early relative to age 70, but 6 months early relative to when you contacted the office! This cost Larry's dentist 9 months of Delayed Retirement Credits. He did receive 6 months of retirement benefits in a lump-sum check. But his monthly payment is forever reduced by 6 percent (nine-twelfths of 8 percent). The *only way*, according to Jerry, to ensure this doesn't happen is to write in the Remarks section of the application form that you don't want to receive retroactive benefits, but instead want your retirement benefit to commence with your 70th birthday. If a Social Security representative completes the application for you, carefully review your copy of the application to make sure this remark is included. The online application is far safer on this score.

31. You Need to Get It in Writing

It's one thing to ask Social Security for a benefit to which you are eligible and to start receiving it when you want. It's another thing to actually get what you asked for when you ask for it. If you don't specify in writing on your benefit application form *in the Remarks sections* exactly what benefits you are filing for and which benefits you aren't filing for and precisely when you want to receive the benefits for which you are applying, you won't have any legal proof to appeal a mistake by Social Security if it makes one. It's very hard to write anything on an application form over the phone. You can file over the phone for some but not all benefits, and Social Security will send you a copy of your application perhaps with the Remarks section properly filled in based on your dictation. The safest way, though, would be to visit your local office and make sure your wishes are properly noted by the claims rep in the Remarks section and make sure you leave with a dated (in effect, time-stamped) copy of your application. Better yet, file online when possible.

32. You Need to Get It in the Right Writing

If the Remarks section contains terms like "at this time" or references future plans to do X, Y, or Z, that won't cut it. You need to make unequivocal statements to Social Security to ensure they do what you want to do no matter how obvious that is. Here's the reference in POMS just to show we aren't making this up:

> The claimant may restrict the application by completing appropriate blocks on the application or by signing an unequivocal statement that he or she does not wish to file for a specific benefit as follows:
>
> "I filed on (DATE) for all benefits for which I may be eligible except _____"; or

"I wish to exclude _____ benefits from the scope of this application."

Only unequivocal statements are acceptable. Qualifying phrases such as "at this time" or he or she plans to file in the future are not acceptable.

33. If You Earn Too Much After You Take Early Retirement Benefits, All Your Earnings Up to the Point That You Take Your Full Retirement Benefit Can Be Counted Under the Earnings Test

We've told you about the Earnings Test and that it's generally over-stated because at least the benefit that is lost due to the Earnings Test is bumped up at FRA thanks to what's called the Adjustment of the Reduction Factor. What we want to emphasize here is that all your earnings, even wages you make in non-covered employment, are counted in applying the Earnings Test. Also, if you become entitled to benefits in the middle of a year, even money that you earned in the months prior to becoming entitled count toward the annual Earnings Test.

34. If Your Child Who Was Disabled Prior to Age 22 Earns Too Much They May Become Disqualified for Receiving Disabled Child Benefits Off of Your Work Record or That of Your Current or Ex-Spouse

Social Security permits disabled children that aren't blind to earn some, but not much, money before declaring them no longer disabled. In 2016, this annual level of earnings, called the level of Substantial Gainful Activity, was only $13,560 per year. For blind children it was $21,840. If the child earns more than this amount even for a single year, they could lose their rights to collect disabled child and child survivor benefits for the rest of their lives!

35. If Your Disabled Child Is Receiving Supplemental Security Income (SSI), This Income Will Be Reduced Dollar for Dollar for Every Dollar Provided by Disabled Child and Child Survivor Benefits

This is yet another Catch-22. So if you are thinking of taking your retirement benefit early to provide your disabled child with a disabled child benefit and, perhaps your spouse with a child-in-care spousal benefit, you need to be aware that some of what you will pick up in the right hand will be taken away from the left hand.

36. If You Begin Your Retirement Benefit After FRA, but Before Age 70, You Have to Wait till the Next January to See a Higher Payment

Delayed Retirement Credits (DRCs) are payable beginning with the January after the year they are earned and then at age 70. So if someone with FRA of 66 files at age 68 for benefits beginning, say, May 2017, the worker's retirement benefit for the rest of 2017 would reflect DRCs earned through 2016. But DRCs for 2017 wouldn't be added until January 2018.

37. If You Take Your Non-Covered Pension in a Lump Sum, Social Security Will Prorate Payments in Order to Apply the GPO

Unfortunately, you can't get around the Government Pension Offset (GPO) by taking your non-covered pension in a lump sum.

38. Disability Benefits Aren't Reduced if Taken Early, but the Excess Benefits of the Disabled Are

If you receive disability benefits on your own record, the benefit amount is unreduced if taken early (before FRA). However, excess spousal and excess widow(er)'s benefits are reduced for age. The same is true of excess divorced or excess divorced widow(er) benefits.

39. Make Sure Your Spouse or Ex-Spouse Doesn't Die Before You Become Disabled

If you are entitled to disability benefits on your own record and then become entitled to a higher widow(er) benefit before full retirement age (FRA), you'll keep collecting the disability benefit and get an excess widow(er) benefit equal to the difference between the two benefits. If you are below full retirement age, the excess widow(er) benefit will be reduced. But at FRA, Social Security will eliminate the reduction factor applied to your excess widow(er) benefit. Things are very different, however, if you are first collecting a reduced widow(er) benefit and then start collecting a disability benefit that is less than your reduced widow(er) benefit. In this event, your disability benefit will offset your widow(er) benefit dollar for dollar, and you'll end up with the same total payment. And the reduction factor applied to your excess widow(er) benefit won't be eliminated when you reach FRA.

40. The Dead Have a Better Benefit Formula than The Disabled

More earnings years are used to calculate the benefit amount for someone who becomes disabled at a young age, as opposed to someone who dies at the same age. For example, the benefit amount for a person who becomes disabled at age 28 is based on their best 5 years of inflation-adjusted earnings, whereas survivor benefits on the record of a person who dies at age 28 are calculated using their best 2 years of inflation-adjusted earnings. A 5-year earnings average is usually much lower than a 2-year average, resulting in significantly lower disability benefits.

WHITHER SOCIAL SECURITY?

We said at the outset that this book would be about how to get what's yours from Social Security, not about its finances or ways we think the program should be changed. We do, however, have strong thoughts about these matters. Here they are, starting with Paul.

PAUL

It's as obvious as it is enervating: coauthorship demands compromise. And indeed the book you have just about finished, unless of course you first opened it to this chapter, represents a negotiated settlement. In writing our first edition and then drafting this one, Larry would rail against the Social Security system, as he occasionally does in his weekly and otherwise excellent "Ask Larry" column for the *PBS NewsHour* Making Sen$e website, suggesting malign intent, a hopeless future, and general fecklessness. I would recoil at what I considered irresponsible hyperbole, animus, and undue pessimism and would then rewrite. Phil would—well, Phil can and will speak for himself when he gets this chapter's last word.

I also worried that Larry's railing would scare people, especially young people, into thinking they would never get any Social Security at all. Millennials are generally defined as Americans born between 1980 and the mid-2000s and are now a larger cohort than baby boomers. When, in my travels as an economics reporter, I ask them about Social Security, they typically say something like, "It won't be there when I retire."

So let me declare at the outset, especially to young people: you *will* get yours—or at the very least, you'll get most of it. This is something we three authors emphatically agree on: the millennials are simply *wrong*.

We do disagree on how *much* they will get from Social Security, and the taxes they—or *someone*—will wind up paying to make sure the checks keep going out. But even the darkest official forecast still assures people as young as 18 today something like 75 percent of the paychecks their elders are currently receiving.

Official forecasts, however, are deeply misleading. That's because they rely on the notion that there's a Social Security "trust fund" that is running out of money; that a so-called Social Security lockbox has been "raided" to pay for other expenditures. Such palaver is misleading, if not arrant nonsense.

First of all, the so-called trust fund is an accounting fiction: the money supposedly stashed away for future generations is nearly $3 trillion worth of U.S. government bonds—Uncle's Sam's IOUs that he gives as a legal promise to pay back what he's borrowed.

The story goes that the trust fund took in Social Security taxes, then "loaned" that money to the government in return for bonds. The trust fund has the bonds; beneficiaries have the cash.

But you see the fiction, right? The government is in effect borrowing money from *itself* by issuing its bonds to the trust fund, meanwhile using the money from current Social Security taxes—more than $913 billion in 2015—plus other taxes, revenues, and borrowed money, to pay government expenses. Phil provides a very good explanation in his contribution to this chapter.

Yes, the official accounting is that because Social Security paid out only $888 billion in 2015, the trust fund wound up $25 billion in the black. But that's just last year. The dire predictions stem from the fact that as baby boomers retire, they will stop paying in, start taking their benefits, and the trust fund will therefore soon sink into the red, shrinking year by year.

But look, this is nothing more than what I call ledger-de-main. Who cares if the trust fund is officially recorded as in the red or in the black? The government *itself* is in the red. The government takes in taxes. It pays out expenses—for defense, science, Medicare, Social Security, and everything else, including the interest on the money it borrows. But since the U.S. government doesn't take in as much as it pays out, it runs an annual federal *deficit*—and has done every year since 1969, with the exception of President Clinton's last three years in office. It covers the annual deficit by borrowing money and handing over its bonds in return. And those bonds, all added together, make up our cumulative national debt.

When the bonds come due, the government simply pays them off and borrows more. So every time the trust fund is supposedly tapped to pay a Social Security benefit, it's really just Uncle Sam saying to himself: "Time for me to redeem one of those bonds in the trust fund with cash, and raise the cash by borrowing some more. Or raising taxes, if Republicans would ever let me."

But here's my point. How likely is it that Uncle Sam is going to renege on his commitments to the elderly? Any more than he's about to renege on his promises to the defense establishment, or to veterans, or to his 2.8 million federal employees, or his Medicare recipients, or to the bondholders of his federal debt?

Larry's lament has been that both Social Security and America are bankrupt. Why? Because both have failed to account honestly for the promises they have made to current and future generations. These promises are essentially off the books, says Larry. To which I say: no kidding. You mean Americans want benefits but don't much like paying for them? You mean human beings borrow against the future and then try to maintain a state of denial about their future obligations? And why single out Social Security? The Medicare promises are even more unrealistic.

But what do we suppose will actually happen with Social Security's promises, and Medicare's promises, and Uncle Sam's debt to pay off those promises? Like every other set of unrealistic promises, they will be finagled, modified, renegotiated.

In 1981, President Ronald Reagan and Congress appointed a commission to "reform" Social Security, chaired by the man who later ran the Federal Reserve Bank, Alan Greenspan. The so-called Greenspan Commission was asked "to study and make recommendations regarding the short-term financing crisis that Social Security faced at that time." The words are those of the Social Security Administration today, but as you can see, the sense of "crisis" was abroad in the land even then.

The commission's recommendations inspired the Social Security Reform Act of 1983, featuring a host of changes, including a delay in cost-of-living benefits, a modest Social Security tax increase, increased tax rates on employee income to match the 6.2 percent that employers already had to pay, making up to 50 percent of Social Security income taxable for the first time (a ceiling later raised to 85 percent for higher earners), and eliminating "windfall benefits" for those with a pension from non-covered employment, as explained in Chapter 15.

Amazingly, Congress then went the commission one better, lengthening the eligibility age for Social Security from 65 to 66, eventually to become 67 by 2027.

The supposed crisis was averted—by changes that reflected the pressure of what was considered unyielding financial reality. That's what's likely to happen again.

Many of us will give a little. Some will give more than others— presumably Americans who earn enough not to need Social

Security's checks. There will be a huge outcry, as there always is when people are asked to pay more or get less. Maybe members of the House will be besieged by seniors, as Congressman Dan Rostenkowski was in 1989. (You should look up the footage on YouTube.) And yes, seniors will vote to protect their benefits, and there will be more seniors than ever.

But though we'll stub innumerable toes in the process, some way, somehow, we will once again kick the can down the road.

How *exactly*? Following the 2005 lead of Nobel laureate economist Peter Diamond and former Clinton budget director Peter Orszag in *A Summary of Saving Social Security: A Balanced Approach* and the more recent book by Martin N. Baily and Jacob Funk Kirkegaard, *U.S. Pension Reform: Lessons from Other Countries*, I'd bet on some combination of the following:

- raising the Social Security (FICA) tax slightly from its current 12.4 percent total for employer and employee. We've referred several times in this book to economist Alicia Munnell of Boston College's Center for Retirement Research. She has pointed out that a tax hike of another 1.2 percentage points on employers and the same hike on employees would completely eliminate the projected Social Security shortfall for the next 75 years. "We've just had a payroll tax cut of 2 percentage points," Munnell said when I interviewed her for the *PBS NewsHour* in 2013. "I couldn't even tell. And then they raised it again by 2 percentage points and I still couldn't tell. There wasn't jubilation when it happened and it wasn't cataclysmic when it went back."
- hiking the ceiling on FICA taxes from 2016's $118,500; it rises annually, but only at the rate of inflation, and didn't rise at all from 2015, because inflation was nonexistent;
- making 100 percent of Social Security benefit income taxable;

- lengthening the retirement age gradually, in line with increased longevity and career spans;
- tinkering with the cost-of-living adjustment to lower it a bit;
- lowering benefits for better-off Americans by what financial expert Robert Pozen has proposed, "progressive indexation";
- increasing immigration because immigrants tend to be younger and thus pay Social Security taxes for decades while not collecting benefits, though I don't think this is happening anytime soon as of this rewriting;
- encouraging more Americans to continue to work later in life, and thus continue to pay more and more FICA taxes, something that's already happening: some 30 percent of baby boomers are working past age 65;
- finally, if the techno-optimists are right, a surge in economic growth will bring in enough taxes to make the system whole.

As it happens, President Obama has already pushed the cost-of-living adjustment and of course, in the Bipartisan Budget Bill of 2015, ended certain benefits.

In fact, after we had finished the manuscript for the first version of *Get What's Yours*, the Social Security Administration's chief actuary issued a report on the impact of various program changes proposed at one time or another (or perhaps concocted by the actuary for purposes of discussion or illustration). So, for example, if we changed, starting in 2021, the way in which benefits are indexed—from using average wage growth to using inflation as the basis—the actuary reports that we would not only wipe out the entire Social Security deficit over the next 75 years but in fact build a substantial *surplus*. Indeed, even over the infinite time horizon Larry favors, 89 percent of the deficit would be eliminated by this one change alone.

Or we could "maintain current-law benefits for earners at the 30th percentile and below" and change the index from wage growth to inflation for everyone else. That would erase 82 percent of the 75-year shortfall—more than half of the deficit over an infinite time horizon.

Alternatively, according to the actuary, we could increase the normal retirement age three months per year starting for those aged 62 in 2017 until it reaches 70 in 2032 and increase it one month every two years thereafter. Deficit reduction? Sixty percent over 75 years; 48 percent, infinite horizon.

Also on the list: "Apply the 12.4 percent payroll tax rate on earnings above $250,000 starting in 2015," says the actuary's report, "and tax all earnings once the current-law taxable maximum exceeds $250,000." That change would eliminate 75 percent of the infinite horizon deficit. Just phasing in, over the next decade, an increase in the taxable maximum such that 90 percent of earnings would be subject to the payroll tax would eliminate a third of the infinite deficit.

Combine a few of these changes, and Social Security insecurity would become a bugaboo of the past.

IS THE FUTURE 75 YEARS
AWAY—OR FOREVER?

Larry and I differ in another way about Social Security's solvency. He insists that we use not 75 years, as most do, but an infinite time horizon when talking about the system's "unfunded liabilities"—its promises of future benefits for which insufficient money has been set aside in the trust fund. By that measure, the system is a depth-defying $23 trillion or so underwater, though I hope I've made clear by now that talking about the trust fund is foolish, practically speaking.

But let me again quote Alicia Munnell, when confronted with Larry's number and infinite time horizon. Her reply?

"When I'm talking about Larry Kotlikoff, whom I love, I need to separate some things that I agree with him on and some things that I don't agree with him on. I think using this trillion-dollar number is not very helpful at all because big numbers happen over a long period of time and other stuff also happens over a long period of time." In other words, things will change—a lot sooner than before we reach the end of the universe.

SOCIAL SECURITY WAS DESIGNED TO PROTECT US, NOT TO DRIVE US MAD

In the dogged struggle between Larry and myself, there has been one further bone of contention: Social Security's supposedly damnable complexity.

Larry likes to say that Social Security was designed to drive us mad. To the contrary, I think it's mad to say such a thing, even in jest.

I can hardly deny that Social Security, like every other piece of complex policy in a large, complicated, and highly politicized economy, has evolved in ways that are often confusing—bedeviling, even. But so has the tax code. The criminal justice code. Dodd-Frank. Ever scrutinize the Americans with Disabilities Act?

And it isn't just a modern American phenomenon. Ever take a look at Blackstone's four-volume *Commentaries on the Laws of England*, published in the eighteenth century? Ever wonder why the Old Testament needed the six-thousand-page Talmud to be interpreted? Why the Scholastics argued endlessly over issues of Christian faith (though never, it turns out, over how many angels could dance on the head of a pin)?

Like any thoughtful polity, we're a nation of laws and rights. They're constantly changing with changing times, with changing mores, changing technology. In the process, they become more fine-tuned, more complicated, more gamed, more byzantine. As a result, they're frequently infuriating. Simplification would be great and often, perhaps, a stunning improvement. Even with the help of TurboTax, however, filing my taxes remains a humiliating hassle. It's simply a fantasy that laws and policy can be made simple.

Tell your neighbor that the right of way through your property is too damned complex to figure out so she had just as well forget about it. Tell someone whose baby has been poisoned by lead paint from an unregulated toy made in China that federal product safety regulations are too damn complicated. Tell the stockholders of a corporation that's gone bankrupt through ledger-de-main that securities law is impenetrable.

American society is often accused of being overly litigious. But is there so much litigation because our rules are *deliberately* complicated? Might it not be that they are complicated because of our insistence on "the rule of law," which is America's widely heralded international competitive advantage? Because of our insistence on the ever more finely tuned checks and balances that have made the United States, for all its infamous flaws, the most stable long-standing democracy on earth?

People love to quote Dick the Butcher from Shakespeare's *Henry VI, Part II*, as he was mapping out the road to utopia: "The first thing we do, let's kill all the lawyers."

But mightn't lawyers be a function of size, pluralism, and profoundly rights-based traditions? *Of course* there are special interests—or "factions," as they were called at the founding of the republic in the Federalist Papers. But isn't that the price we pay for liberty? As James Madison put it in the most famous of the papers, Federalist 10: "Liberty is to faction what air is to fire, an ailment without which it instantly expires. But it could not be less folly to abolish liberty, which is essential to political life, because it nourishes faction, than it would be to wish the annihilation of air, which is essential to animal life, because it imparts to fire its destructive agency."

You want *simple*? Well, Social Security started out simply enough. Almost no women or minorities, excluded because they dominated job categories not covered by the original act, as were workers in agriculture, domestic service, and many teachers, nurses, hospital employees, librarians, and social workers. Moreover, if you were still working, you couldn't collect benefits.

So we adjusted, adapted, and modified the law and in the process, made it more complex. Just two years after the Social Security Act came the recession of 1937, even at the time blamed on the government having cut back on its New Deal largesse and the austerity effects of the $2 billion that had been collected in Social Security taxes that were then sitting in a reserve fund—an actual "lockbox"—that is, not being spent.

So, to reprime the economy, Social Security benefits were moved forward two years—to 1940 instead of 1942—and benefits increased for everyone eligible for them. And there was more *complexity* to come. *Family* protection also became a priority, so in 1939, other amendments to the Social Security Act added wives, elderly widows, and dependent survivors of covered male workers. If a married wage-earning woman's own benefit was less than 50 percent of her husband's, she was now treated as a wife, not a worker, and got the 50 percent. Thus the birth of the spousal benefit . . . and of yet more complexity.

There's one more dynamic in a competitive market system like ours: people are forever trying to push the envelope, test the rules, game the system. That's what Larry's hypothetical character in Chapter 8, William H. Gigolo, exemplifies. As a result, Social Security plays the never-ending game of cat-and-mouse that is the fate of all regulators.

Let me conclude with a journalistic anecdote.

More than twenty-five years ago, I called a Wall Street hotshot about whom I'd read in the *Wall Street Journal*—for a story that I never wound up doing (too complicated to explain). It had to do with a technique in which shares of stock were converted into debt. The debt would then be tax deductible, reducing corporate profits and, therefore, corporate taxes—in effect, converting the tax payments into interest payments. Could such financial engineering be good for the American economy circa 1988, when leveraged buyouts—since rechristened "private equity"—were taking corporate America by storm and depriving the U.S. Treasury of perhaps billions of tax dollars in a time of ballooning federal deficits?

"Hey look," the very frank Wall Street big shot said to me, "if you've got a problem with profits being transformed into interest payments and thus depriving the government of taxes, the answer is simple: just rewrite the law to eliminate the tax deductibility of interest."

"Oh sure," I scoffed. "That's easy to do!"

"It *would* be if you gave the job to me and six of my smartest guys," the fellow shot back defiantly. "We could write an airtight law in months."

And then followed one of the most memorable questions and answers of my reportorial career.

"When you go back into private practice," I asked, "could you beat the law that you'd written?"

His answer, as God is my witness: "I should certainly hope so."

Can we simplify? I suppose. Larry has his own so-called Purple Plan. It is well thought out. And few, if any, people on earth know more about the mechanics of the Social Security benefits system than Larry. He claims the plan is simplicity itself. And, as he wrote in a column on our PBS website: "We don't need to keep the current system around for another day, let alone another 80 years. Were I in charge, I'd freeze it, pay off, over time, everything it now owes, and replace it with a *modern version* of Social Security that's fully funded, fair, simple, and efficient."

From whom have I heard promises like that before? Just about every politician ever.

But I don't think I'm skeptical just because I'm a journalist who's kicked around for decades. Many Americans have *good reason* for keeping the Social Security system as it is. Many, in fact, want to improve it by *addition*. And the status quo isn't just a function of bureaucrats looking to protect their turf, protected, as most bureaucracies are, by rules that reward fidelity over competence. Because of the antigovernment bias so stoked by conservatives, the bureaucrats in sectors like Social Security are woefully understaffed and over-matched, as we've pointed out again and again.

The point is, Social Security has evolved as our country has. We write rules. People complain about their lack of fairness and clarity. So we expand the rules, make exceptions to them. That's because we're a large, pluralistic democracy. Those with a stake in the rules put up a fight. That's what they're *expected* to do. The administrators respond, just as *they* are expected to.

To the extent that Social Security is a hard-to-navigate system, it's due at least in part to our constant attempt to balance what we feel is fair against what we think we can afford—and because writing laws and regulations is hard, never-ending work.

Let me end with this promise: the next time I hear someone railing about the complexity of our Social Security system, or our legal system, or our regulatory system, I will simply ask: so how come just about everyone in the world wants to immigrate to America? Is it just the weather?

LARRY

Our Social Security system is a disgrace, not in its objectives or in the tremendous help it has provided older people over the years, but in the way it's been designed and the way it's been financed.

Its complexity is beyond belief. The formula for the Social Security benefits of a married spouse involves ten complex mathematical functions, one of which is in four dimensions! It leads all kinds of people to make all kinds of mistakes in deciding when to take benefits and what benefits to take. And the good folks at Social Security will far too often tell you things that are one hundred percent untrue with one hundred and fifty percent conviction. That's why we wrote this book—to help people get what's theirs. The new law makes the Social Security benefit collection decision even more difficult. You now have to figure out if and to what extent you have been grandfathered. And if you haven't been grandparented, there is no full spousal or full divorced spousal benefit to tide you over until you take your retirement benefit at age 70. So the economic decision about waiting to collect and how to deal with the cash flow issues associated with waiting has become more difficult.

Paul, I love you dearly, but you almost fell victim to the system's caprice to the tune of $50,000. I wonder how you would feel today had we never discussed your Social Security strategy and had you then discovered that you'd lost upward of $50,000 of benefits you'd paid for but didn't know about.

Would you be saying, "No problem. This is the price of democracy"?

I think you'd be outraged, and properly so. But there are people who are losing out every day on their benefits because they can't figure out what they are actually owed and the best way to get what's theirs.

The truth is, our democracy was and is very deeply flawed. Social Security's complexity and fiscal condition confirm this. Democracy is collective choice by the people. But having indecipherable institutions, be they our Social Security system, our tax system, our health-care system, or our financial system, deprives the people of the knowledge they need to make choices. Instead it leaves social choice not to the people but to the bureaucrats, who get to decide what's best. The way the new Social Security law was passed is about as good an example as one can have of the incredibly nondemocratic processes that suffuse "America's democracy."

I say bureaucrats rather than elected officials because our representatives are also at the mercy of the bureaucrats. Indeed, there is, I'd wager, not a single member of Congress with detailed knowledge of Social Security's 2,728 rules or its tens of thousands of rules about those rules. And when it comes to Social Security, the big picture is the sum of all the small pictures.

To be clear, this doesn't mean, for example, that the new Social Security provisions were written by someone working at Social Security. Indeed, top officials at Social Security seemed to be as surprised as anyone by the new provisions. My strong sense is that some congressional staffer with a law degree who thought he understood what he was doing wrote the changes to the law. Had Phil and I not pointed out in print some of the most glaring features, including the fact that checks would stop in six months for certain households, the grandparenting amendments would probably never have been enacted.

Bureaucracy is not a sine qua non of democracy. New Zealand is a pretty good democracy from everything I can discern. Its social security system has one rule: you reach retirement age and you get a monthly check—the same check as everyone else.

I'm not advocating New Zealand's system for the United States. Instead, I'm proposing we freeze the current Social Security system and replace it with the Purple Social Security Plan presented at www.thepurplesocialsecurityplan.org, which is a remarkably simple, progressive, compulsory saving system. Phil views me as politically naïve for proposing radical reforms like this. But if you look across countries and over time, you see huge changes by governments in their old-age pension systems. And, gee, we just saw a huge, in many ways unimaginable change included in the federal budget bill signed by President Obama on November 2, 2015. So who's naïve?

Radical change in our Social Security system is inevitable for the simple reason that the system is broke—indeed, in worse fiscal shape than Detroit's pensions when that city declared bankruptcy.

My evidence for this?

It's the $26 trillion infinite-horizon fiscal gap shown in table IVF1 of the 2015 Social Security Trustees Report. This present value shortfall is net of the system's trust fund and is almost $1 trillion larger than the system's fiscal gap reported in 2014. The table shows that Social Security is 31 percent underfunded. Paul, you and Alicia Munnell, whom I love dearly, may not approve of looking out to the "end of the universe" in measuring today's Social Security unfunded liability. But that characterization is off base for the simple reason that the fiscal gap is a *present value* measure that more heavily *discounts* the system's future cash flows the farther out they are in the future. The reason we need to look out to the infinite-horizon fiscal gap is due to an economics labeling problem. This problem exists because government can label its receipts and expenditures in a myriad of ways, each of which changes the 75-year fiscal gap, on which you and Alicia are focused, but leaves the infinite horizon fiscal gap unchanged. The economics labeling problem is the reason that the Inform Act has been endorsed by more than 1,200 economists, including 17 Nobel laureates (see www.theinformact.org).

The Inform Act mandates infinite-horizon fiscal gap accounting by government agencies for the entire fiscal enterprise. My own estimate based on the Congressional Budget Office's Alternative Fiscal Scenario Projections puts the country's overall fiscal gap at $199 trillion for 2015. This is 53 percent of the present value of all future federal taxes, so our federal government, taken as a whole, is 53 percent underfunded. Stated differently, we need a 53 percent hike in *all* federal taxes to permit our federal government to meet all its expenditure commitments. And if one focuses just on Social Security, the requisite immediate and permanent Social Security FICA tax hike to ensure that Social Security pays all scheduled benefits is 31 percent!

Paul, I know you love your children and grandchildren more than life itself. But what you seem to be ignoring is that paying for what the government spends is, generationally speaking, a zero-sum game. The less our generation pays, the more your kids and grandkids will have to pay; mine, too. And we are moving full speed ahead to leave our kids and grandkids with fiscal bills that are far, far beyond their capacity to pay. This transformation of the American dream into the American nightmare is a terrible act of immortality, which, quite frankly, you, Phil, and Alicia appear to be condoning. Yes, Paul, I know you and Phil feel this will never happen and that small adjustments will be made and that all will be fine. This is Panglossian in the extreme, as a quick glance at Argentina's century-long economic decline confirms. Yes, things that can't go on will stop. But they will stop too late. The fact that the Social Security actuaries raised their, *not my*, measure of the system's unfunded liability by almost $1 trillion in one year shows how quickly things are changing and why small, slow changes won't work any better for Social Security than they did for Detroit.

SOCIAL SECURITY VERBATIM

THE DECK MAY APPEAR SLIGHTLY STACKED

"Even if we caused the [benefits] overpayment, you must show that you are without fault."

ALL QUOTES FROM OFFICIAL SOCIAL SECURITY RULES

PHIL

Larry has interesting ideas for replacing Social Security with a fairer and better program. They're never going to happen. We're not going to replace an eighty-year-old program that has become an enormous bureaucracy, with rules to match, and that touches the lives of virtually every American.

Can you imagine, for example, that tax reform—if it ever happens—would include replacing or reinventing the Internal Revenue Service? The IRS is a hundred-plus-year-old creature that has become the giant squid of bureaucracies. Our tax system is so complicated that an army of lawyers, accountants, tax experts, and other financial advisers has become necessary to comply with provisions that are impenetrable to untrained eyes.

And, unfortunately, you can add health care to the list of essential components of an advanced society that are increasingly too complicated to be understood by the public they are supposed to serve.

Such is the nature of national government. It is a major failing of the United States. It is a source of rising public anger and disaffection toward government that weakens our democracy and provides oxygen to the fires that are stoked by antigovernment extremists. It debases political discourse and puts needed political compromises out of reach. This situation is not about the welfare state, nor is it an indictment of the aims of these programs. It is an inescapable truth of complexities—of the systems we've built to govern ourselves, of the technology that has evolved to do so, and of the underlying challenges our social, economic, and political problems present.

LET'S KEEP SOCIAL SECURITY
MOSTLY THE WAY IT IS

Still, short of a societal collapse of dystopian proportions, I hope not to see a Social Security program in fifty years that looks a whole lot different from the one we have today. And while Larry and other brilliant and civic-minded reformers might lament this observation, I do not.

We've spent an entire book telling you about the complexities and shortcomings of Social Security. But it's appropriate here to take a big step back from these details, see the larger picture, and, just perhaps, gain some perspective.

Social Security is paying our benefits at the rate of roughly $900 billion a year. It does so very efficiently and with a cost structure that would be impossible for any private company to match.

It is an economic lifeline for most older Americans. Today, people who are 65 and older have the *lowest* poverty rate of any age group in the nation. Before Social Security was adopted, older citizens had the nation's *highest* poverty rate. It's not the tooth fairy that caused this hugely important shift. It's been Social Security and, for the past fifty years, Medicare.

Social Security retirement and disability benefits (not including the SSI program) have been self-funded and have not added a penny to the U.S. budget deficit. I'm going to spend some time on this topic. It's important and, further, I encounter many well-meaning critics of Social Security who rail about the way it's added to unsustainable budget deficits.

SOCIAL SECURITY AND
BUDGET DEFICITS

Major changes were made to Social Security in 1983 as part of the nonpartisan commission led by then future Federal Reserve Board chair Alan Greenspan. The baby boomers were a big deal even thirty-plus years ago. We knew then what today's age wave would look like. And so the 1983 changes created (among other things and not always on purpose) a funding system for Social Security that has built big surpluses to prepare for the years when millions of boomers would be taking Social Security benefits.

These program surpluses are invested in a special series of U.S. Treasury securities, which have generated interest income to the program. Many books have been written about whether Social Security would have been better off placing its surpluses in nongovernment stocks and bonds. That's an interesting discussion, to be sure, but the point here is that Social Security did not fritter away its surpluses. That work was done by a succession of shortsighted Congresses and presidents, who spent the dollars they received from Social Security on other government programs. This is hardly the fault of Social Security, and blaming it for Washington's fiscal besottedness is way off base.

Social Security's self-sufficiency has been essential to its success. Whatever we do, it would be an enormous mistake to commingle its funding with the rest of the federal budget, and thereby expose it to annual political popularity contests. This has been, in fact, what has happened to the Social Security Administration's annual operating budget in recent years. The result has been huge cuts in staffing, a reduction in the number of Social Security offices around the country, and a reduction in hours that the remaining offices are open to the public. It is just madness to have done these things to the agency just as its workload was poised to soar, courtesy of the front end of the boomer generation turning 65, at a rate averaging 10,000 a day during the period 2011–29.

The SSA has responded with a big push to move its services online, to call centers, and even to remote video feeds. What choice does it have? But as we explained earlier, online tools have significant limitations. The public served by the agency does not use online tools very much and is not about to become digitally savvy anytime soon. Even if it raised its online IQ a lot, the fact remains that millions and millions of Social Security claiming decisions are too complicated to be made using online tools. So, whatever else we do about Social Security, we must improve the agency's ability to serve the public and to communicate more clearly.

THE HUBRIS OF FORECASTING THE FUTURE

The standard for evaluating the financial soundness of Social Security and any possible reforms of the program is to evaluate their impact over the coming 75 years. There is nothing magical about 75-year time frames. This is just the one we use for Social Security. Larry and a thousand other economists have signed on to an effort to use an infinite time horizon for looking at the budget implications of Social Security and other government programs. This proposal is worth serious discussion but such debates rarely happen these days in Washington, and this one is no exception.

It turns out that the life span of the 1983 changes will, instead, be closer to 50 years than 75. Program payouts have been sweetened without compensating revenue increases. The projections of economic growth and inflation made 35 years ago have not been flawless. Projections of retirement and claiming patterns were also fallible. And then there were inflation and recession and sluggish growth and, well, you get the picture. Larry says those 1983 reforms fell far short of being an honest look at the ensuing 75 years. Today's huge pressures on old-age benefits caused by the baby boom were well known in 1983, and the reforms could have more honestly anticipated these pressures by some combination of revenue increases and benefit adjustments. But selling even limited reform was a tough task and there was no stomach for more severe changes. As Jack Nicholson famously said in *A Few Good Men*, "You can't handle the truth!"

Similar shortcomings are likely in any politically feasible Social Security reforms today that look at the 75-year window ending around 2090. But it's been known for years and years that Social Security needs adjustments in its mix of benefits and revenues to be placed again on a self-sustaining path. These changes must be gradual to avoid ruining the retirement plans and dreams of people now receiving benefits and approaching retirement age. As an example, recall that the program's Full Retirement Age will not begin rising from 66 to 67 until 2020—a rule change made more than three decades ago. This is a financial supertanker, and its course should not be changed abruptly.

Unfortunately, the longer Congress dithers over changing Social Security, the more severe such changes will have to be to prevent the program from running out of money. I pray we have no more surprise changes to the program as happened in November 2015. As this new edition persuasively argues, this is not the way to restore either the program or, especially, public confidence that it will be there for future generations.

Still, there are many, many plausible scenarios for reforming Social Security without either breaking the bank or simply hiking payroll taxes on high-income earners. Higher earners should pay more, but those increases shouldn't be the only or even largest source of program revenue changes. The SSA is not the IRS, nor should it be. The broad public support for the program is, in large measure, due to its near universality. Social Security benefits are already highly progressive, meaning that low-income recipients get payments that replace a much higher percentage of their pre-retirement incomes than do high-income beneficiaries. It's possible to make the program self-supporting through a broad array of benefit, timing, and payroll tax changes.

Among these, we must acknowledge the cumulative and continuing effect of longevity, but not for everyone. Extending the FRA to 68, 69, and even 70 over the next 30 to 40 years makes sense, but people with low levels of education and low incomes are not participating fully in the longevity revolution. The support we provide them at the earliest claiming age of 62 should be strengthened, not weakened. So, anything we do to "reform" Social Security must recognize that longevity gains are not being enjoyed equally.

WE NEED TO FIX 401(K) PLANS, TOO

Lastly, any effort to address the future of Social Security also must address the future of the nation's private retirement savings industry. The 401(k) and its related tax-advantaged retirement savings vehicles have not worked well. Too few people have participated, they have saved too little, and their investment decisions have been unwise. Major changes have been made to 401(k)s in recent years, and today's plans are producing big improvements on all fronts—participation, savings rates, and investment performance. But these better results, by and large, are limited to higher-earning employees. The people who need the help the least are thus getting the lion's share of the tax benefits of these accounts, while half of the nation's workers can't even participate in a 401(k), and many of those who could simply do not make enough money to do so.

Private retirement firms have defended their turf aggressively and there is clearly a role for these plans. However, we need to have an honest and serious debate about how we use tax dollars to promote private retirement savings. If file-and-suspend strategies were seen as undesirable upper-income benefits, can't the same be said about tax-deferred retirement accounts?

Instead of cutting Social Security, we need to have a *very* serious debate about increasing its role. Again, as we've noted in *Get What's Yours*, Social Security was never designed to be a provider of most of an older person's retirement income. But it has become so for most retirees. We need to recognize this reality as well as the limited success of the private retirement savings industry.

What makes more sense—an expansion of a voluntary retirement savings program that hasn't worked well, or expansion of Social Security, which has worked well, is already available to nearly all workers, is very inexpensive to administer, and offers guaranteed payments that include inflation protection?

SOCIAL SECURITY AND YOUNGER GENERATIONS

Make no mistake. There is no free lunch here. Expanding Social Security would mean higher payroll taxes for ordinary working Americans and their employers. It would limit the growth of private savings and investment plans. It would represent further nationalization of our retirement system. All of this bothers me a lot, but not nearly as much as the prospect of millions of Americans facing longer lives with insufficient financial resources to enjoy them. And that is clearly the future we will have unless we make major improvements in our retirement programs.

It's also a future that will be felt primarily by younger generations. Paul, Larry, and I already know what our retirements will look like, at least in terms of our retirement incomes. Changing Social

Security will mean very little if anything to us or to most people already in their 50s and 60s. But it will mean a lot to those who are younger.

The health of Social Security is really a younger person's game, and people under 40 overwhelmingly believe it's game over for them. Opinion polls show that younger people don't believe Social Security will be there when they retire. So, my last requirement for changing the program is to make sure that whatever we do, younger generations can once again feel confident that they can plan their lives and their retirements around a solid Social Security program.

ACKNOWLEDGMENTS

I thank our editor, Bob Bender, and agent, Alice Martell, for so adroitly and gracefully shepherding the publication of this book. And I thank Boston University for its enduring and significant support of my research and efforts to make my research of direct value to the public, the private sector, and policy makers. I thank my wife, Bridget Jourgensen, for her steadfast support in what was an intense period of writing.

—LAURENCE KOTLIKOFF

The responsibility for the contents of this book rests solely with its authors. But there are many researchers and journalists whose work has helped me immensely in understanding the issues addressed in *Get What's Yours*. Special thanks to Nancy Altman, codirector of Social Security Works and cochair of the Strengthen Social Security project; David C. John, deputy director for the Retirement Security Project at the Brookings Institution and a senior strategic policy adviser with AARP's Public Policy Institute; and Eugene Steuerle at the Urban Institute. Many thanks also to the Center for Retirement Research at Boston College, directed by Alicia Munnell, which has produced an invaluable stream of research and clear analysis about Social Security and its many claiming challenges. That center, the University of Michigan Retirement Research Center, and the National Bureau of Economic Research make up the Retirement Research Consortium, which has conducted extensive research on Social Security (much of it funded by the agency). The Employee Benefit Research Institute is a treasure trove of data and insights on retirement topics. Reports from the Congressional Budget Office and Government Accountability Office are must-reads. Morningstar is the gold standard of consumer-oriented research about retirement investments. Financial service firms regularly churn out solid research on individual retirement savings and spending habits; Fidelity and Vanguard stand out, but there are many, many others doing terrific work here.

Kimberly Castro, managing editor for money and health at *U.S. News &*

World Report, provided time and support for my own articles about Social Security from 2008 to 2013. More recently, Penelope Wang, editor at large at *Money*, has been equally generous and supportive of my writing there. I am thankful to them, and also appreciative of the efforts by other journalists who track important retirement and Social Security topics. There is a cadre of experienced journalists who follow these topics. With apologies for the inevitable omissions. I have been a faithful reader of Emily Brandon, *U.S. News & World Report*; Scott Burns, a longtime financial journalist and friend who later built his own asset management company, AssetBuilder; Mary Beth Franklin, *Investment News*; Michael Hiltzik, *Los Angeles Times*; Stan Hinden, AARP; Mark Miller, Reuters and Morningstar; Janet Novack, *Forbes*; Robert Powell, *MarketWatch*; and Anne Tergesen, *Wall Street Journal* (and before her, Kelly Greene, who left the *Journal* in 2014).

The Social Security Administration is, far and away, the most extensive and valuable resource for information about its programs. It has a deep and accessible website. It posts research and reports online, including its rules and its detailed Program Operating Manual System (POMS). It provides upward of 100 forms on its website and is moving as quickly as it can to place more and more of its public communications capabilities online. Among federal bureaucracies, Social Security stands out for being transparent and accessible. Still, *Get What's Yours* would have been a more complete book had the Social Security Administration seen fit to allow me to interview its experts and managers. For reasons never provided to me, it declined to do so. Given the complexity of Social Security, there is a wealth of knowledge that officials could have imparted. Public information officer Dorothy Clark did respond dutifully to many of my questions. She also declined to respond to many other questions I posed, without explaining why. Her colleague Kia Anderson, who left the agency in 2014, was also most helpful. Thanks to them both. Despite wanting more access, I came to understand the agency's sensitivity to its public statements and its reluctance to provide comments. Nearly every American who works or has worked during the past eighty years, not to mention their family members, is affected by Social Security rules. Any public comment by an authorized representative of the agency literally can affect—and potentially confuse and alarm—millions of people.

—PHILIP MOELLER

As for me, I'm grateful for those in the acknowledgments above, to the coauthors who wrote them, and to *PBS NewsHour* (originally *The MacNeil/ Lehrer NewsHour*), which has employed me for more than thirty years now, giving me unparalleled encouragement—and ample time—to cover the news from an economics perspective. The program also encouraged me to initiate an online page—Making Sen$e—where Larry first posted on Social Security in the summer of 2012 and where he has generously answered viewer questions every Monday since. The Making Sen$e website, as well as our coverage over the past nine years, was made possible by the support of the Sloan Foundation. And, of course, viewers like you, though I trust you won't mind that I don't acknowledge each of you by name.

—PAUL SOLMAN

GLOSSARY

Average Indexed Monthly Earnings (AIME)

When Social Security computes an insured worker's benefit, it first adjusts or "indexes" his or her earnings to reflect the change in general wage levels that occurred during the worker's years of employment. Such indexation ensures that a worker's future benefits reflect the general rise in the standard of living that occurred during his or her working lifetime. Up to 35 years of earnings are needed to compute Average Indexed Monthly Earnings. If a worker has more than 35 covered years, Social Security chooses those years with the highest indexed earnings, sums such indexed earnings, and divides the total amount by the total number of months in those years. It then rounds the resulting average amount down to the next-lower dollar amount. The result is the AIME. If a person has fewer than 35 years of covered earnings, Social Security takes the actual years, enters 0 for the rest, and divides by 420 (the number of months in 35 years).

Bend Point

Bend points divide your AIME into portions that contribute varying percentages to your PIA: 90 percent of the lowest portion under the first bend point, 32 percent of the middle portion between the bend points, and 15 percent of the amount above the second bend point. The dollar levels of these bend points are adjusted for inflation. In 2016, they are $856 and $5,157. A description of how bend points are used is found below in the entry for Primary Insurance Amount (PIA).

Child Benefit

A child can claim child insurance benefits on a parent's record if the child is dependent on that parent as defined by Social Security and if the child is not married. The child also must either be under 18, or be no older than 19 and a full-time elementary or secondary school student. The parent on whose record the claim is based must be entitled to disability or retirement insurance. The child insurance benefit is equal to 50 percent of the insured parent's PIA if the insured parent is currently entitled to a retirement benefit.

Child-in-Care Spousal Benefit

Having a child in care may allow you to claim spousal benefits if you have not yet reached 62 and may also make you eligible for mother's and father's insurance. You have a child in care if you have parental control, as defined by Social Security, over a child who is under 16 or who is 16 or older and is disabled.

Child Survivor Benefit

A child is eligible for a surviving child insurance on a deceased parent's record if all the conditions to receive child insurance benefits are met and the child was also dependent on the deceased parent and the deceased parent was either fully or currently insured at the time of death. The surviving child insurance benefit is equal to 75 percent of the deceased parent's PIA at the time of death.

Cost of Living Adjustment (COLA)

COLAs are applied to years after you become eligible to receive benefits in order to maintain the purchasing power of retirement benefits. They become effective in December of each year and reflect the rise in the Consumer Price Index (CPI) for urban wage earners during the 12 months ending the previous September. There was no COLA for 2016 because the CPI declined during the measurement period.

Covered Earnings

These are the maximum amount of wages on which you pay Social Security taxes. Earnings covered by Social Security are those for which you paid Social Security taxes, either by having them withheld from your paycheck or by paying Social Security taxes on earnings from self-employment. The ceiling for covered earnings rises each year to adjust for inflation. The ceiling in 2016 is $118,500.

Death Benefit

A onetime payment of $255 paid in addition to any monthly survivor benefits that are due. This benefit is paid only to a widow(er) or minor children.

Deeming

The deeming provision states that if you are eligible for both reduced retirement and reduced spouse's benefits—meaning you've filed for them before your Full Retirement Age (FRA)—then you cannot restrict your application to just one of these types of benefits. By filing for either benefit, you are deemed by law to have filed for both types of benefits. You will collect an amount equal to or close to the greater of the two benefits.

Delayed Retirement Credit (DRC)

Between Full Retirement Age and age 70, monthly benefits will rise by 8 percent a year plus the COLA for people who defer taking their retirement benefit.

Disabled Child Insurance Benefit

A child can claim disabled child insurance benefits on a parent's record if the child meets all of the conditions to receive child insurance benefits and if he or she is 18 or older and under a disability as defined by Social Security. This disability must also have begun before the child reached age 22. The disabled child insurance benefit is equal to 50 percent of the insured parent's PIA if the insured parent is currently eligible for a retirement benefit. The benefit amount might be reduced by the Family Maximum Benefit (FMB; see below). The benefit amount also might be reduced if a disabled child is eligible for a disability or retirement insurance benefit based on his or her own record, in which case only the amount by which the child's monthly benefit rate exceeds his or her retirement or disability insurance amount is paid as the disabled child insurance benefit.

Divorced Spouse's Insurance Benefit

You can claim divorced spouse's insurance benefits if your ex-spouse is currently entitled to retirement or disability insurance benefits. You must be single and 62 or over and you must have been married to your ex-spouse for at least 10 years. Also, you cannot claim this benefit if your PIA exceeds or equals one-half of your ex-spouse's PIA and you are currently entitled to retirement or disability insurance. If your ex-spouse is not currently entitled to retirement or disability insurance benefits, but he or she has attained age 62 and is fully insured, you can become independently entitled to benefits on your ex-spouse's record if you meet all of the other requirements in the preceding paragraph and have been divorced for at least two continuous years.

Divorced Widow(er)'s Insurance Benefit

You may be eligible for divorced widow(er)'s insurance benefits if you were married to your deceased ex-spouse for at least 10 years. You must also be age 60 or over, or at least age 50 but under 60 and meet the disability requirements as defined by Social Security. Your deceased ex-spouse must also have been fully insured; you must be single; and you must not be entitled to a retirement insurance benefit equaling or exceeding your deceased ex-spouse's PIA. The same limitations as above apply to divorced widow(er)'s benefits if your deceased ex-spouse was ever entitled to reduced retirement benefits.

Early Retirement Reduction

People who claim Social Security benefits before reaching FRA are subject to a range of potentially large and permanent reductions depending on their claiming ages and the type of benefit involved. The table below illustrates the effect of early retirement for both a retired worker and the spousal benefits to which his or her spouse is eligible. For this illustration, Social Security used a $1,000 PIA.

Year of birth[a]	Normal (or full) retirement	Number of reduction months[b]	Monthly Primary Amount	Percent Reduction[c]	Monthly Spouse Amount	Percent reduction[d]
1937 or earlier	65	36	$800	20.00	$375	25.00
1938	65 and 2 months	38	791	20.83	370	25.83
1939	65 and 4 months	40	783	21.67	366	26.67
1940	65 and 6 months	42	775	22.50	362	27.50
1941	65 and 8 months	44	766	23.33	358	28.33
1942	65 and 10 months	46	758	24.17	354	29.17
1943–1954	66	48	750	25.00	350	30.00
1955	66 and 2 months	50	741	25.83	345	30.83
1956	66 and 4 months	52	733	26.67	341	31.67
1957	66 and 6 months	54	725	27.50	337	32.50
1958	66 and 8 months	56	716	28.33	333	33.33
1959	66 and 10 months	58	708	29.17	329	34.17
1960 and later	67	60	700	30.00	325	35.00

a. If you are born on January 1, use the prior year of birth.

b. Applies only if you are born on the 2nd of the month; otherwise the number of reduction months is one less than the number shown.

c. Reduction applied to PIA ($1,000 in this example). The percentage reduction is ⅚ of 1 percent per month for the first 36 months and $5/12$ of 1 percent for each additional month.

d. Reduction applied to $500, which is 50 percent of the PIA in this example. The percentage reduction is $25/36$ of 1 percent per month for the first 36 months and $5/12$ of 1 percent for each additional month.

Earnings Test

People collecting benefits who continue to work are subject to an Earnings Test until they've reached Full Retirement Age (FRA). Social Security withholds benefits if the worker's earnings exceed a certain level, called a retirement Earnings Test exempt amount. One of two different exempt amounts applies—a lower amount in years before the year you attain FRA and a higher amount in the year you attain FRA. These exempt amounts generally increase annually with increases in the national Average Wage Index. It's important to note, however, that benefit reductions caused by the Earnings Test usually will be restored once the worker reaches FRA. At that age, his or her monthly benefit will be increased permanently to account for the months in which benefits were withheld.

For people attaining FRA after 2016, the annual exempt amount in 2016 is $15,720. For people attaining FRA in 2016, the annual exempt amount is $41,880. This higher exempt amount applies only to earnings made in months prior to the month of FRA attainment. Social Security withholds $1 in benefits for every $2 of earnings in excess of the lower exempt amount. It withholds $1 in benefits for every $3 of earnings in excess of the higher exempt amount. Earnings in or after the month the worker reaches FRA do not count toward the retirement test.

Family Maximum Benefit (FMB)

The FMB is a ceiling on the total Social Security benefits that may be collected based on a single worker's earnings record. It is not a fixed percentage but varies depending on the worker's earnings and even the kinds of benefits involved. If your Primary Insurance Amount (PIA) is very low, your FMB will be 150 percent of your PIA. With a somewhat higher PIA, the FMB rises to 187 percent of your PIA. Then the multiple drops, ending up at 175 percent of your PIA. Auxiliary benefits—those available to other family members—are subtracted from the worker's PIA and thus are 50 percent of the very-low-income worker's PIA, 87 percent of the moderate-income worker's PIA, and 75 percent of the high earner's PIA.

Second, if the worker takes her benefits early, say, at 62, her retirement benefit will be reduced to 75 percent of her PIA. In this case, the most that the family, including the worker, would receive is 75 percent of her PIA (her reduced retirement benefit) plus 50 percent of her PIA—the most left over for the spouse and kids after subtracting the PIA, not her actual benefit received from the FMB. In this case, the total amount the very-low-earner family, including the earner herself, can receive is only 125 percent of the worker's PIA.

Next, suppose the worker is a moderate earner and has a FMB equal to 187 percent of her PIA. Further assume this worker waits until 70 to collect her retirement benefit. In this case her own retirement benefit is 1.32 times her PIA and the maximum Auxiliary Benefits are 87 percent of her PIA. Hence, the largest amount the moderate earner family, including the earner herself, could receive is 219 percent of the worker's PIA.

The formula used to compute the FMB is similar to that used to compute the PIA. The formula sums four separate percentages of portions of the worker's PIA. For 2016, these portions are the first $1,093, the amount between $1,093 and $1,578, the amount between $1,578 and $2,058, and the amount exceeding $2,058. These dollar amounts are the "bend points" of the FMB formula. For the family of a worker who became age 62 or died in 2015 before attaining age 62, the total amount of benefits payable will be computed so that it does not exceed:

a. 150 percent of the first $1,093 of the worker's PIA, plus
b. 272 percent of the worker's PIA over $1,093 through $1,578, plus
c. 134 percent of the worker's PIA over $1,578 through $2,058, plus
d. 175 percent of the worker's PIA over $2,058.

Full Retirement Age (FRA)

FRA is the age at which a person may first become entitled to full or unreduced retirement benefits. The FRA for those born between 1943 and 1954 is 66. For those born before 1943, it is lower. For cohorts born after 1954, it will gradually rise to age 67 for those born in 1960 or later. (Also called Normal Retirement Age by Social Security.)

Full Retirement Benefit

This is the retirement benefit available to a worker based on his or her own work history, assuming the worker applies for a retirement benefit at their FRA. Social Security also refers to a worker's full retirement benefit as their Primary Insurance Amount.

Government Pension Offset (GPO)

If you receive a pension based on your employment by the U.S. government, state governments, or other political subdivisions not covered by Social Security, then any spouse's, divorced spouse's, widow(er)'s, divorced widow(er)'s, or deemed spouse's benefits may be reduced if you receive pension payments based on that employment. For everyone who began receipt of his or her government pension in December 1984 or later, the GPO reduces your Social Security benefit by two-thirds of the amount of your government pension.

Primary Insurance Amount (PIA)

This is a worker's full retirement benefit. It is calculated via a progressive benefits formula based on your Average Indexed Monthly Earnings. The PIA is the sum of three separate percentages of portions of the AIME (see bend point, above, for further details). For an individual who first becomes eligible for old-age insurance benefits or disability insurance benefits in 2016, his or her PIA will be the sum of:

a. 90 percent of the first bend point of $856 in AIME, plus
b. 32 percent of the second bend point for AIME over $856 and through $5,157, plus
c. 15 percent of AIME in excess of $5,157.

Recomputation of Benefits

Social Security will automatically increase your benefit if warranted. This is most often caused by continued wage earnings after reaching age 60 that qualify to become one of your 35 highest years of earnings included in calculations to determine your AIME, on which your PIA is based. There can be other causes for recomputation, but whatever they are, your PIA might be increased, but will never be decreased. The recomputation becomes effective in January of the year after the earnings were generated. For example, an increased benefit due to a recomputation based on 2015 earnings will first be applied to the payment for January 2016.

Retirement Insurance Benefit Limit (RIB-LIM)

This limit applies to widow(er) benefits claimed on the earnings of spouses who filed for their retirement benefits before reaching FRA. The RIB-LIM computation can be very complex. The benefit you can claim as a widow(er) on your deceased spouse's earnings record is limited to the higher of either 82.5 percent of their retirement benefit at his or her FRA, or the amount your deceased spouse was collecting at the time of death.

Social Security Disability Insurance (SSDI)

SSDI is the program providing monthly benefits to disabled workers and their eligible family members. It is supported by a separate disability insurance trust fund within the Old-Age, Survivors, and Disability Insurance program.

Spousal Insurance Benefit

At FRA, a spouse is eligible for the larger of his retirement benefit based on his own record or half of the retirement benefit his spouse will be eligible for at her FRA based on that spouse's record. (Do not feel bad if you need to read this over again—we've read it a lot!) If the retirement benefit a spouse would receive based on his own record is less than half of the retirement benefit his spouse would receive at her FRA based on that spouse's record, the excess spouse's insurance benefit at FRA is the difference between the retirement benefit a spouse is entitled to and half of the benefit his spouse would receive at FRA. The spousal benefit eligibility rule stipulates that no matter their age, a spouse is not eligible for spouse's benefits until the spouse whose earnings the claim is based on files for his or her retirement benefits. If you are eligible for both reduced retirement and reduced spouse's benefits and you file for either, you will be deemed by law to have applied for both (see deeming, above).

Supplemental Security Income (SSI)

SSI is funded by general tax revenues, not Social Security taxes, and provides monthly cash payments to aged, blind, and disabled people who have limited income and resources. It is administered by the Social Security Administration.

Widow(er)'s Insurance Benefits

If you were married to your deceased spouse at least 9 months and you are 60 or older, or if you are at least age 50 but under 60 and you meet the disability requirements as defined by Social Security, you may be eligible for widow(er)'s benefits. If divorced, you must not have remarried before age 60. Your deceased spouse or ex-spouse must have achieved fully insured status, and you must not be eligible for a retirement insurance benefit that equals or exceeds your deceased spouse's PIA. Your unreduced widow(er)'s benefit is equal to your deceased spouse's PIA at FRA plus any increases to his or her retirement insurance benefit from Delayed Retirement Credits earned by delaying receipt of retirement benefits past his or her FRA. Your widow(er)'s benefit is limited if your deceased spouse claimed retirement benefits early before reaching FRA. (See Retirement Insurance Benefit Limit above for further details.)

Windfall Elimination Provision (WEP)

You will be subject to the WEP if you earned a pension in any job not covered by Social Security and you also have enough Social Security credits for covered quarters due to other employment and are therefore eligible for Social Security retirement benefits. The WEP may reduce your Social Security benefits unless you have worked 30 or more years in covered employment (in jobs that levied Social Security payroll taxes). In 2016, the WEP cannot reduce your monthly Social Security payments by more than $428 or half of your non-covered pension, whichever amount is less.

THE BASICS

EMPLOYMENT AND EARNINGS	
Workers in Old-Age, Survivors, and Disability Insurance covered employment	163 million
Average earnings (2013)	$43,786
Earnings required in 2016 for:	
1 quarter of coverage	$1,260

Earnings Test exempt amounts for 2016:

Under Full Retirement Age for entire year	$15,720
For months before reaching Full Retirement Age in 2015	$41,880

AVERAGE MONTHLY BENEFIT (OCTOBER 2015)

Retired workers

Workers	$1,338
Spouses	$686
Children	$649

Survivors of deceased workers

Nondisabled widow(er)s	$1,284
Disabled widow(er)s	$720
Widowed mothers and fathers	$939
Surviving children	$831
Parents	$1,128

Disabled workers

Disabled Workers	$1,165
Spouses	$318
Children	$350
Cost of Living Adjustment for 2016:	0.0 percent

NUMBER OF BENEFICIARIES (OCTOBER 2015)

OASDI	59.8 million

Old-Age Insurance

Total	42.9 million
Retired workers	40.0 million
Spouse	2.3 million
Child	0.6 million

Survivor Insurance

Total	6.1 million
Widows and widowers	4.1 million

Disability Insurance

Total	10.8 million
Disabled workers	8.9 million

TOTAL BENEFIT PAYMENTS (ANNUALIZED AS OF OCTOBER 2015)

Old-Age, Survivors, and Disability Insurance	$879.8 billion
Old-Age and Survivors Insurance	$747.2 billion
Disability Insurance	$132.6 billion

TAX RATES

5.30 percent of covered payroll each for employee and employer for retirement insurance.

0.90 percent of covered payroll each for employee and employer for disability insurance.

1.45 percent of TOTAL payroll each for employee and employer for Medicare Part A (hospital) insurance. High-income households pay additional 0.9 percent Medicare tax mandated by Affordable Care Act.

Total is 15.30 percent, all of which a self-employed person must pay.

ANNUAL TAXES PAYABLE IN 2016

Maximum earner: $7,347 for OASDI (includes $1,718 for Medicare) plus 1.45 percent in Medicare payroll taxes on all earnings exceeding $118.500

2016 payroll tax ceiling: $118,500 in annual earnings

Maximum taxable annual earnings: $117,000 in 2014; $118,500 in 2015

APPENDIX

ACTUALLY FILING TO GET WHAT'S YOURS

Okay. You may need a few deep breaths before tackling this next piece of advice. At some point, you actually will need to file for your own Social Security retirement benefit. We're here to help.

It will come as no surprise by this point in *Get What's Yours* that there is a seemingly endless array of reasons why you might file for some form of Social Security at many different ages. Move with deliberate speed. Go online first and search out as much as you can.

During your online journey, you will come across articles, advice, and, of course, commercial messages from any number of groups and people who want to "help you." Use them as a guide and, when you inevitably wind up at the Social Security website, which you will, compare what these sources say with what Social Security says. Larry owns a Social Security software company that provides claiming advice; there are others as well. Check them out. But in the end, the official word, perhaps hard to find and harder still to understand, will be somewhere at ssa.gov. So will most of the forms you will need. The agency is, after all, the Hallmark of benefits and has a form or application for every occasion (smiley faces not included).

While we regularly take Social Security to task, its website can be very helpful *if you know where to look*. You can actually file online. But if that scares you, or even if you just want someone to talk to as you go through the process, by all means call or visit your local Social Security office. Just be sure to have a copy of this book close at hand, lest a disagreement arise. We suggest putting a Post-it on any pages you hope to act on.

If you decide to defer your benefits, the odds are you will need to file for Medicare before you file for Social Security. Medicare, of course, often seems as complicated as Social Security. That's a book for another day, and in fact Phil has written one for release later in 2016. For now, just make sure that you file for Medicare alone and do not accidentally file for your Social Security benefit, too. Take your time. Make sure you understand ahead of time anything you sign or are asked to sign.

And while Social Security has just about every form you'll need online, we can't walk you through an online application here, given all the permutations of individual circumstances. To actually file for benefits online, you'll need to create your personalized My Social Security account and provide the agency with your personal information. Many of the forms are interactive—the information you provide on one screen will trigger the display of the next screen, taking you step-by-step through the application. We asked Social Security to provide us the text for all these screens so we could see what the agency wanted to know and whether its wording was clear. The agency declined our request.

But it did provide us the basic printed application form that is used if you go to a local office in person. It is extensive and, while it may not ask for the information in the same way or sequence that would occur online, it provides an inventory of what you'll be expected to tell the agency when you apply for your own retirement benefit. It also provides information on filing for Medicare, some agency disclosure standards, and a list of personal events that Social Security wants you to communicate to the agency.

The form we're presenting here is *Form SSA-1-BK.* It was last updated in February 2014. The agency regularly updates forms, but the information requested here will not have changed greatly since then.

As you make your way through this form, you'll see our guidance and comments inserted in italics, centered, just like this sentence.

Ready? Here goes.

APPLICATION FOR RETIREMENT
INSURANCE BENEFITS

1. (a) PRINT your name: FIRST NAME, MIDDLE INITIAL, LAST
    NAME
   (b) Check (X) whether you are: ❑ Male ❑ Female
2. Enter your Social Security number:

Answer question 3 if English is not your language preference. Otherwise, go
to item 4.

3. Enter the language you prefer to: Speak Write
4. (a) Enter your date of birth: Month, Day, Year
   (b) Enter name of city and state, or foreign country where you were
       born.
   (c) Was a public record of your birth made before you were age 5?
       ❑ Yes ❑ No ❑ Unknown
   (d) Was a religious record of your birth made before you were age 5?
       ❑ Yes ❑ No ❑ Unknown

*Shades of birthers going after President Obama? Hardly. But the agency regu-
larly encounters applicants who are not who they seem. Even people who already
have a Social Security card number may be asked to provide proof of their birth
and residency. And while we don't know how often the statements on these forms
are aggressively checked for accuracy and truthfulness, providing false information is a strategy we would label "suboptimal."*

5. (a) Are you a U.S. citizen? Yes (Go to item 7.) ❑ No (Go to item (b).)
   (b) Are you an alien lawfully present in the U.S.? ❑ Yes (Go to item
       (c).) ❑ No (Go to item 6.)
   (c) When were you lawfully admitted to the U.S.?
6. Enter your full name at birth if different from item 1(a): FIRST
   NAME, MIDDLE INITIAL, LAST NAME
7. (a) Have you used any other name(s)? ❑ Yes (Go to item (b).) ❑ No
       (Go to item 8.)
   (b) Other name(s) used:

8. (a) Have you used any other Social Security number(s)? ❑ Yes (Go to
        item (b).) ❑ No (Go to item 9.)
    (b) Enter Social Security number(s) used:

*Millions of people have inadvertent inconsistencies in their work records. They
may be Bob on one payroll form and Robert on another. A middle initial may pop
up on one W-2 and not on another from a second employer. Women who change
their names upon marriage may have earnings that Social Security is not including in their benefits calculations. Helping the agency track down possible duplica-
tions makes sense.*

Do not answer question 9 if you are one year past full retirement age or
older; go to question 10.

9. (a) Are you, or during the past 14 months have you been, unable to
        work because of illnesses, injuries or conditions? ❑ Yes ❑ No
    (b) If "Yes," enter the date you became unable to work: MONTH,
        DAY, YEAR
10. (a) Have you (or has someone on your behalf) ever filed an
        application for Social Security, Supplemental Security Income, or
        hospital or medical insurance under Medicare? ❑ Yes (If "Yes,"
        answer (b) and (c).) ❑ No (If "No," go to item 11.) ❑ Unknown
        (If "Unknown," go to item 11.)
    (b) Enter name of person(s) on whose Social Security record you filed
        other application: FIRST NAME, MIDDLE INITIAL, LAST
        NAME
    (c) Enter Social Security number(s) of person named in (b). (If
        unknown, so indicate.):
11. (a) Were you in the active military or naval service (including Reserve
        or National Guard active duty or active duty for training) after
        September 7, 1939 and before 1968? ❑ Yes (If "Yes," answer (b)
        and (c).) ❑ No (If "No," go to item 12.)
    (b) Enter date(s) of service: From—Month, Year; To—Month, Year
    (c) Have you ever been (or will you be) eligible for monthly benefits
        from a military or civilian Federal agency? (Include Veterans

Administration benefits only if you waived Military retirement pay.) ❑ Yes ❑ No

People who've served in the military can get wage credits that may increase their Social Security benefits. They also can receive a military pension and Social Security benefits. So, you should know your service record. You can find more details at http://www.ssa.gov/retire2/veterans.htm.

12. Did you or your spouse (or prior spouse) work in the railroad industry for 5 years or more? ❑ Yes ❑ No

There is a special retirement program for railroad workers, begun independently of Social Security at a time when railroads played a much larger role in the nation's economy than they do today. The program is run by the Railroad Retirement Board (https://secure.rrb.gov/). Be aware that a railroad retirement pension can be affected by a person's Social Security work history and benefits.

13. (a) Do you (or your spouse) have Social Security credits (for example based on work or residence) under another country's Social Security system? ❑ Yes (If "Yes," answer (b) and (c).) ❑ No (If "No," go to item 14.)

     (b) List the country(ies):

     (c) Are you (or your spouse) filing for foreign Social Security benefits? ❑ Yes ❑ No

The United States has agreements with 25 other nations to help people get proper retirement credit if they've earned wages from work in multiple countries. These so-called totalization agreements are explained at http://www.ssa.gov/interna tional/agreements_overview.html.

Answer question 14 only if you were born January 2, 1924, or later. Otherwise go on to question 15.

14. (a) Are you entitled to, or do you expect to be entitled to, a pension or annuity (or a lump sum in place of a pension or annuity) based on your work after 1956 not covered by Social Security? ❑ Yes (If "Yes." Answer (b) and (c).) ❑ No (If "No," go to item 15.)

(b) I became entitled, or expect to become entitled, beginning: month/year

(c) I became eligible, or expect to become eligible, beginning: month/ year

I agree to promptly notify the Social Security Administration if I become entitled to a pension, an annuity, or a lump sum payment based on my employment not covered by Social Security, or if such pension or annuity stops.

The previous questions refer to our old friends WEP and GPO. Check them out in Chapter 14 or in the Glossary.

15. Have you been married?
    (a) Yes. (If Yes, answer item 16.)
    (b) No. (If No, go to item 17.)

We have devoted much effort to talking about spousal benefits, divorce benefits, and survivor benefits. So does Social Security. The agency is gathering marital information here that could be crucial in any future benefit issues involving your spouse (present, former, or deceased) and your children. Remember the old ad campaign about it not being nice to fool Mother Nature? Well, it's even worse to try to fool Social Security. We know one thing about a program based on possibly paying benefits for the rest of your life, your present and former spouses' lives, and even the lives of your children: it has a very long institutional memory.

16. (a) Give the following information about your current marriage. If not currently married, write "None." Go to item 16(b).

    Spouse's name (including maiden name)

    When (Month, day, year)

    Where (Name of City and State)

    How marriage ended (If still in effect, write "Not Ended.")

When (Month, day, year)

Where (Name of City and State)

Spouse's date of birth (or age)

If spouse deceased, give date of death

Spouse's Social Security number (If none or unknown, so indicate.)

(b) Enter information about any other marriage if you:
- Had a marriage that lasted at least 10 years; or
- Had a marriage that ended due to death of your spouse, regardless of duration; or
- Were divorced, remarried the same individual within the year immediately following the year of the divorce, and the combined period of marriage totaled 10 years or more.

Use the "Remarks" space to enter the additional marriage information. If none, write "None." Go on to item 16 (c) if you have a child(ren) who is under age 16 or disabled or handicapped (age 16 or over and disability began before age 22); and you are divorced from the child's other parent, who is now deceased, and the marriage lasted less than 10 years.

Spouse's name (including maiden name)

When (Month, day, year)

Where (Name of City and State)

How marriage ended

When (Month, day, year)

Where (Name of City and State)

Marriage performed by:
- Clergyman or public official
- Other (Explain in "Remarks.")

Spouse's date of birth (or age)

If spouse deceased, give date of death

Spouse's Social Security number (If none or unknown, so indicate.)

(c) Enter information about any marriage if you:
- Have a child(ren) who is under age 16 or disabled or handicapped (age 16 or over and disability began before age 22); and
- Were married for less than 10 years to the child's mother or father, who is now deceased; and
- The marriage ended in divorce. If none, write "None."

To whom married

When (Month, day, year)

Where (Name of City and State)

How marriage ended

When (Month, day, year)

Where (Name of City and State)

Marriage performed by:
- Clergyman or public official
- Other (Explain in "Remarks.")

Spouse's date of birth (or age)

If spouse deceased, give date of death

Spouse's Social Security number (If none or unknown, so indicate.)

Use the "Remarks" space for marriage continuation or explanation.

If your claim for retirement benefits is approved, your children (including adopted children and stepchildren) or dependent grandchildren (including step grandchildren) may be eligible for benefits based on your earnings record.

17. List below FULL NAME OF ALL your children (including adopted children, and stepchildren) or dependent grandchildren (including stepgrandchildren) who are now or were in the past 6 months UNMARRIED and:
    - UNDER AGE 18
    - AGE 18 TO 19 AND ATTENDING SECONDARY SCHOOL OR ELEMENTARY SCHOOL FULL-TIME
    - DISABLED OR HANDICAPPED (age 18 or over and disability began before age 22)

Social Security payments may be available to qualifying children and their parents if the children are young, in school, or are disabled, and became disabled before age 22.

Also list any student who is between the ages of 18 to 23 if such student was both: 1) Previously entitled to Social Security benefits on any Social Security record for August 1981; and 2) In full-time attendance at a post-secondary school.

(IF THERE ARE NO SUCH CHILDREN, WRITE "NONE" BELOW AND GO ON TO ITEM 18.)

18. (a) Did you have wages or self-employment income covered under Social Security in all years from 1978 through last year? ❑ Yes (If "Yes," go to item 19.) ❑ No (If "No," answer item (b).)

(b) List the years from 1978 through last year in which you did not have wages or self-employment income covered under Social Security:

Social Security retirement benefits normally require at least 40 quarters of earnings large enough to qualify as representing a "covered quarter" for the purposes of calculating benefit entitlements. Current information on required earnings levels may be found at http://www.ssa.gov/oact/cola/QC.html. As you know by now, unless you first opened the book to this page, the agency uses up to 35 years of covered earnings to calculate your Annual Indexed Monthly Earnings, a figure that is used to calculate your Primary Insurance Amount. If you have more than 35 years of earnings, the agency uses the highest 35 in calculating your AIME. See Chapter 3 for more details.

19. Enter below the names and addresses of all the persons, companies, or government agencies for whom you have worked this year, last year, and the year before last. IF NONE, WRITE "NONE" BELOW AND GO ON TO ITEM 20.

    NAME AND ADDRESS OF EMPLOYER (If you had more than one employer, please list them in order beginning with your last (most recent) employer.)

    Month Year   Month Year

    (If you need more space, use "Remarks.")

20. May we ask your employers for wage information needed to process your claim? ❑ Yes ❑ No
21. THIS ITEM MUST BE COMPLETED, EVEN IF YOU ARE AN EMPLOYEE.
(a) Were you self-employed this year and/or last year? ❑ Yes (If "Yes," answer (b).) ❑ No (If "No," go to item 22.)
(b) Check the year or years in which you were self-employed:
    In what kind of trade or business were you self-employed?
    (For example, storekeeper, farmer, physician)

Were your net earnings from your business $400 or more? (Check "Yes" or "No.")

❑ This year ❑ Yes ❑ No

❑ Last year ❑ Yes ❑ No

22. (a) How much were your total earnings last year? Amount: $

An accurate earnings record, including any self-employment income, is essential to Getting What's Yours. This includes a record of months in which you did not work—information that Social Security needs to know to process your application accurately. Be aware that there's a 1- to 2-year lag time for the agency to gather your formal earnings records from the IRS.

   (b) Place an "X" in each block for EACH MONTH of last year in which you did not earn more than *$ in wages, and did not perform substantial services in self-employment. These months are exempt months. If no months were exempt months, place an "X" in "NONE." If all months were exempt months, place an "X" in "ALL."

*Enter the appropriate monthly limit after reading the instructions, "How Work Affects Your Benefits" (http://www.ssa.gov/pubs/EN-05-10069.pdf).

❑ NONE ❑ ALL

Jan. Feb. Mar. Apr. May Jun.

Jul. Aug. Sept. Oct. Nov. Dec.

23. (a) How much do you expect your total earnings to be this year? Amount: $

   (b) Place an "X" in each block for EACH MONTH of this year in which you did not or will not earn more than *$ in wages, and did not or will not perform substantial services in self-employment. These months are exempt months. If no months are or will be exempt months, place an "X" in "NONE." If all months are or will be exempt months, place an "X" in "ALL."

*Enter the appropriate monthly limit after reading the instructions, "How Work Affects Your Benefits" (http://www.ssa.gov/pubs/EN-05-10069.pdf).

❑ NONE   ❑ ALL
Jan. Feb. Mar. Apr. May Jun.
Jul. Aug. Sept. Oct. Nov. Dec.

Answer this item ONLY if you are now in the last 4 months of your taxable year (Sept., Oct., Nov., and Dec., if your taxable year is a calendar year).

24. (a) How much do you expect to earn next year? Amount: $
    (b) Place an "X" in each block for EACH MONTH of next year in which you do not expect to earn more than *$ in wages, and do not expect to perform substantial services in self-employment. These months will be exempt months. If no months are expected to be exempt months, place an "X" in "NONE." If all months are expected to be exempt months, place an "X" in "ALL."

*Enter the appropriate monthly limit after reading the instructions, "How Work Affects Your Benefits" (http://www.ssa.gov/pubs/EN-05-10069.pdf).

❑ NONE   ❑ ALL
Jan. Feb. Mar. Apr. May Jun.
Jul. Aug. Sept. Oct. Nov. Dec.

25. If you use a fiscal year, that is, a taxable year that does not end December 31 (with income tax return due April 15), enter here the month your fiscal year ends. _____

DO NOT ANSWER ITEM 26 IF YOU ARE FULL RETIREMENT AGE AND 6 MONTHS OR OLDER; GO TO ITEM 27.

PLEASE READ CAREFULLY THE INFORMATION ON THE BOTTOM OF PAGE 8 AND ANSWER ONE OF THE FOLLOWING ITEMS:

26. (a) I want benefits beginning with the earliest possible month, and will accept an age-related reduction. ❑

(b) I am full retirement age (or will be within 12 months), and want benefits beginning with the earliest possible month providing there is no permanent reduction in my ongoing monthly benefits. ❏

(c) I want benefits beginning with (enter date). ❏

MEDICARE INFORMATION

If this claim is approved and you are still entitled to benefits at age 65, or you are within 3 months of age 65 or older you could automatically receive Medicare Part A (Hospital Insurance) and Medicare Part B (Medical Insurance) coverage at age 65. If you live in Puerto Rico or a foreign country, you are not eligible for automatic enrollment in Medicare Part B, and you will need to contact Social Security to request enrollment.

COMPLETE ITEM 27 ONLY IF YOU ARE WITHIN 3 MONTHS OF AGE 65 OR OLDER.

Medicare Part B (Medical Insurance) helps cover doctor's services and outpatient care. It also covers some other services that Medicare Part A does not cover, such as some of the services of physical and occupational therapists and some home health care. If you enroll in Medicare Part B, you will have to pay a monthly premium. The amount of your premium will be determined when your coverage begins. In some cases, your premium may be higher based on information about your income we receive from the Internal Revenue Service. Your premiums will be deducted from any monthly Social Security, Railroad Retirement, or Office of Personnel Management benefits you receive. If you do not receive any of these benefits, you will get a letter explaining how to pay your premiums. You will also get a letter if there is any change in the amount of your premium.

While Get What's Yours *is not about Medicare, we can't stress here too strongly that this program, like Social Security, can be very complicated and that you should not take decisions about it lightly or, worse, assume you don't have decisions to make. Please take the time—beginning at least several months before you sign up—to carefully explore the program and your options. In particular, use the online tools at medicare.gov to find the best insurance plans for your needs. This often involves carefully entering the specific drugs and dosages you take into*

Medicare's "formulary" tool to find insurance plans that will give you the best pricing deal.

You can also enroll in a Medicare prescription drug plan (Part D). To learn more about the Medicare prescription drug plans and when you can enroll, visit www.medicare.gov or call 1-800-MEDICARE (1-800-633-4227; TTY 1-877-486-2048). Medicare can also tell you about agencies in your area that can help you choose your prescription drug coverage. The amount of your premium varies based on the prescription drug plan provider. The amount you pay for Part D coverage may be higher than the listed plan premium, based on information about your income we receive from the Internal Revenue Service.

If you have limited income and resources, we encourage you to apply for the Extra Help that is available to assist you with Medicare prescription drug costs. The Extra Help can pay the monthly premiums, annual deductibles, and prescription co-payments. To learn more or apply, please visit www.socialsecurity.gov, call 1-800-772-1213 (TTY 1-800-325-0778) or visit the nearest Social Security office.

One last Medicare tip: this is not a "set and forget" program. Insurers change their coverage terms and prices every year. Most Medicare beneficiaries stick with the same plan from year to year, even after it has ceased being the best plan for them. Take advantage each fall of the annual enrollment period when you can change Medicare plans. If you find a plan that has received Medicare's highest quality rating of five stars, you will be able to switch into that plan anytime during the year. (Medicare frees top-rated plans from annual enrollment limitations.)

27. Do you want to enroll in Medicare Part B (Medical insurance)?
    ❏ Yes ❏ No

Filing for Medicare should not trigger a claim for Social Security benefits but make sure Social Security does not accidentally think you've filed for both (unless, of course, that's exactly what you want to do).

28. If you are within 2 months of age 65 or older, blind or disabled, do you want to file for Supplemental Security Income? ❑ Yes ❑ No

REMARKS (USE A BLANK SHEET OR SHEETS FOR ANY EXPLANATIONS.)

I declare under penalty of perjury that I have examined all the information on this form, and on any accompanying statements or forms, and it is true and correct to the best of my knowledge. I understand that anyone who knowingly gives a false or misleading statement about a material fact in this information, or causes someone else to do so, commits a crime and may be sent to prison, or face other penalties, or both.

SIGNATURE OF APPLICANT

Date (Month, day, year)

SIGNATURE (First Name, Middle Initial, Last Name) (Write in ink.)

Telephone number(s) at which you may be contacted during the day:

DIRECT DEPOSIT PAYMENT INFORMATION (FINANCIAL INSTITUTION)

Routing Transit Number: _____

Account Number: _____
❑ Checking
❑ Savings
❑ Enroll in Direct Express

Applicant's Mailing Address (Number and street, Apt No., P.O. Box, or Rural Route) (Enter Residence Address in "Remarks," if different.):

_____

City and State: _____

ZIP Code: _____

County (if any) in which you now live: _____

Witnesses are required ONLY if this application has been signed by mark (X) above. If signed by mark (X), two witnesses who know the applicant must sign below, giving their full addresses. Also, print the applicant's name in the Signature block.

1. Signature of Witness: _____

Address (Number and Street, City, State and ZIP Code)

_____

2. Signature of Witness: _____

Address (Number and Street, City, State and ZIP Code)

_____

COLLECTION AND USE OF INFORMATION FROM YOUR APPLICATION/PRIVACY ACT NOTICE/PAPERWORK REDUCTION ACT NOTICE

Sections 202, 205, and 223 of the Social Security Act, as amended, authorize us to collect this information. We will use the information you provide to determine if you or a dependent are eligible for insurance coverage and/or monthly benefits.

The information you furnish on this form is voluntary. However, if you fail to provide all or part of the requested information it may prevent us from making an accurate and timely decision concerning your or a dependent's entitlement to benefit payments.

We rarely use the information you supply for any purpose other than determining benefit payments for you or a dependent. However, we may use it for the administration and integrity of our programs. We may also disclose information to another person or to another agency in accordance with approved routine uses, which include but are not limited to the following:

Read this privacy section carefully. Although the agency says it rarely uses your information for anything save benefit decisions, you should assume that other government agencies could see the information you've provided to Social Security.

1. To enable a third party or an agency to assist us in establishing right to Social Security benefits and/or coverage;
2. To comply with Federal laws requiring the release of information from our records (e.g., to the Government Accountability Office and Department of Veterans Affairs);
3. To make determinations for eligibility in similar health and income maintenance programs at the Federal, State, and local level; and
4. To facilitate statistical research, audit, or investigative activities necessary to assure the integrity of Social Security programs (e.g., to the Bureau of Census and to private entities under contract with us).

We may also use the information you provide in computer matching programs. Matching programs compare our records with records kept by other Federal, State, or local government agencies. Information from these matching programs can be used to establish or verify a person's eligibility for federally funded or administered benefit programs and for repayment of incorrect payments or delinquent debts under these programs.

A complete list of routine uses for this information is available in our Privacy Act Systems of Records Notices entitled, Earnings Recording and Self Employment Income System (60-0059) and Claims Folders Systems (60-0089). Additional information regarding these and other systems of records notices, are available on-line at www.socialsecurity.gov or at your local Social Security office.

Paperwork Reduction Act Statement—This information collection meets the requirements of 44 U.S.C. 3507, as amended by section 2 of the Paperwork Reduction Act of 1995. You do not need to answer these questions unless we display a valid Office of Management and Budget control number. We estimate that it will take about 11 minutes to read the instructions, gather the facts, and answer the questions. **SEND OR BRING THE COMPLETED FORM TO YOUR LOCAL SOCIAL SECURITY OFFICE. You can find your local Social Security office through SSA's website at www.socialsecurity.gov. Offices are also listed under U.S. Government agencies in your telephone directory or you may call Social Security at 1-800-772-1213 (TTY 1-800-325-0778).** You may send comments on our time estimate above to: SSA, 6401 Security Blvd., Baltimore, MD 21235-6401. Send only comments relating to our time estimate to this address, not the completed form.

CHANGES TO BE REPORTED
AND HOW TO REPORT

Failure to report may result in overpayments that must be repaid, and in possible monetary penalties.

- You change your mailing address for checks or residence. (To avoid delay in receipt of checks you should ALSO file a regular change of address notice with your post office.)
- Your citizenship or immigration status changes.
- You go outside the U.S.A. for 30 consecutive days or longer.
- Any beneficiary dies or becomes unable to handle benefits.
- Work Changes—On your application you told us you expect total earnings to be $_____ a year.

You ❏ (are) ❏ (are not) earning wages of more than $ _____ a month.

You ❏ (are)(are not) self-employed rendering substantial services in your trade or business.

(Report AT ONCE if this work pattern changes)

- You are confined to a jail, prison, penal institution or correctional facility for more than 30 continuous days for conviction of a crime, or you are confined for more than 30 continuous days to a public institution by a court order in connection with a crime.
- You have an unsatisfied warrant for more than 30 continuous days for your arrest for a crime or attempted crime that is a felony of flight to avoid prosecution or confinement, escape from custody and flight-escape. In most jurisdictions that do not classify crimes as felonies, this applies to a crime that is punishable by death or imprisonment for a term exceeding one year (regardless of the actual sentence imposed).
- You have an unsatisfied warrant for more than 30 continuous days for a violation of probation or parole under Federal or State law.

Okay. We doubt that Social Security will be on your list of pen pals if you wind up in the slammer or are fleeing from the gendarmerie. But other change-of-life events can, as we've stressed, have a big impact on the Social Security benefits due you and other present and even former family members. So, before informing Social Security of such changes, take a lap or two through Get What's Yours *and make sure you understand the benefit implications of these changes, including the timing of any indicated benefit applications.*

- You become entitled to a pension, an annuity, or a lump sum payment based on your employment not covered by Social Security, or if such pension or annuity stops.
- Your stepchild is entitled to benefits on your record and you and the stepchild's parent divorce. Stepchild benefits are not payable beginning with the month after the month the divorce becomes final.
- Custody Change—Report if a person for whom you are filing or who is in your care dies, leaves your care or custody, or changes address.

- Change of Marital Status—Marriage, divorce, annulment of marriage.
- If you become the parent of a child (including an adopted child) after you have filed your claim, let us know about the child so we can decide if the child is eligible for benefits. Failure to report the existence of these children may result in the loss of possible benefits to the child(ren).

HOW TO REPORT

You can make your reports online, by telephone, mail, or in person, whichever you prefer.

If you are awarded benefits, and one or more of the above change(s) occur, you should report by:

- Visiting the section "my Social Security" at our web site at www.socialsecurity.gov
- Calling us TOLL FREE at 1-800-772-1213.
- If you are deaf or hearing impaired, calling us TOLL FREE at TTY 1-800-325-0778; or
- Calling, visiting or writing your local Social Security office at the phone number and address shown on your claim receipt.

For general information about Social Security, visit our web site at www .socialsecurity.gov.

For those under full retirement age, the law requires that a report of earnings be filed with SSA within 3 months and 15 days after the end of any taxable year in which you earn more than the annual exempt amount. You may contact SSA to file a report. Otherwise, SSA will use the earnings reported by your employer(s) and your self-employment tax return (if applicable) as the report of earnings required by law, to adjust benefits under the earnings test. It is your responsibility to ensure that the information you give concerning your earnings is correct. You must furnish additional information as needed when your benefit adjustment is not correct based on the earnings on your record.

In nearly all cases, the W-2 that your employers file with the IRS or, if you're self-employed, your tax returns, will be sufficient documentation of this reporting requirement. But we do have a problem with Social Security's statement that it's your responsibility to furnish additional information when "your benefit adjustment is not correct." How, we ask, are you going to know if it's not correct unless the agency tells you? And how would it know the information is not correct in the first place? Benefit adjustments based on the Earnings Test may not be apparent to you for years after the earnings were received and disclosed to Social Security. Our advice here (and, unlike Social Security, we do give advice) is to keep very careful records of your earnings. If you are affected by the Earnings Test, make sure any benefit reductions (which, you'll recall, are later restored to most beneficiaries) agree with your earnings records. If they don't, contact the agency right away.

PLEASE READ THE FOLLOWING INFORMATION CAREFULLY BEFORE YOU ANSWER QUESTION 26.

- If you are under full retirement age, retirement benefits cannot be payable to you for any month before the month in which you file your claim.
- If you are over full retirement age, retirement benefits may be payable to you for some months before the month in which you file this claim.

This is a very oblique reference to the Social Security rule that most people who delay filing for benefits past full retirement age can receive a lump-sum payment equal to up to six months of their benefits. The period may be up to a year for some filers. But the entitlement period does not include periods before reaching full retirement age. So, if you filed for spousal benefits at age 66 and 4 months, your lump-sum payment would be for only four months of benefits. Check out Chapter 3 for further details and exceptions.

- If your first month of entitlement is prior to full retirement age, your benefit rate will be reduced. However, if you do not actually receive your full benefit amount for one or more months before full retirement age because benefits are withheld due to your earnings, your benefit will be increased at full retirement age to give credit for this withholding. Thus, your benefit amount at full retirement age will be reduced only if you receive one or more full benefit payments prior to the month you attain full retirement age.

With modest apologies for piling on, the Get What's Yours *language police politely requests that the SSA rewrite the above paragraph.*

RECEIPT FOR YOUR CLAIM FOR SOCIAL SECURITY RETIREMENT INSURANCE BENEFITS TO BE COMPLETED BY SOCIAL SECURITY REPRESENTATIVE

TELEPHONE NUMBER(S) TO CALL IF YOU HAVE A QUESTION OR SOMETHING TO REPORT

BEFORE YOU RECEIVE A NOTICE OF AWARD:

AFTER YOU RECEIVE A NOTICE FOR AWARD:

SSA OFFICE:

DATE CLAIM RECEIVED:

Establishing the time you filed for benefits may be crucial if any questions later occur about your eligibility for benefits or the amount of benefits due you. You can establish this time most securely by applying for benefits at a Social Security office and having the agency's representative enter the time of your application. You also can file by mail. We recommend a certified letter requiring agency acknowledgment. If you file for benefits over the phone or online, and do not receive written confirmation of your claim after a few weeks, we recommend you write a certified letter to your local SSA office. You can find a ZIP code office locator at https://secure.ssa.gov/ICON/main.jsp. *Include the date of your claim and the details of how it was filed. If any dispute later arises, this letter can help establish a record of your actions.*

Your application for Social Security benefits has been received and will be processed as quickly as possible.

You should hear from us within _____ days after you have given us all the information we requested. Some claims may take longer if additional information is needed.

In the meantime, if you change your address, or if there is some other change that may affect your claim, you—or someone for you—should report the change. The changes to be reported are listed above.

Always give us your claim number when writing or telephoning about your claim.

If you have any questions about your claim, we will be glad to help you.

CLAIMANT: _____

SOCIAL SECURITY CLAIM NUMBER: _____

NOTES

Chapter 1. Why We Bothered

1. "Changes in U.S. Family Finances from 2010 to 2013: Evidence from the Survey of Consumer Finances," Federal Reserve Board, September 2014, http://www.federalreserve.gov/pubs/bulletin/2014/pdf/scf14.pdf.

2. "Proposed budget bill would have devastating effects on millions' Social Security Benefits," October 27, 2015, http://www.pbs.org/news hour/making-sense/houses-proposed-budget-bill-will-devastating-effects-millions-social-security-benefits/.

3. $B(a) = PIA(a) (1 - e(n)) (1 + d(n)) Z(a) + max((.5 \, PIA^*(a) - PIA(a) (1 + d(n))) E(a), 0) (1 - u(a,q,n,m)) D(a)$. This is the "simple" formula for the benefit, B, of a spouse at age a that prevailed prior to the change in the law. There are ten separate mathematical functions on the right-hand side. We wonder what would happen if members of Congress were asked to explain this formula to constituents.

Chapter 2. Life's Biggest Danger Isn't Dying, It's Living

1. http://www.prnewswire.com/news-releases/over-one-in-five-ameri cans-expect-to-die-in-debt-300190301.html.

2. Annual Statistical Supplement to the Social Security Bulletin, 2015, Table 6.B5.1.

3. http://www.federalreserve.gov/econresdata/2014-report-economic -well-being-us-households-201505.pdf.

4. Jeffrey R. Brown, Aries Kapteyn, and Olivia S. Mitchell, "Framing Effects and Expected Social Security Claiming Behavior," NBER Working Paper 17018, May 2011.

5. "Social Security Consumer Study," Nationwide Financial Retirement Institute, June 2014.

6.

	MALE	FEMALE
Exact age	**Life expectancy**	**Life expectancy**
62	19.90	22.68
63	19.15	21.85
64	18.40	21.03
65	17.66	20.22
66	16.93	19.42
67	16.21	18.63
68	15.51	17.85
69	14.81	17.09
70	14.13	16.33
71	13.47	15.59
72	12.81	14.86
73	12.18	14.14
74	11.55	13.44
75	10.94	12.76
76	10.34	12.09
77	9.76	11.44
78	9.20	10.80
79	8.66	10.18
80	8.13	9.58
81	7.62	9.00
82	7.14	8.43
83	6.68	7.89
84	6.23	7.37
85	5.81	6.87
86	5.40	6.40
87	5.02	5.94
88	4.65	5.52
89	4.31	5.12
90	4.00	4.75
91	3.70	4.40
92	3.44	4.08
93	3.19	3.79
94	2.97	3.53
95	2.78	3.29
96	2.61	3.08
97	2.46	2.89
98	2.33	2.72
99	2.21	2.56
100	2.09	2.41

Note: The period life expectancy at a given age is the average remaining number of years expected prior to death for a person at that exact age, born on January 1, using the mortality rates for 2011 over the course of his or her remaining life.

Source: http://www.ssa.gov/oact/STATS/table4c6.html.

7. "Risks and Process of Retirement Survey Report," Society of Actuaries, 2012.

8. Melissa A. Z. Knoll, "Behavioral and Psychological Aspects of the Retirement Decision," *Social Security Bulletin* 71, no. 4 (2011).

9. https://www.ssa.gov/planners/retire/agereduction.html#chart&sb=0.

10. In particular, for most plausible real interest rates, two-earner households with average life expectancy maximize the present value of Social Security benefits when the primary earner delays claiming until age 70. Primary earners in one-earner couples can also maximize the present value of their household's benefits by delaying, though the actuarially advantageous delay period is shorter and the gains are smaller. Delaying is less attractive for secondary earners in two-earner couples, and for singles. However, at real interest rates of 1.6 percent or less, two-earner households maximize present value when secondary earners delay as well.

    Single men and women benefit from at least a short delay (to age 64) for real interest rates of, respectively, 3.5 percent or less and 4.1 percent or less. "The Decision to Delay Social Security Benefits: Theory and Evidence," National Bureau of Economic Research, http://www.nber.org/papers/w17866.

11. http://www.moneychimp.com/features/market_cagr.htm.

Chapter 3. Social Security—from A to Zzzzzzzz

1. These steps are explained in the statement but it does not provide numerous other basic details about your benefits that we believe it should.

2. Of course, a dollar received at age 100 is not as valuable as a dollar received today because you could bank the dollar received today and have more, potentially much more, money at age 100. It's even less valuable if you have to be alive to receive it. Using a reasonable 2 percent real interest rate to discount—make less of all future Social Security benefits that you might receive through age 100—produces lifetime benefits of $556,088 from taking benefits immediately versus $712,411 from waiting till 70. This means that waiting to collect is equivalent (apart from tax issues) to finding $156,323 ($712,411 less $556,088) on the sidewalk!

3. The precise formula is the smaller of the widow(er) benefit reduction factor times the decedent's PIA and an amount we'll call x. This amount x is the larger of (a) the decedent's retirement benefit inclusive of any Delayed Retirement Credits (if the decedent suspended their retirement benefit after reaching FRA) or (b) 82.5 percent of the decedent's primary insurance amount.

4. https://secure.ssa.gov/poms.nsf/lnx/0300615770.

5. Every year, the agency and others who oversee its programs issue extensive reports. One is called the *Annual Report of the Board of Trustees of the Federal Old-Age and Survivors Insurance and Federal Disability Insurance Trust Funds*. A second is called the *Annual Statistical Supplement to the Social Security Bulletin*. Many of the tables and charts presented here are taken from the most recent versions of these documents. However, to make sure you're seeing the most current data, you might want to look up these documents in a search engine and download the current versions.

Chapter 4. The New Social Security Law

1. Recall that Jan, Paul's wife, filed for her retirement benefit when Paul reached full retirement age. But then Jan immediately suspended it. Doing so let Jan wait till 70 to collect her highest possible retirement benefit. It also permitted Paul to file for only his spousal benefit while also waiting till 70 to get his largest retirement benefit.

2. By the way, it's January 2, because Social Security treats someone whose birthday is today as having changed ages the day before. So someone born on January 1, 1954, is viewed as having become 62 in 2015 since their Social Security birthday was December 31!

Chapter 5. Three General Rules to Maximize Your Lifetime Benefits

1. Social Security also reduces excess benefits if taken early.

2. The current FRA for purposes of calculating spousal or retirement benefits is 66. That age will rise by two months beginning in 2021 (for someone born in 1955) and will keep going up by two months every year until FRA reaches 67 in 2027 (for those born in 1960 and later years).

3. To be clear, there is no compounding before full retirement or after, just across these two multiyear periods.

4. http://www.nber.org/aging/rrc/papers/orre13–04.pdf.

Chapter 6. Be Careful Taking Social Security's Advice and Help

1. https://www.ssa.gov/oact/TR/2015/V_B_econ.html#292722.

Chapter 7. The Benefits of Not Retiring

1. Not everyone will see their AIME rise if they continue working, of course. Many older persons seek part-time jobs or shift into encore careers where compensation is secondary to the appeal of the job. And for people who in the past earned near the national average wage, the end of indexing might not have much of an impact. In short, if the prospect of higher Social Security benefits is an important component of your decision to keep working, you should analyze your earnings years and see how continued work would affect your AIME.

Chapter 9. Married or Divorced with Benefits

1. These are "plain vanilla" choices. As we've gone to great lengths to stress, claiming ages can be as early as 60 for survivors, 50 for disabled survivors, and much younger for disabled claimants and qualifying children.

2. A little more contemplation produces a third revelation. Only one spouse and only one ex-spouse can collect an excess spousal benefit in this context. The reason: if spouse A's excess spousal benefit is positive, his PIA must be less than half of his partner, spouse B's, PIA. But the flip side of this coin is that spouse B must have a PIA that is more than twice the size of spouse A's. Hence, for spouse B, the excess spousal benefit must be zero. Substitute ex-spouse for spouse and you have the same story about divorced spousal benefits.

Chapter 10. Widowed? Why Social Security Is a Major Women's Issue

1. Widows whose husbands died before age 62 may be entitled to a slight bump-up in benefits due to a provision in the law enacted in 1983. It tried to at least partially equalize their survivor benefits with those of

women whose husbands died at later ages. This provision does so by assuming the deceased husband's benefits were calculated at a later age, using an alternative computation called Widow(er)'s Indexing, or WINDEX for short (gotta love those clever acronym wizards at the SSA).

Chapter 11. Never Married or Divorced Too Soon

1. http://www.census.gov/hhes/families/files/cps2014/tabA1-all.xls.

Chapter 12. Hidden Benefits for the Disabled

1. "A worker who becomes disabled before the quarter in which he or she attains age 31 satisfies the recency-of-work requirement if credits have been earned for at least one-half of the quarters during the period beginning with the quarter after the quarter the worker attained age 21, and ending with the quarter in which the disability began. If this period contains 12 or fewer quarters—that is, if the disability begins in the quarter the worker attains age 24 or earlier—then a minimum of six credits must be earned in the 12-quarter period ending with the quarter in which the disability began."

2. www.ssa.gov/policy/docs/quickfacts/stat_snapshot/.

3. For nondisabled workers now age 62, taking benefits immediately comes at a 25 percent reduction relative to their full retirement benefit. Hence, a disabled worker is receiving $1/(1 - 0.25)$ or 1.33 times what the nondisabled worker would receive.

Chapter 13. Social Security and Medicare

1. https://www.socialsecurity.gov/oact/cola/QC.html.
2. https://secure.ssa.gov/poms.nsf/lnx/0601101020.
3. https://www.ssa.gov/forms/ssa-44.pdf.
4. https://www.irs.gov/pub/irs-pdf/p969.pdf.
5. http://www.pbs.org/newshour/spc/new-older-workers/chapter-1-re thinking-retirement.

Chapter 14. Government Pensions and Windfall Penalties

1. Now, because you are an eagle-eyed reader, you probably noticed the use of the phrase "substantial earnings" in the WEP adjustment table. It turns out that you need to have earned a fair amount of covered earnings in a year for it to qualify as "substantial" under the WEP provisions. The agency defines substantial as 25 percent of each year's payroll tax ceiling. But in a trip down one of Social Security's numerous rule-making rabbit holes, it doesn't use the current law's ceiling but what the ceiling would be under laws in effect prior to 1976. You can find annual figures for substantial earnings at http://www.ssa.gov/OACT/cola/yoc.html.

Chapter 15. 60 Good-News Secrets to Higher Lifetime Benefits

1. Technical aficionados will find a flaw in this language. Social Security doesn't literally consider the date that you file for your retirement, i.e., the date that you walk into their office or call them on the phone and request your retirement benefit. Instead, they consider the date at which you become entitled to receive a retirement benefit. You can file for a retirement benefit up to 4 months before you are eligible to collect it, and if you do so file you become entitled to the benefit on the date at which you become eligible to collect it. You become entitled even if you suspend your benefit; hence, even though you have filed for your retirement benefit, have become eligible for it, and have become entitled to receive it, you have, nonetheless, elected to suspend its receipt.

2. She would receive the smaller of (a) his full PIA reduced by the survivor benefit reduction factor if the widow takes her survivor benefit early and (b) an amount we'll call x. So what's x? It is the larger of (c) what he was collecting when he died and (d) 82.5 percent of his PIA. The earlier the deceased worker took survivor benefits, the smaller is his actual benefit entering into part (c). So, up to a point, the sooner the decedent spouse took his retirement benefit, the less his widow will collect.

Chapter 16. 40 Bad-News Gotchas That Can Reduce Your Benefits Forever

1. This is not precisely correct. What you'll get is the sum of your reduced retirement benefit plus the difference between the reduced

excess spousal benefit, defined as half of your spouse's full retirement benefit minus 100 percent of your full retirement benefit augmented by any Delayed Retirement Credits. The reduction applied to the entire excess spousal benefit is based on the spousal benefit reduction factor. And because the retirement and spousal benefit reduction factors aren't identical, the total benefit is not exactly just the reduced spousal benefit.

INDEX

Page numbers in *italics* refer to tables.

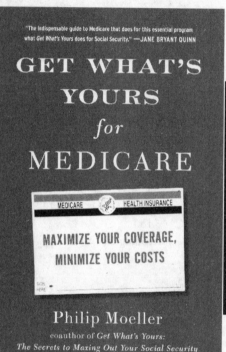